'This book comes at an important time for the corporate world. Having graduated with a Harvard MBA and with seven years of consulting experience, I was well prepared for the strategic content of my role and my mission to develop a turnaround strategy for the company. However, this training did not prepare me for navigating the corporate culture and psychology. I was offered the support of having a corporate coach and John O'Brien's Jungian psychology background stood out for me. Since then, John has been by my side, helping me develop, understand the landscape and have an impact during each of my subsequent roles. He has taught me how to apply corporate analytical psychology and to understand the unconscious forces at play in the board room.

Business schools and consulting firms train people to only focus on results and that can lead to blind spots. To be effective we also have to understand the culture, the mindset of leaders and the psyche. There are organizational scars from previous failures.

This book, grounded in Jungian psychology, provides a comprehensive user guide for navigating corporate systems and understanding what drives people to take certain actions.'

Sadiq Gillani, Senior Vice President at Emirates,
Stanford University Lecturer, former Vice President Group Strategy
with Lufthansa, Harvard MBA, Cambridge University M.Phil.,
Financial Times Top 100 Executive List

I0121525

The Professional Practice of Jungian Coaching

O'Brien and O'Brien and their collection of international contributors introduce the historical and current theory and practice of Corporate Analytical Psychology. Uniquely and practically bringing Jungian ideas to the corporate world, the chapters discuss the increasing need for ethical corporations in the context of individuation and moral hazard, demonstrate how to manage and define complexes that inhibit creativity and productivity, and shows practitioners how to recognise and connect with symbols as an active and living manifestation of the personal and collective psyche. The book is illustrated with practical examples and case studies encountered by the authors during their 30 years of experience consulting the world's leading companies and institutions.

Nada O'Brien, PhD, has consulted for more than 20 years with leaders and groups across a wide scope of industries, including the Nordic Council of Ministers, the Norwegian National Health Service, international financial services organizations and pharmaceutical companies in the UK, Europe and USA. She is an accredited Jungian analyst and an alumnus of the C. G. Jung Institute, Switzerland.

John O'Brien, MBA and MA, has over 30 years of top-level experience as a consultant and coach to senior leaders, boards, leading banks and institutions, and executive teams in global corporates in the UK, USA, Europe and Asia. John, a former social worker, is an alumnus of the C. G. Jung Institute, Switzerland, an analyst of the C.G. Jung Dallas Institute and a member of the United Kingdom Council for Psychotherapy.

The Professional Practice of Jungian Coaching

Corporate Analytical Psychology

Edited by Nada O'Brien and
John O'Brien

Routledge
Taylor & Francis Group

LONDON AND NEW YORK

First published 2021
by Routledge
2 Park Square, Milton Park, Abingdon, Oxon OX14 4RN

and by Routledge
52 Vanderbilt Avenue, New York, NY 10017

Routledge is an imprint of the Taylor & Francis Group, an informa business

British Library Cataloguing-in-Publication Data
A catalogue record for this book is available from the British Library

Library of Congress Cataloging-in-Publication Data
A catalog record has been requested for this book

ISBN: 978-0-367-40411-6 (hbk)
ISBN: 978-0-367-40412-3 (pbk)
ISBN: 978-0-429-35598-1 (ebk)

Typeset in Bembo
by Swales & Willis, Exeter, Devon, UK

Contents

Contributors

Virginia Cochran Angel, PhD, JD, MA, LPC, is a Jungian Analyst in Houston, Texas. She received her Doctor of Jurisprudence from the University of Houston Law Center, her MA in Counseling Psychology from Pacifica Graduate Institute and her Diploma in Analytic Psychology from the C. G. Jung Institute in Zürich. Virginia is a member of the IAAP and the C. G. Jung Institute Dallas. She is on the board of trustees of the C. G. Jung Educational Center Houston, and the board of directors of the Jung Foundation Zürich.

Laurence Barrett has worked in senior roles for a number of global organizations, focusing on leadership development and organizational transformation. He holds an MSc in the Psychodynamics of Human Development from the British Psychotherapy Foundation and an MBA from the University of Lancaster. He trained as a coach and a coach supervisor with the Tavistock Institute and has completed the Foundation in Group Analysis at the Institute of Group Analysis. He also currently works as a Practicum Coach Supervisor with the INSEAD Executive Masters in Change.

Teresa Castleman, MA, is a Diplomate Jungian Analyst, Training Analyst for the C. G. Jung Institut of Zürich, the C. G. Jung Institute of Dallas and Vice President and Training Analyst for the C. G. Jung Institute of Colorado. Tess is an author, analyst, educator and retreat facilitator for over 30 years.

Frances V. Dare, MBA, is an Organizational and Leadership Consultant with specialties in executive coaching, organizational development, individual and team processes, diversity and inclusion, governance and change leadership. During her career she has served as a leader within, and a consultant to: Fortune 500 firms across multiple industries, health systems, trade associations, government ministries and social service agencies. Based in the US, she works globally. She holds a BA from Stephens College, an MBA from Southern Methodist University and is a certified coach. Frances is an affiliate coach with Executive Coaching Connections and practices through her own consultancy, Dare Advisory Group.

Michael Escamilla, MD, is a Professor of Psychiatry and Department Chair at the University of Texas Rio Grande Valley in Edinburg, Texas. He is board certified in Psychiatry and is also a member of the International Association of Analytical Psychology. He completed his undergraduate degree at Harvard, his MD at UT Southwestern and his Psychiatry training at the University of California at San Francisco. Dr Escamilla completed his training in Analytical Psychology at the C.G. Jung Institute of Zürich. He was an American Psychiatric Association Fellow in Psychiatric Genetics, also at UCSF, and has conducted seminal studies in the genetics of bipolar disorder and schizophrenia in Latino populations, funded by the National Institute of Mental Health (NIMH). He has served as an advisor to NIMH on psychiatric genetics research and has worked to teach recovery oriented psychiatric practice across the state of Texas. He was the founding director of the Center of Excellence in Neurosciences at Texas Tech University Health Science Center in El Paso, Texas. He has published over 100 journal articles and is the author of the book *Bleuler, Jung and the Creation of the Schizophrenias* (2016).

Carlos Ferreira has worked with global companies in business executive roles for the last 20 years. For the last decade he has focused his work on supporting global leaders, teams and organizations in Europe, Latin America and the US. With special expertise in analytical development and corporate cultural complexes, Carlos helps executives to increase self-awareness, creating and delivering balanced strategies and actions for meaningful, expressive and sustainable results. Carlos holds a MSc in Clinical Psychology and he is a Psychoanalyst and alumnus of the C. G. Jung Institute, Switzerland.

Sadiq Gillani is a Senior Vice President at Emirates, heading up their in-house consulting and transformation group. He is also a Lecturer in Management at Stanford University. Formerly a Senior Vice President Group Strategy with Lufthansa Group and Senior Vice President Network & Fleet Planning at Eurowings, he serves on the World Economic Forum's Global Future Council for Travel & Mobility. He completed his M.B.A. at Harvard Business School and holds a B.A. and M.Phil in Management Studies from Cambridge University. He was selected for the Financial Times Top 100 executives list, Capital Magazine's Top 40 under 40 and by the World Economic Forum as a Young Global Leader. He has visitied 120 countries and worked on 5 continents.

Dominique Lepori lives and works in her private practice in Zürich. Dominique is a Training Analyst, Supervisor and Lecturer of the C. G. Jung Institute, SGAP and IAAP Member, Sandplay Therapist, Supervisor and Teaching Member of the Sandplay Society, SGSST and ISST Certified Group Analyst, Member of SGAZ. She is a GAS MSc Psychologist and MA Economist HSG and CFA Member.

Janis Maxwell, PhD, is a Training Analyst and Supervisor at the C. G. Jung Institute, Kuesnacht, Switzerland. She has served as President and Director of Training of the Philadelphia Jung Institute, as well as Director of Training for the Inter-Regional Society of Jungian Analysts in the US. She holds degrees in mathematics and counselling psychology from the University of Central Arkansas.

Ms Maxwell also served as Corporate Assistant Secretary for a major Fortune 500 Company for several years before training to become a Jungian analyst. She is a member of IAAP, C. G. Jung Institute, Philadelphia Jung Institute, Inter-Regional Society of Jungian Analysts and Schweizerische Gesellschaft für Analytische Psychologie (SGAP, Swiss Society for Analytical Psychology).

Danijel Pantic is the Founder and Managing Director of ECG Summit and Eastern Bridge (Brussels) public sector consulting firms supporting cross border business change management initiatives in Western Europe. He graduated with an MA degree at the Law Faculty in Belgrade and received specialist education at Law School of the University in Leiden (Netherlands) and University in Vienna. With a corporate background as an Advisor and Researcher for Deloitte and the Economy Institute, Danijel became a significant contributor to the development of civil society organizations in Serbia. In the aftermath of the Yugoslav wars of the 1990s, between 2001 and 2006 he was Secretary General of the European Movement. A founder of the Serbian Association of Managers, Danijel was also Researcher in the Institute for European Studies in Belgrade.

Foreword
Sadiq Gillani

This book comes at an important time for the corporate world, as it starts to embrace diversity in senior leadership. Whilst every region is at a different stage of embracing diversity, this change is disrupting the organizational psyche and traditional model of leadership. I was appointed to be Chief Strategy Officer of Deutsche Lufthansa, Europe's largest airline, in 2011 at the age of 32 and not yet speaking a word of German. As I looked around at my first meeting of the top fifty leaders, I saw forty-five white German men over the age of 50 and the meeting language was switched to English for the first time so that I could participate. The corporate culture was very German and very conservative and enabled people with similar backgrounds to succeed. The new CEO also appointed five female leaders within a few months to try to modernise the culture. This was in stark contrast to the traditional corporate culture of promoting from within and we were seen as outsiders.

Having graduated with a Harvard MBA and with seven years of consulting experience, I was well prepared for the strategic content of my role and my mission to develop a turnaround strategy for the company. However, this training did not prepare me for navigating the corporate culture and psychology. I was offered the support of having a corporate coach and John O'Brien's Jungian psychology background stood out for me. Since then, John has been by my side, helping me develop, understand the landscape and have an impact during each of my subsequent roles. He has taught me how to apply corporate analytical psychology and to understand the unconscious forces at play in the board room.

I learned (the hard way) that the organizational psyche didn't like surprises or change. I learned that when a senior colleague was emotionally upset at me for not being consulted, that responding with rational arguments would be counterproductive. I learned how to apply Jungian type psychology to understand the personalities of my senior stakeholders to interact in a way which would resonate with them. I learned how common narcissists are in senior leadership positions, what drives them and how to work with them. Organizational politics are hard to understand as an outsider and it requires a lot of effort to build trust among your new colleagues. This book provides a comprehensive user guide to navigating corporate systems, grounded in Jungian psychology and understand what drives people to take certain actions.

Business schools and consulting firms train people to only focus on results and that can lead to blind spots. To be effective we also have to understand the culture, the mindset of leaders and the psyche. In organizations there are often repeating patterns of family structures playing out. There are organizational scars from previous failures. There is often an inherent risk aversion, built up over many years. Coming in fresh into an organization, one has to learn the culture whilst convincing people to trust us. As a leader with a diverse background, it becomes even harder to gain trust as people tend to like those who are similar. The 20/60/20 rule applies quite accurately in these situations: 20% of people can be convinced to support you, but 20% of people will be at best sceptical and at worst out to destroy you. The real challenge is to work on the middle 60%, using your supporters to help. In most companies trust comes with time rather than fresh ideas, making it challenging for newcomers.

As the trend of diversity in any sense or form continues to influence corporations, organizational cultures and psyches are being disrupted for the better. However, it takes a lot of time to embed the new leaders and there will be casualties along the way. Often the organization rejects them, like a foreign object inside the body. It takes a lot of resilience for the new leaders to overcome these challenges as well as to understand corporate psychology to positively transform the energy unleashed.

Introduction

The untapped alchemy of organizations: a 21st-century vision for human development and organizational transformation within corporations

Frances V. Dare

Two books published in the early 1990s captured the public imagination. One focused on organizational transformation through systems thinking, new mental models and team learning. The second focused on personal transformation by reconnecting with instincts, passion, creativity and wisdom through myths, fairy tales, folktales and stories. The first, *The fifth discipline: the art and practice of learning organizations* by Peter Senge (1990), would sell more than 1million copies. The second, *Women who run with the wolves: myths and stories of the wild woman archetype* by Clarissa Pinkola Estés (1992), spent 2 years on the New York Times bestseller list. Clearly, the desire to reinvent the organizations within which people spend their working lives and a parallel desire to restore personal vitality and creativity were active in what psychologist Carl Jung would call 'the collective unconscious'.

Thirty years later, the work of reinventing corporations and organizations continues in earnest. That work is supported by a pantheon of professional consultants, and an array of business publications, leadership approaches and management theories. In the private realm, self-help books, seminars and coaches for everything from diet, exercise, life balance and professional success abound. What does that say about collective and individual progress toward organizational success and personal fulfilment? Why do business performance and personal fulfilment remain in separate realms?

In a career spanning the same three decades I've seen, experienced and wrestled with the challenges of optimising business performance while also providing fulfilling work and personal growth for my teams. As a leader within several global corporations, and a consultant to many respected 'big logo' companies, I've led initiatives for growth and transformation utilising a range of practices and methodologies. Yet something has almost always seemed missing. In recent years, applying Jung-based approaches to individual, team and corporate development has provided a crucial missing piece and helped achieve deeper, more lasting transformation.

And so, two decades into the new century, it's important to ask a number of crucial questions. How fully have business and organizational transformation approaches responded to critical professional and personal questions of our time? Are most corporations fully capable of successful growth and evolution? How can corporations build adaptable organizations as they evolve? How do corporations and their leaders sustain the human creativity and passion that fuels top performance and innovation? Are most corporations truly structures of value for their investors, the people they employ and the consumers they serve? A few examples from modern corporate life illuminate the current answers. They also light a path to the future.

Most founders starting a business are passionate about the core service or product as well as the company they hope to build. In recent decades it has become fashionable to state foundational values for the new enterprise. Those values are meant as North stars for meaningful work and a socially committed venture. They are often displayed on posters and T-shirts, memorialised in slides and highlighted in investor pitches. At best, the values are deeply shared, aligned with workers' and consumers' personal values, and lived by all. More commonly, they are more press release platitudes than soulful realities.

As a nascent organization grows and evolves, the intimacy found among early employees with shared experiences wanes. The communication of passion, commitment and values is relegated to new hire orientation, organized corporate meetings, team retreats and organizational development consultancy; often with diminishing success over time. Employees may feel disconnected from the 'heart' of the business but cannot explain why. And of course, the corporation evolves. Products and services multiply. Geographic expansion happens. Mergers and acquisitions take place. Corporations face the seeming paradox of how to retain spirit and values, essentially the corporate soul, while evolving and adapting for business and financial success. A modern-day parable shows how the journey may unfold.

This mythical company was founded in the middle of the past century. The founders were not types to sit in a conference room defining core values. Instead values emerged, as the most meaningful values often do, through the actions, ethics and beliefs of the early leaders. If asked, employees would describe values such as: 'work incredibly hard but always take care of your people, especially in times of crisis'; 'compete fiercely but always ethically and with integrity'; 'do not let anything get in the way of serving customers'. Less scripted and more organic, the values were real and lived across the organization. Contact with leaders, especially the legendary CEO, was frequent and often informal.

Thirty years into the company's growth the founder passes the CEO baton to another early leader. The core values remain alive and central to continued success. Yet as early employees retire and the first CEO from outside the company arrives, the founding values and culture fade. Frequent layoffs to deliver bottom-line numbers result in fear and uncertainty countering the original value of people care. Complexity and bureaucracy make serving customers more and more of a challenge with less empowered front line employees. The best efforts of external consultants are made. These included the CEO's personal leadership coach. A new mission and values are developed but morale wanes. Employee passion fades. At the same time, many leaders and managers remain committed to the company, customers and workers. Examples of high-performing individuals, teams and business units remain. Yet company performance suffers. In the end, the mythical corporation's decline continues and it's acquired by a competitors. The once-storied brand vanishes. What lessons can be learned from this tale? How might the values and vitality from the corporation's early life have lived on even as the company evolved and expanded?

Creating an intrinsic, 'change-able' capability across an enterprise has many dimensions, again grounded in key questions. How are effective leaders at all levels and across the organization best identified, nurtured, rewarded and promoted? How do leaders generate and sustain a consistent organizational culture? Every organization has both exemplary and toxic leaders, high-performing and low performing employees. Paradoxes abound. How can it be that one leader's superstar employee is another leader's below-par performer? Like the tale of the Ugly Duckling, are employees expected to look and act just like all others in the flock (despite a proclaimed commitment to diversity)? What accounts for wildly different reviews of a leader from various direct reports?

Investments the size of small nation GDPs are spent each year identifying individual leadership styles and strengths through tools such as StrengthsFinder, the Myers-Briggs Type Indicator, and Leadership Practices Inventory®. Skills training for active listening, effective feedback and team-building abound, as does diversity training. Optimal leadership behaviours are described, taught and evaluated. Early and mid-career leaders who show promise are mentored and coached. Despite all the training and development, what is missing? What gets in the way of being a consistently good leader? Why does one leader click with some employees and conflict with others? How do varying interpersonal relationships and interactions impact the corporate culture?

Organizations with good success in the 'up, down and across' leadership realm have a foundation for change. When specific initiatives are planned, new services designed, or business acquired, many organizations believe they are ready to embrace the new. Most recognise and implement well-studied and widely adopted change leadership practices. Change champions are identified, communication campaigns created and training programmes designed. Often these are sufficient and successful. Just as often the desired change is inconsistent across the organization, slower than hoped for, or even a failure that sets the organization back. With all the tremendous research behind change management and leadership effectiveness what may still be missing?

A close cousin to change and adaptability, the art and science of innovation is also well studied. From ideation through implementation, multiple approaches and best practices have been published and deployed. At the same time, many organizations wrestle with a seeming loss of creativity. Innovation is seen as grand breakthroughs. Innovation often becomes the domain of dedicated teams rather than a corporate capability that keeps the energy and soul of the enterprise alive. The equally important enterprise-wide creativity that delivers delighted customers and energised workers wanes. The energy and spontaneity of work can be lost in process standardisation and diminished by poor leadership and unfulfilling work. Many executives worry about the future and how the next wave of products, customers and passionate, engaged employees will be found.

Jung's depth psychology offers solutions for many of the unanswered questions to organizational dilemmas. The individual and collective unconscious can be revealed by working with archetypes, stories, symbols and lived experience. More fully aware and creative organizations can successfully innovate, evolve and grow. By applying criteria less about behaviours and more about underlying beliefs, emotions and values, effective teams and leaders can be nurtured. By understanding individual and group complexes, community can be strengthened and healthy cultures sustained.

There is no question that corporations of all kinds have evolved significantly since the closing decade of the past century. Many provide rewarding environments for workers, financial returns for investors and business success measured by efficiency and quality. For these organizations, a core question is how to go beyond the success achieved with traditional business and management approaches. Other corporations struggle to engage workers, remain competitive and achieve the financial performance expected by investors and markets. These organizations wrestle with the problem of how to transform when available business and management approaches have been tried and exhausted. Most important for all is the critical question of the 21st century of how to reinvent corporations or to create entirely new corporate models reflecting the societal, environmental and ethical demands of this era. Demographic, geographic, political and social forces demand more of 21st-century corporations. The growing global Benefit Corporation movement signals a sea change in organizational archetypes and business models. In the midst of powerful prevailing forces can be heard a new clarion call. The call is to integrate and apply business science, systems theory, psychology, cultural anthropology, neuroscience and more to catalyse adaptable, innovative high-performing corporations. Organizations that also fill and fuel the human soul. Enterprises that embrace both human and corporate development will chart the course. The promise of 21st-century corporations is one of organizations in which personal and professional, individual and corporate, flourish for generations to come.

This book presents readers with both theoretical foundations and supporting evidence for corporate development based upon Carl Jung's analytic psychology. Throughout, readers will find examples of the practical application of *corporate analytic psychology* along with the professional practice of Jungian coaching and consulting. Combined, the chapters that follow provide theoretical and practical guidance for the art of corporate analytical psychology as a catalyst to create 21st-century corporations and achieve the promise of fully human, dynamic enterprises.

References

Estés, CP 1992, *Women who run with the wolves: myths and stories of the wild woman archetype*, Ballantine Books, New York.
Senge, PM 1990, *The fifth discipline: the art and practice of the learning organization*, Doubleday/Currency, New York.

Part I

Corporations and psyche

Chapter 1

The corporate soul

Janis Maxwell

Author's dreams

I am on the thirty-fifth floor of the tallest building in Baltimore. The building begins to shake and I know that a devastating earthquake is happening. I also know that the building will collapse. I grab white sheets, tie them together and lower myself to the ground. I run. I survive.

I am summoned to the basement of the company. Armed ninja-type soldiers, men and women, have taken the workers hostage and line them up. I ask colleagues, 'what is going on?' 'We are being taken over by a Japanese army', is the answer. 'Just do what they tell you to do'. I look around and see 'trust coupons' on a chair. I know that these will be my ticket out.

Shifting realities

A few years after the dreams cited above, the Fortune 500 company that had been the pride of a city and a state for generations, and in which I was an executive officer, was acquired by an overseas company and subjected to asset stripping. This is a process of buying and dismantling companies, and selling the parts to achieve net gains. The previous CEO and upper management had lost sight of what a healthy organization should have been and had paved the way for the sale and dismemberment. It became a portrait of the disintegration of a corporation that had lost its way. It had lost its soul. On one level, the dreams seemed to have warned that the organization would be taken over by an alien energy and would not survive. In this respect, the dreams were personal but also had a collective meaning.

These dreams occurred before there was any indication that massive changes were about to take place in my world and in the corporate culture of which I was a part. They indicated a world of shifting realities where nothing was what it appeared to be. The maladies that followed in this organization and every organization with which it was affiliated became matters of great concern not only of their leaders, but to every person connected to them.

What happened then and since resulted in much soul searching by the many leaders who sought ways to adapt to the changing world. What had once been functional seemed to be caught in the currents of time and no longer worked in many cases. Taking into account not only a corporate view, but a universal world view, new paradigms were on the horizon. Leadership needed new ideas to meet the changing times, but old paradigms were difficult to change. What could have been the cause of such a dysfunctional situation which affected so many?

It seems that the connection between the body corporate, the spirit of the organization and its soul had been lost. Loss of soul and disconnection from the spirit that rules individuals and corporations contributed to loss of meaning, violence and disintegration. This has affected many of the institutions that have guided and supported culture to unimaginable heights in some parts of the world. Foundational beliefs have been shaken to the core. Perhaps a missed opportunity was the potential connection to a new paradigm.

My view is that caring for the soul of the individual parts of the corporate body is inextricably linked to the generation of profit and could actually increase it. It follows that individuals and world leaders must reflect on how to recover the soul. Some seem to unable to 'hear' and 'see' the coming age. Many seem to have no meaningful connection to the unconscious, to dreams or imagination which could point out the avoidable dangers and perhaps show alternative ways forward.

Idea of the corporate soul

What do we mean when we talk about the soul? It is an idea that is traditionally associated with religions, supported by the underlying myths and the archetypes embedded in them. It often seems that the word 'soul' has been 'relegated to the fringes of the worldview, banished to the marginal existence of the private sphere or has otherwise disappeared altogether' (Gieser 2005, p. 197). But today, many of the foundation myths of corporate culture, while not necessarily religious in nature, still suggest both the presence of a corporate soul and the dangers inherent in the soul's journey.

Corporate culture is based primarily on the lure of the 'bottom line'. A primary goal has been to take care of stockholders by delivering short term profit. This may now be changing in so far as more corporate leaders realise that the automatic drive for short term profit does not necessarily make a healthier organization. Companies such as Microsoft seem to see that taking care of the parts that contribute to their success is vital. For every corporate leader under the sway of greed who possesses a limited understanding of the wise use of wealth, there are others who contribute to making the world a better place. Companies that treat their employees well, making certain that they address the 'bottom line' of people, planet and profit, are more likely to be healthy enterprises, assured of success.

Since leaving the company and becoming a Jungian analyst, I have often thought about how a corporation is like an individual. In fact, the Supreme Court of the United States has decided that corporations have legal rights and responsibilities called by some 'corporate personhood' (Torres-Spelliscy 2014). US courts have thus extended certain constitutional protections to corporations similar to those granted to individuals. What became obvious to me was that the concepts that C. G. Jung used to describe the individual psyche, the soul, were also applicable to organizations. In the corporate structure, one can imagine an ego, a Shadow, an Anima, an Animus and the higher organizing function, the Self (CW 9i). For example, the ego energy of the ruling conscious attitude can be seen in the leadership functions responsible for the health and well-being of the corporate structure and its constituent parts. These are usually formally represented by the CEO and executive team. For Jung, the centre was the Self, the organizing function of the psyche. When an individual or other organizational leader loses touch with that centre, disintegration starts to occur and the body begins to fall apart. Individuals in such an environment often become ill. Leaders who become disconnected from their soulful source of initial success run the risk of suffering neurosis or symptoms of disease. Sometimes they are described as the 'walking dead'.

Recognising that behind the ego, there is an active organizing function which Jung called the Self, is important. H. G. Baynes (1940), in *Mythology of the soul*, illustrates the power of an organizing centre with reference to an example drawn from the insect world. Baynes tells the story of a species of termite in South Africa which consists of communities of thousands of individual termites. These insects, which are both blind and deaf, build architectural structures, make aqueducts to depths of 100 feet for water supply, make gardens for cultivation of fungus which are necessary for digestion and heat, repair walls and make structures which defend the community from invasion. There is no organ which could serve as a brain in which instinctual apprehension can reside. Yet, however distant the termites might be from the queen's cell, the instant the queen is killed every member of this vast organization ceases work and dissolution begins. The power emanating from the queen cannot be conceived in concrete terms. There is no demonstrable path of communication. If a steel plate is driven through the termitary, so that one half is completely separated from the other, the highly coordinated activity goes on as if no obstacle were present. The queen has never performed any of these specialised activities of the sexless termites. Her life is confined and she is immobile in a cell from which she can never emerge. The workers and soldiers have no organs of generation. Therefore, the pattern of activities which they represent is not handed down by them. (Baynes 1940, pp. 754–755).

We might consider this analogous to Jung's concept of the Self as a universal power which includes the physical world. Similarly, the corporate organism,' be it an individual or an organization, is a psychic whole. The Self could also be described as the guiding energy that informs the ego. When thus guided and in harmony, these elements of the psyche, the soul, create a life of meaning and connection to the common good. When we speak of the corporate soul, we are speaking of business, economics, politics, religion and individuals. We are speaking of an entity that is held together and ruled by leaders who have the interest of the 'body' at heart and that rules with those factors in mind. In my experience, effective leadership understands the changing patterns and is open to guidance from dreams and synchronicities, and from those invisible spirits that lead into the future.

A healthy leader is critical for a healthy corporation. In mythology and fairy tales, the king represents the conscious ruling attitude. If the king is healthy, the kingdom thrives. If not, then the kingdom becomes barren. There are numerous tales about sick kings, where the land becomes barren, where nothing can live and thrive. In this respect, King Saul and Nebuchad-nezzar of Biblical lore can be considered as examples of psychic illness. There also is the legend of King of Arthur and Holy Grail. These are all stories that provide guidance about what happens and what to do when leadership becomes sick and out of touch with the soul. The body (corporate) must be connected to the soul and the spirit to be healthy and to thrive.

Healthy corporations

What is a corporation? How would we describe its soul if we agree it should or does have one? As C. G. Jung and others have demonstrated, an individual human being is constituted of many parts which work together as a whole to function in a healthy way. The world soul, the Anima Mundi, operates in a similar way. According to several systems of thought, the world soul is an intrinsic connection between all living things on the planet, and relates to the world in much the same way as the soul is connected to the human being. Plato (1937) adhered to this idea which became an important continuity in most Neoplatonic systems. The belief that the world is indeed a living being endowed with a soul and intelligence, a single visible living entity containing all other living entities which by their nature are all related, accords with Jung's idea of the Self.

So how might we address these issues of loss of soul? Begg (1972) argues that there are three things that must come together to affect and transform culture: an archetypal aspect, an individual aspect and an historical aspect with its profound virtue of the human soul. When one of these is ignored, then the whole cultural structure suffers and eventually dies, as evidenced by the company in which I worked. The archetypal aspect is the energy behind the outer reality, the Zeitgeist, the structuring elements and the fuel for a meaningful life. Archetypes are the powers behind these realities. They manifest in accordance with the culture in which they appear. This aspect can be imagined as a war in heaven, for example, by St. Michael and his angels fighting the dragon, attempting to bring harmony to the world. In the soul, this battle is the urge toward wholeness, harmony and balance. The individual aspect is what carries this energy into the world. The historical aspect is especially important as much of the information that we need to connect body, soul and spirit has been lost in the mists of time.

The prevailing myth that has supported the corporate soul has been much like the fabled dragon that hoards its gold. It is hidden in the depths of a mountain or, in a modern manifestation, in offshore accounts, unavailable to support the soul, the body and the spirit of an organization. But perhaps we can also imagine an Oriental dragon, a life-giving and a beneficent source of power.

Organizational psychologist Jerry Harvey (1988, 1999) writes about corporate life and what happens when an organization goes down a wrong road, losing its connection to soul and spirit. Its people become depressed. They are separated from something that has supported them emotionally and has provided meaning to life. Many become ill like the children who develop anaclitic depression as a result of early loss. If not reconnected to a source of emotional life (a mother symbol) within a short period, they can die or remain permanently injured in body and soul. A company that values its employees by providing them not only with material reward but also an environment where individual spirit and soul can unite with the corporate body to become whole is a healthy corporation. Its parts work together for the common good, just as the different parts of the psyche work together with the different parts of the body to be a healthy human being. The dragon then becomes beneficent and life-enhancing.

Theodore Abt (1989) indicates that man can handle many life issues, but cannot tolerate a meaningless life. He believes that the soul and dreams that issue from a soul place cannot be ignored in development planning. He believes that messages from the unconscious must be taken concretely in many instances:

> I hope to make it evident that the hinterland of our soul, our emotional background, is a reality that absolutely must be given its full due when we set to work on collective problems. If this is not done, the background of our soul will make its demands felt in the form of all sorts of irrational disturbances and spiritual epidemics.
>
> (Abt 1989, p. 19)

He advocates a more holistic approach in which we are connected to each other, to the earth and to the universe. We no longer live in a bounded world. The internet has connected us to each other, to the world and to the depths of the universe in unimaginable ways, both creative and destructive. It could be that the internet has changed the prevailing myths that hold the archetypal energies that organise life on this planet. Perhaps it is possible to progress, to go forward in a soulful way, if we become aware of the reality of the soul.

Bottom line

What is the 'bottom line'? Could it be that we must develop a new world view that recovers forgotten truths, and retrieves the soul from the fringes of modern society? In my view, we must bring a more feminine view, being more receptive, creating a container that holds and bears life, and hearing and nurturing the voice from the unconscious. We can communicate this voice of the potential of the future to leadership in corporate and institutional life. The body corporate cannot survive without change. We must return to retrieve what has been lost, a connection to the soul.

Thomas Moore's (1992) bestseller *Care of the soul*, has been described as a book for troubled times. Moore writes that 'care of the soul touches another dimension (…) we honor its expressions' (p. 304). For me, that dimension is the realm of dreams, visions and imagination. Leaders who take seriously their task of caring for the soul pay careful attention to the messages from this realm.

My dreams of the demise of the corporation, which had supported me and thousands of others for years and which had provided an environment in which soul could thrive, were instructive. That I would survive to take a different path in life was not evident at the time. Only years later would I understand that the dreams were prophetic. C. G. Jung's work and his journeys into the world of the soul have both informed and enabled me to approach leadership in a more holistic manner. I listen to dreams in a new way, and use imagination as a partner to bring new ideas and understanding to whatever group with which I am involved. As a result, I have been privileged with leadership roles in the Jungian world, which allow me to facilitate new understandings of the depth process necessary for success.

Ancient wisdom tells us that when the time is right, transformation can become a reality. Leaders in institutions are looking for ways to transform leadership in a changing world. That time may be now.

References

Abt, T 1989, *Progress without loss of soul: toward a holistic approach to modernization planning*, Chiron, Wilmette.
Baynes, HG 1940, *Mythology of the soul*, Bailliere, Tindall and Cox, London.
Begg, I 1972, 'The theme of the turning point in Lord of the Rings', final thesis, C. G. Jung Institute, Kusnacht.
Gieser, S 2005, *The innermost kernel: depth psychology and quantum physics. Wolfgang Pauli's dialogue with C. G. Jung*, Springer, Berlin.

Harvey, J 1988, *The Abilene paradox and other meditations on management*, Maxwell Macmillan International, New York.

Harvey, J 1999, *How come every time I get stabbed in the back, my fingerprints are on the knife? and other meditations on management*, Jossey-Bass, San Francisco.

Jung, CG 1968, 'The archetypes of the collective unconscious', in HRead, MFordham, GAdler and WMcGuire (eds.), *The collected works of C. G. Jung* (CW), trans. RFC Hull, CW 9i, Princeton University Press, Princeton. pp. 341.

Moore, T 1992, *Care of the soul*, Harper Collins, New York.

Plato 1937, 'Timaeus', in *The dialogues of Plato*, trans. B. Jowett, vol. 2, Random House, New York. p. 34.

Torres-Spelliscy, C 2014, 'The history of corporate personhood', Brennan Center for Justice, viewed on 9 December 2019, www.brennancenter.org/our-work/analysis-opinion/history-corporate-personhood.

Chapter 2

Corporations and psyche

John O'Brien

The corporate world is a seeming paradox. It feeds clothes and provides shelter for the greater part of the human race. It globalises provision of goods and services, vocational opportunities and human rights. And it is the opposite. It deprives, dehumanises and destroys. A phenomenon of human organization it is also the source of economic, diplomatic, military and information power which both fuels and decides the fates of governments.

What then is a corporation? Is it an embodiment of a noble spirit which animates the finest endeavours of the human race? Is it an instrument of self-interest, power and warfare? What forces are invoked when a corporation is formed and whom does it serve?

Our modern understanding of a corporation derives from its 17th-century definition as a trading organization chartered by the state, in some cases with a licence to kill. The Online etymology dictionary (2019) gives the definition of a 'legally authorised entity, artificial person created by law from a group or succession of persons'. It can include 'municipal governments and modern business companies' and can be regarded as 'a whole composed of united parts, a structure, system, community, corporation, political body, a guild' (Online etymology dictionary 2019).

In the early 20th century, Machen (1911) explained the legal tenet that 'from the earliest period of our judicial history, lawyers and judges have reiterated the doctrine that a corporation is an intangible legal entity, without body and without soul' (p. 1). He further noted the argument that they are created by the law. But he also drew attention to the seemingly opposite view that corporations are formed by groups of real people gathered together for a common purpose. Having reflected upon both positions, judicial and real, he concluded that corporations should correctly be regarded as recognised by the law but not created by it (1911, p. 262). Thus, corporations are real bodies of people which can act with will, and as argued by Dewey (1926), are therefore legally regarded as having moral personality.

Definitions from the 15th century given in the Online etymology dictionary (2019) include 'persons united in a body for some purpose', and the 'assumption of a body'. The incorporation of spirit is implicit in the supporting dictionary example given of the incarnation of Christ. Furthermore, the Latin verb 'corporare' means not only to 'embody, make or fashion into a body' but also 'to make into a corpse, kill' (Online etymology dictionary 2019).

In order to understand and engage with corporate groups and individual members from a psychological perspective which embraces both human and legal points of view, the term 'corporate psyche' will be introduced. This term will help to build a framework within which we can ask, 'To what extent should legal and real approaches be regarded as a healthy tension of opposites, or a potential symptom of a dissociation of personality?' We can also consider whether the different definitions make a cogent whole.

At first glance, the elements of legality, body of individuals with a purpose, spiritual incarnation and killing seem somewhat disparate, and the possibility of a combination into a useful definition of corporation seems quite remote. The different definitions arise from discrete fields of discourse. But a closer examination of the history of corporations provides an empirical basis for an integrated definition.

The East India Company

We find the essential elements above in the prototypes for modern corporations such as the British East India Company. According to Sicard (2015) earlier prototypes can be found in the Toulouse Mills of 14th-century France, which were financed by an elementary partnership structure.

The East India Company, however, was a formed society, legally authorised as an artificial person created by law. It had a body which was separate to its investors, and it was licensed to wage war, to kill. The incorporation of spirit is implicit in its Royal Charter granted in 1600 by Queen Elizabeth I being 'Defender of the Faith' and the Charter granted by 'special Grace' of the monarch (Shaw 1887). In those times in England, grace was understood in terms of Protestant Christianity. Initially a trading organization, over time the company built its own military force and administrative functions and effectively ruled large parts of India. Carson (2012) argues that in order to safeguard its assets and trade successfully across diverse cultures and beliefs, the company had initially adopted a policy of freedom of worship. Towards the end of the 18th century it came under increasing pressure to Christianise India, and this together with other factors such its diversification into the opium trade and its rapid expansion contributed to the Indian Rebellion of 1857. This resulted in the abolition of the company in 1858 and the establishment of the Raj, which lasted until 1847.

Sreni

A similar but different example is given by Khanna (2005) who states that the earliest forms of corporation are to be found in Ancient India, before

800 BCE in the form of *sreni* (early trade associations or guilds). He argues that they meet four of today's legal criteria for corporations; separate legal personality, centralised management, transferability of interest and limited liability. In this case, the spiritual element was assumed in so far as the *sreni* imposed laws of conduct upon their members in the form of *sreni dharma*, which derived from the various religious precepts at that time by which hunting and the killing of animals was a prohibited *sreni* activity. For example, Hindu dharma signified accordance with the original rhythmic order of life, or *Rta*, expressed in a code of conduct. Jainism dharma included the codes for purification and moral transformation.

Spirit in Roman corporations

The question of the spirit of the corporation was carefully considered in Rome, and particularly in Justinian's Code (529 to 565 CE), the *Corpus Juris Civilis* (Frier, 2016), which provided the context for the concept of corporation, or 'corpora' derived from Stoic philosophy. Patterson (1983) noted that the general theory states that objects which appear to be separate have an inner *spirit* and that it is this *spiritus* which gives identity to the material object. This force was considered to operate independently of the material object. Organizations were regarded as a special class of corpora, which would remain intact regardless of the longevity of constituent members. They were treated with greater or lesser restriction according to the exigencies of the state. These types of corpora were not intended as legally personalities as 'were not meant to be fictitious persons or simply entities with state endowed artificial personalities' (Patterson 1983, pp. 87–98).

For clarity, this chapter assumes an overlap of meaning between the terms 'psyche', 'spirit' and 'soul' and *The concise Oxford dictionary* (2011) definitions of the latter two terms are used for reference. Soul is defined as 'the spiritual or immaterial part of a person, regarded as immortal', and spirit is defined as 'the non-physical part of a person which is the seat of emotions and character'.

Example: spirit in a national government

The spiritual question appears to be pertinent to the operation of corporations of all kinds, including governments. For example, the flow through of spiritual authority from individuals and groups, to government, to the law and onward to corporate governance is perhaps most apparent in the relationship between the United States Declaration of Independence (1776) and the Constitution (1787). The former is based on the social and spiritual premise that 'all men are created equal, that they are endowed by their Creator with certain unalienable Rights, that among these are Life, Liberty and the pursuit of Happiness'. The spirit is carried through to Constitution in the next phrase; 'That to secure these Rights, Governments are instituted among Men, deriving their just Powers from the Consent of the Governed'. The Declaration of Independence and Constitution appear to be linked analogously to the first and second tablets of Mosaic Law as described by Roger Williams, the first table representing Divine Law and the Second, its interpretation and application to the secular the governance of human behaviour (Hall 1998, p. 77).

What is a corporation?

Taking into account the above examples, for the purpose of this book the author now gives the following working definition. *A corporation is an organized body incorporated from spirit, created by people bonding together for a specific purpose, chartered and therefore legally recognised and restricted by the law of the state.* In accepting this definition, it should be noted that there are corporate bodies which are not recognised in law, such as criminal organizations, revolutionary and terrorist movements, secret sects and so on. While worthy of consideration, they are beyond the scope of this book.

Questions

We might now pose a number of the questions. What happens if the flow of spiritual authority is diverted? What happens if the use of law becomes disconnected with the spirit upon which it is founded? Similarly, what happens if a business corporation loses connection with its spirit, expressed in values statements such as 'we respect and value our employees'? In this case, could this hazard be a factor contributing to the waves of mental illness suffered by workers in some of today's companies? According to the World Health Organization (2019) the estimated cost of depression and anxiety to the global economy is $1 trillion in lost productivity, with harassment and bullying at work being commonly reported problems. Work related issues include

> inadequate health and safety policies, poor communication and management practices, limited participation in decision-making or low control over one's area of work; low levels of support for employees, inflexible working hours; and unclear tasks or organizational objectives.
>
> (World Health Organization 2019)

It is doubtful whether these outcomes relate to the founding spirit and are consistent with the espoused values of the companies in question.

The motto of the City of London is 'Domine Dirige Nos' (Lord guide us). How can we then account for the fact that there were no successful criminal prosecutions of UK banks in the period January 2008 to

December 2018, whereas in the same period nearly twenty U.S. criminal actions against New York and London based banks succeeded? (Thompson 2019). A great deal of effort and cost is involved in recruiting and developing corporate leaders. So, what is happening? What forces are at work in corporations which produce such predatory outputs as economic crime, exploitative labour practices, infringements of human rights and so on?

What differentiates those corporations which take humanity forward with leaps of scientific advancement, and are also wellsprings of creativity, generating wealth for all concerned? How can corporations continually refresh and renew their vitality and their animating forces? The questions are critical for all areas of corporate activity: making a profit and/or creating social benefit; efficiently delivering goods and services; maintaining adaptive capability; attracting and retaining talent; avoiding corruption; and behaving morally in a complex and demanding world.

Is it not curious that corporations sometimes base decisions on the delusion of actually being an intangible entity, without body and soul? Could this be regarded as a form of legalism, i.e. using the law to pursue power and control without a spiritual or moral reference? Could it be that this confusion or abuse of terms destroys integrity? What would be the consequences of real people and groups behave as intangible entities? Might such behaviour meet the diagnostic criteria for mental conditions such as antisocial personality disorder (DSM-5, p. 661)?

As contributors to the field of study and practice of Jungian coaching and consulting, we are concerned with the psychological realities of all systems from which emanate declarations, constitutions, expressed values, visions and missions, behaviours, goods and services, and social influence. These are indeed powerful forces which require consciousness, alertness, and self-awareness. Without considerable effort we are left in the grip of forces unknown which produce consequences neither understood nor wished for by the well-intended rational mind, or the morally informed corporate will. How can we now start to explore these forces? More importantly, how can integrity be strengthened where it is found and restored where it has been lost?

References

Carson, P 2012, 'The East India Company and religion, 1698–1858', in *Worlds of the East India Company series*, vol. 7, Boydell Press Woodbridge, Cambridge University Press, Suffolk, p. 7.

Declaration of Independence: a transcription 1776, The US National Archives, viewed on 5 December 2019, www.archives.gov/founding-docs/declaration-transcript.

Dewey, J 1926, 'The historic background of corporate legal personality', *Yale Law Journal*, vol. 35, no. 6, pp. 655–673.

Frier, B (ed) 2016, *The Codex of Justinian*, vol. 3, Hardback Set: A new annotated translation, with parallel Latin and Greek text (English, Ancient Greek and Latin edition), trans. F. Blume, Cambridge University Press, Cambridge.

Hall, TL 1998, *Separating church and state: Roger Williams and religious liberty*, University of Illinois Press, Chicago.

Khanna, V 2005, 'The economic history of the corporate form in Ancient India', discussion papers, Michigan University, viewed on 17 December 2019, www.law. umich.edu/centersandprograms/lawandeconomics/abstracts/Pages/05-014.aspx.

Machen, JR 1911, 'Corporate personality', *Harvard Law Review*, vol. 24, no. 4, pp. 253–267, DOI:10.2307/1324056.

Patterson, JL 1983, 'The development of the concept of corporation from earliest Roman times to A.D. 476', *Accounting Historians Journal*, vol. 10, no. 1, pp. 87–98.

Shaw, J 1887, *Charters relating to the East India Company from 1600–1761*, Madras Government Press, Madras.

Sicard, G 2015, *The origins of corporations: the mills of Toulouse in the Middle Ages*, trans. M Landry, Yale University Press, New Haven.

Thompson, B 2019, 'UK's poor record on corporate crime comes under attack', *Financial Times*, viewed on 5 December 2019, www.ft.com/content/52101b3e-3f51-11e9-b896-fe36ec32aece.

World Health Organization 2019, *Mental health in the workplace: information sheet*, viewed on 5 December 2019, www.who.int/mental_health/in_the_workplace/en/.

Chapter 3

Introducing corporate analytical psychology

Nada O'Brien

Since the development of coaching and corporate consulting services to organizations during the early 1990s, there has been a proliferation of approaches, theories, methods and techniques trying to explain and deal with the underlying patterns which govern organizational life. During that time we have studied, applied and developed practical coaching in accordance with the evolutionary pressure of adding measurable added value to individuals and organizations in many countries around the world. Working with various types of organizations within the framework of analytical psychology, a particular framework for grasping the complex, multidimensional dynamic of organizational life began to crystallise.

Discussions with colleagues, clients and experts from similar and different disciplines have greatly contributed to the articulation of a framework for the emerging scientific discipline. This process has coincided with the popularisation of coaching and consulting approaches, tools and practices labelled as 'Jungian'. While such interest in analytical psychology is most welcome, bearing in mind the risks associated with depth psychology we strongly advocate that at this point in time, practice must be professionalised to safeguard client welfare, professional integrity and ethics. A fundamental requirement is a full clinical analytic training which filters and prepares those willing to undertake the rigours of personal analysis and the responsibilities of professional practice.

Corporate analytical psychology is the science of analytical psychology applied to corporate life. It is interdisciplinary by nature, involving scientific fields such as business management, economics and finance, education, law, technology and politics. The corporate analytical psychology field of enquiry is concerned with all areas related to corporate life. Applying Jungian lenses to the study of corporate phenomena includes observations of the embodied energy, the energy transformation process and the underlying principles governing corporate life and spirit of the time. The aim of corporate analytical psychology is to develop a theoretical and practical framework for understanding and facilitating the individuation process on the individual, group and collective levels in relation to corporate phenomena. As with analytical psychology, corporate analytical psychology is hermeneutic and synthetic in the nature of its approach with a concept of development based on the mutual influence of applied experience and research (Jones & Mehr 2007).

The main topics are listed below and are studied in the relevant chapters of the book:

- Principles of the energy transformation process in organizations
- Structure of psyche in individuals, groups and organizations
- The individuation process in individuals, groups and organizations
- Corporate complexes
- Trauma
- The *field* in organizations
- Corporate culture
- Corporate analytical psychology practice: Jungian coaching and consulting
- Methods
- Ethics

Research methodology and practice methods are based on the analytical psychology framework. Specific features of corporate analytical psychology methods are described in the book chapters of this volume: 'Corporate analytical psychology topics', 'Corporate analytical psychology methods', 'Application of corporate analytical psychology: Jungian coaching and consulting' and 'Ethics'.

An understanding of the principles of organizational life is relevant to all corporate stakeholders. The role of corporate analytical psychology practitioners is to facilitate the individuation process on the individual, group and organizational level within the corporate context. Corporate analytical psychology will therefore be examined within the framework of Jungian coaching and consulting, the practical form it has taken during recent years. Corporate analytical psychology is a base from which practical methods and tools for professional practice of Jungian coaching and consulting are researched, designed and developed for use in the corporate world.

Part I of this book 'Corporations and psyche' introduces actual dilemmas and challenges regarding corporations and their role in the present Zeitgeist, taking the reader through the historical definitions of what corporation is. Part II outlines the fundamentals of analytical psychology and post Jungian research, setting the ground for the introduction of the theoretical framework of corporate analytical psychology. A brief historical overview of the development of corporate analytical psychology, together with the main topics and methods, are presented in Part III of the book.

The professional practice of corporate analytical psychology begins with a description of Jungian coaching and consulting concepts and describes the practice through different categories. Discussion of ethics of Jungian coaching and consulting with an archetypal perspective follows in Part V. Separate attention is given to practice in organizations which are corporate by definition but do not fall into the category of business corporations. These include examples of prisons, forensic investigators and international football. Examples from different categories have been selected for their potential to show new perspectives which might cross fertilise.

Closing reflections include observations of corporations in the spirit of the times and the emerging, transformative role of Jungian coaches and consultants. New developments and potential realities as yet unknown are considered in the final chapter.

Reference

Jones, R & Mehr, S 2007, 'Foundations and assumptions of the scientist-practitioner model', *American Behavioral Scientist*, vol. 50, pp. 766–771.

Part II

Carl Jung's analytical psychology and post Jungian research

Chapter 4

Fundamental concepts of analytical psychology

Nada O'Brien

It is curious that we tend to base our decisions, reality checks and actions in important aspects of life upon our conscious reasoning while actually we are mostly unconscious. Neuroscience informs us that we are only aware of a very small percentage of our cognition, while in fact our ways of being are overwhelmingly dependent upon the brain activity rooted in the unconscious. US News and World Report state:

> According to cognitive neuroscientists, we are conscious of only about 5 percent of our cognitive activity, so most of our decisions, actions, emotions, and behaviour depend on the 95 percent of brain activity that goes beyond our conscious awareness.
>
> (Szegedy-Maszak 2005)

A century ago, working with psychiatric patients and exploring his own inner challenges, Carl Gustav Jung came to a similar realisation, acknowledging not only the existence of something much larger and more powerful than consciousness but also the intrinsic laws governing human life. This set him on a journey of profound scientific and personal discovery of the unconscious. As such, he was mapping a whole new world for humanity. Like Beethoven whose music, delivered from the unknown, mapped the new paths of the music up until the present day, Jung chose to dive deeply and alone into the unknown, armed only with an open mind and faith in guidance by the mystery of his soul. His discoveries, made over a lifetime, still unfold in new forms of ground-breaking scientific research. These are not limited to psychology and some are still awaiting examination through future scientific lenses.

It would be a daunting task to select and categorise the main discoveries in Jung's work. Each carries singular importance and they are interconnected. Each has multifaceted relevance to vast areas of life. Our choice of key concepts below is based on their essential importance over several decades of helping our clients meet the practical challenges of corporate life. It is thus offered as a contextual reference.

The principle of opposites

The essential framework for understanding Jung's analytical psychology is the principle of opposites. 'The opposites are the ineradicable and indispensable preconditions of all life' (CW 14, para. 206). Jung conceptualised life as a flow of psychic energy between the opposite poles, using the framework of the laws of thermodynamics. Applying this energy view, the conscious and the unconscious are seen as a pair of opposites and their relationship is a key factor of human development, growth and transformation. The intrinsic development of personality which Jung terms *individuation* is a lifelong and natural journey occurring in every individual, and it is governed by natural laws. Its geography, directions, intensity and highs and lows, among others, are modelled by the relationship of the opposites primarily between the conscious and the unconscious. It applies to all landmarks of the life opus, and uniquely to 'Homo Sapiens'. What do these terms actually mean and why are they so pivotal for our existence?

We could imagine the individual conscious self as a small island in the ocean and that all our experiences, perspectives and conscious knowledge come from the perspectives of that island. We could imagine the unconscious as the ocean, the sky and all other visible and invisible entities that are not the island. When we remember a dream or have a special experience of an irrational nature, when we register a specific mood or a strong bodily reaction, we interact with the tokens from the unconscious. We receive the coded information and knowledge from different dimensions of the unconscious, compensating the naturally limited and one-sided perspective of consciousness. The ego, or centre of consciousness, has registered an impact of a force from the unconscious. These inputs are unknown to consciousness because their source is beyond conscious radius and appears in unknown forms to it. And yet, there is something peculiar, almost familiar about them, as if carrying the distant echo of a siren call to dive into the depths and explore. Alas, the very nature of the unconscious is evasive. Its messages sometimes reach the shores of the island. A dream might be remembered. But in most cases, it washes away quickly leaving only faint traces on the sands of memory. Therefore, making the unconscious conscious seems to be an *opus contra naturam*. It is as if the unconscious wants to be seen and engaged with but then disappears. However, opposites reside together in the unconscious. Thus, paradoxical reasoning finds its home in the discourse of analytical psychology.

The central actors in this relationship between the conscious and unconscious pair of opposites are the ego and the Self.

The ego and the Self

Jung considers ego as the centre of consciousness (CW 9ii, para. 1) and he attributes it with analytical powers, cognition, reality checking, personal identity and the vital ability to mediate between the conscious and unconscious. Ego consciousness is related to the unconscious in the sense that that 'the greater the degree of ego-consciousness, the greater the possibility of sensing what is not known' (Samuels, Shorter & Plaut 1986, p. 51). Ego thus has the ability to engage with the superior forces of the personality which, to the greatest degree, are the Self, the central ordering and unifying principle of the entire personality. The Self is attributed with the central authority of the psyche; a human being's fullest potential. It presents the utmost goal and meaning of life. Furthermore, 'the Self is not only the centre, but also the whole circumference which embraces both conscious and unconscious; it is the centre of this totality' (CW12, para. 44). It is as if the ego is created to realise, to the extent of its capacity, the potential of the Self. The Self needs the ego in order to realise itself in the realm of consciousness. The Self resides in the unfathomable depths of the unconscious, but is also the whole system comprising conscious and unconscious. The relationship between the ego and the Self is a lifelong one, demanding from the ego continuous enlargement and fulfilment of the potential of the relationship. Over the course of a lifetime, when in each developmental cycle birth is given to new consciousness, the realm of consciousness is thereby enlarged. In other words, the unconscious is made more conscious. According to Jung, this changes the overall ratio between conscious and unconscious and thus affects the big picture in and of the world. Every such act of illumination (making the unconscious conscious) is a creative act par excellence. These dynamics are found in universal narratives of the fight between light and darkness evoking the eternal topic of good and evil (Evans 1964, pp. 47–49). The process of the Self realising its potential through an individual ego is unique to each person and could be experienced as a life task or mission. Jung called this lifelong journey *individuation* and it is the central reference of his work. The realisation of human potential calls for 'talent management' to be informed by and aligned with individuation.

Energy view

The relevance of mathematical concepts might not be readily apparent to our considerations of inner world life. Likewise, ideas from classical and quantum physics might seem remote from topics concerning emotions, instincts and unusual events. Science and the soul might seem odd bedfellows. Yet dream analysis or work with music and symbols can lead to ground-breaking scientific discoveries and Jung's work, strongly characterised by such ideas, contains many examples.

Jung focused his observations on the *movement* of psychic energy, which is only possible if oppositional poles are constellated. The movement, however, is as multifold and complex a phenomenon as one can imagine. Its descriptions are informed by rich contemporary perspectives in the sciences such as quantum physics, astronomy and biology. The movement, or flow of psychic energy is regulated by natural laws. Remarkably, this implies that our inner reactions, experiences, behaviour and also life events are not simply a haphazard sequence of random occurrences, but are in fact deeply regulated and meaningful. How are they regulated and how can our understanding of the regulating principles help us in our everyday lives and professional endeavours?

Jung came to the discovery of these regulating principles by devotedly working with his patients, examining his inner life and observing human relations and life phenomena. Despite being surrounded by leading medical professionals and scientific minds, he could not ignore the observations which were inexplicable within the scientific paradigm of his time. This sparked a lifetime of research which resulted in a science which articulates the regulating principles and provides a framework for understanding the hidden forces which form patterns of human behaviour in individuals, groups and globally. It also suggests a methodology for consciously engaging with and participating in the energy of life. Spanning this vast territory, Jung developed a scientific discourse which includes medicine, psychology, psychiatry, physics, anthropology, mythology, comparative religion and linguistics, to name just a few.

Jung articulated the regulating principles of the psychic energy flow in terms of the first and second laws of thermodynamics. He considered psyche as 'a relatively closed system in which transformations of energy lead to an equalization of differences' (CW 8, para. 49). Therefore, the process of development, maturation or the entire life cycle is regarded as an energy transformation process. The process starts with an imbalance and tends to end with a higher degree of balance. The focus is on the motion or more precisely on the 'relations of movement' (final or teleological view) rather than on the 'moving substance' (causal view) (CW 8, para. 5). These perspectives invite interpretation directed towards the goal and purpose of the movement rather than its causes. An example of the relations of movement is Fibonacci's sequence as a pattern of growth in botany or music, or the behavioural patterns of individuals, groups and collective. Observing the relations of movement, Jung directed attention to the principle of equivalence: 'for a given quantity of energy expanded or consumed in bringing about a certain condition, an equal quantity of the same or another form of energy will appear elsewhere' (CW 8, para. 34). Psychologically, it means that a certain amount of libidinal energy 'disappears' (withdraws to the unconscious) and, following the equivalence principle, a substitute is formed in the unconscious. The substitute bears peculiar common features to the conscious contents from which the energy withdrew. This newly created value soon reveals signs of unconscious activity which indicate the way forward towards potential integration with the consciousness. For example, people find that certain occupations, routines or patterns of life which worked well for a while either lose their meaning or there is a significant lack of motivation or resistance to conduct them. Furthermore, as moods start swinging, feelings of unease, anxiety, flatness or anger accompany the change, and the body reacts with minor or more intense disorders. Peculiar dreams, events and behaviour can also occur in the luminal space of change. They carry the features of the lost energy, as well as the germs and patterns of the new energy ready to be integrated into the dimension of consciousness. Therefore, equivalent qualities in and relations between single and series of occurrences reveal a profound multidimensional symmetry of interrelatedness and meaning in the liminal space of becoming, between the old and the new. This invites consideration of phenomena such as nonlocality and coherence, which are not only significant research topics of modern physics but also practical tools for understanding and navigating our universe. Remarkably, these relational patterns of movement seem to appear in all realms of life, for example, in numerical patterns, biological structures, human behaviour, dreams, historical occurrences, music, art, fairy-tales and organizational culture. In whichever form they manifest, they are tokens of the energy transformation process, the flow of energy regulated by natural generative principles.

Focusing on psychic energy, Jung observed different types of energies manifesting to consciousness in certain differentiated ways based on common features. This informed his articulation of the structure of the psyche.

Structural view

As with forces in nature which are recognised and articulated in the discourse of natural sciences, different forces inhabiting the psyche are differentiated according to a number of factors including locus, direction, way of interaction, intensity and impact. Jung discovered that there are particular forces which relate to the ego and which perform defined functions in the energy transformation process. Some of these (animus and anima) connect the ego with the unconscious, while others (persona) connect the ego with the external world. They come from the realm of shadow, which is in oppositional tension with consciousness. These forces reside in the deepest layer of the psyche, which Jung called the *collective unconscious*. He described this as 'a source in which all the past and all the future lie, it does not belong to the individual, but to mankind' (Jung 2018, p. 113). From that source wherein dwell all generative principles, all potential springs into form, shaping and affecting energy flow for individuals, groups and the collective. Forces from this deepest layer communicate with consciousness through the personal unconscious, which contains the unique biographical unconscious material of an individual. All these interactions serve the purpose of stimulating ego adaptation towards the inner and the outer worlds. The forces in the collective unconscious operate and interact as patterns and are themselves fundamental generative principles of the psyche. Jung sees them as archetypes:

Typical attitudes, modes of action – thought processes and impulses which must be regarded as constituting the instinctive behaviour typical of the human species. (...) These patterns of experience are by no means accidental or arbitrary; they follow strictly preformed conditions which are not transmitted by experience as contents of apprehension but are the preconditions of all apprehension. (...) We may think of them (...) as schemata, or as inherited functional possibilities which, nevertheless, exclude other possibilities or limit them to a very great extent. This explains why even fantasy, the freest activity of the mind, can never roam into the infinite (...) but remains anchored to these preformed patterns. (...) Even the images that underlie certain scientific theories – energy, its transformation and constancy, the atomic theory (...) are proof of this restriction.

(CW 6, para. 512)

Archetypes are irrepresentable in themselves and evident only through their manifestations as images, relational patterns to life (inner and outer), patterns of thought and behaviour. Not only do archetypal patterns structure our thinking, but they are also recognisable in life events, typical situations and 'plots'. Together with the theoretical physicist and Nobel Prize winner, Wolfgang Pauli, Jung advanced the scientific view on the connection between psyche and matter. This deepened his understanding of archetypes in the context of physics. Pauli, as a result of his collaboration with Jung, adopted an archetypal view of science and of life phenomena in general. Jung analysed more than 1300 of Pauli's dreams and these contributed to some of Pauli's scientific discoveries. For example, a repetitive music dream prompted his ground-breaking understanding of the spin concept. Pauli placed a strong emphasis on the connection between phenomena in physics, biology and the unconscious: 'Psyche and matter are governed by common (...) not in themselves ascertainable ordering principles' (Meier 2014). Observing the connection between energy and matter, the transformation of energy and the analogous relationship between unconscious and material occurrences, Jung and Pauli noticed the acausal connecting principle, synchronicity. They discerned meaning in the symbolic common to psychic phenomena, physical processes and material events. Card summarises the archetypal hypothesis based on Jung and Pauli's propositions:

1) Physics and psyche represent complementary aspects of the same transcendental unitary reality, the Unus Mundus.
2) Archetypes act as fundamental dynamical patterns whose various representations characterise all processes whether mental or physical.
3) Archetypes acting simultaneously in both the realms of matter and mind account for synchronistic phenomena.

(Card 1996 in Morariu & Card 1998, p. 74)

Although there can be any number of archetypes, in current literature advocating partial applications of Jung's work we increasingly note postulations of definite numbers of archetypes without precise reference to Jung. As with Jung's terms of complexes and typology, the concepts of archetypes, in particular animus, anima, persona and (especially) shadow are becoming more commonly used in literature dealing with organizational life. The combination of popular and simplistic application carries significant risk. These concepts have been a focus of clinical research from different perspectives of Jungian and post Jungian authors and could be of great value in practical work on any level if approached with careful scientific thought backed with openness and personal and professional experience.

Jung's view of anima, animus, persona and shadow which he recognised as empirical concepts based on related psychic phenomena (CW 9i, para. 114) provide kaleidoscopic lenses on the core facets of identity in terms of human essential makeup and potential, the roles we play in life, gender issues and the phenomena of good and evil.

The archetypes of animus and anima represent the core masculine and feminine principles in attitudes, beliefs, inspirations, moods, impulses and modelling of ideas. In the process of individuation, they carry the great potential of connecting and guiding towards the centre of personality and self-realisation. At the same time, they carry the serious dangers of identification and possession, which accompany every archetypal force or complex. There are intrinsic patterns in the ways that animus and anima manifest in consciousness and impact personality both as separate forces and as 'a couple' as the Self is approached.

Libidinal energies around persona carry adaptive potential in the external world in terms of the variety of social and professional roles needed for human life in a community. 'We are masks (*personae*) through which the gods sound (*personare*)' (Hillman 1990, p. 82). As with any adaptation process, as well as with the overall tendency towards a higher degree of balance, there is always the challenge of the genuine voice being sounded through the mask. This allows the actor to don different masks without identifying with or being possessed by them.

One of the most valuable and sobering lessons from Jungian work is that the source of evil is not the dark side of personality. It is a person not acknowledging and dealing with the dark side of personality (Jensen & Mullen 1982). *Shadow* is psychic content which is out of different reasons unacceptable to consciousness and comprises personal, familial, cultural, national and collective dimensions. Taking into consideration that shadow is a psychic force, it connotes that a substantial amount of energy is unavailable to the conscious personality and can threaten to overpower consciousness. This is why conscious attempts to integrate the shadow are important. The consequences of not engaging with one's shadow could be catastrophic, and exemplified in the atrocities of the WWII:

If this unconscious disposition should happen to be one which is common to the great majority of the nation, then a single one of these complex-ridden individuals, who at the same time sets himself up as a megaphone, is enough to precipitate a catastrophe. The good people, in their innocence and unconsciousness, do not know what is happening to them when they are changed overnight into a 'master race' (…) and an amazed Europe is hard put to accommodate itself to the 'new order' where anything so monstrous (…) is not merely a possibility but a *fait accompli*.

(CW 18, para. 1374)

What is not conscious is projected and acted out, which means that we do not take control or responsibility for certain aspects of our personalities, which at their core carry the potential for unthinkable evil. 'The Shadow is a living part of the personality and therefore wants to live with it in some form' (CW 9i, para. 44). The analogy of evil characters in fairy tales suggests that they are necessary challenges for the hero to discover his core potential and to eventually become king of a new land (thus integrating a new awaiting territory of the psyche). Mephistopheles words echo at this point: 'I am part of that force that always wills the evil and always produces the good' (Goethe, *Faust*, Part One, line 1335). Furthermore, once when the seven heads of a monster are cut off, a dove or a magical creature of moving beauty is freed, informing that in the core of a frightening force resides a noble power. Neurosis, psychopathology and certain diseases could be usefully understood as shadow forces which have accumulated power over time being kept in the unconscious. Not having been engaged with, they seek redemption by being witnessed and understood with compassion. Indeed, this is the very path for their energy transformation and integration into consciousness. And only then do the riches which they had guarded become available to the hero.

How to observe these structural actors of the psyche in organizational life is examined more closely in the parts III, IV, V and VI of this book.

Symbol

Archetypes appear to consciousness as images and symbols. Image is a result of the spontaneous activity of the unconscious and momentary conscious situation, thus 'the interpretation of its meaning, therefore, can start neither from the conscious alone nor from the unconscious alone, but only from their reciprocal relationship' (CW 6, para. 745). Jung uses the term *image* in order to mark a representation of psychic content. Representations of psychic content can take any type of medium or form, for example, visual, auditory and feeling. Image contains and amplifies the symbol (Samuels, Shorter & Plaut 1986, p. 72), and is the best expression for something unknown (Sharp 1991, p. 131). The hidden riches delivered to humanity through the symbolic communication of psyche are illustrated by Einstein's description of his scientific discoveries: 'The theory of relativity was a music thought that came to me' (Suzuki & Suzuki 1969, p. 90). 'My new discovery is the result of musical perception. (...) I very rarely think in words at all. A thought comes, and I may try to express it in words afterwards' (Wertheimer 1945, p. 213). These impressive examples show how the wisdom ready to be integrated into the conscious realm of humanity communicates from the unconscious in an unknown but discernible form (symbol) to the carrier.

The process of symbol formation designates a process of energy transformation. The psychic development is occasioned by the attraction of the symbol, which happens when the conditions for energy transformation are met. The transformation process occurs as energy flows between the poles of instinct and culture (often also called 'spirit'). Impulses, which come from the instinctual spectrum of the psyche, find their form and meaning in images: 'Image represents the meaning of the instinct' (CW 8, para. 398). Emotions (Latin 'emovere', to *move out*) play an important role in this process, designating an inward symbol. Inwardly, symbols are lived out as emotions; outwardly, emotions are apprehended as symbolic qualities. 'The symbol is thus the emotion itself in the aspect of an exciting image' (Hillman 1961, p. 258). Symbols, unlike signs, always possess a certain amount of libidinal charge and are emotionally meaningful. Thus, in analytical psychology we always look for a symbol. Psyche speaks in symbols and it is in symbols where the clues of the development and energy transformation lie. In symbols we find the encapsulated vital energy which disappeared from consciousness (substitute formation). They provide the most precious encoded diagnostic insights into the core causes of seemingly intractable problems. Containing the germs of future movement of the transformational process, they also indicate the way forward. In symbols we find the 'middle ground'. They appear as the transcendence of the psychological crucifixion on opposite poles. As they appear, new energy might flow.

> When there is full parity of the opposites, attested by the ego's absolute participation in both, this necessarily leads to a suspension of the will, for the will can no longer operate when every motive has an equally strong countermotive. Since life cannot tolerate a standstill, a damming up of vital energy results, and this would lead to an insupportable condition did not the tension of opposites produce a new, uniting function that transcends them. This function arises quite naturally from the regression of libido caused by the blockage.
>
> (CW 6, para. 824)

The form of this new development is a *living symbol* and represents a *transcendent function* which results from the oppositional tendencies of the conscious and unconscious and 'makes the transition from one attitude to another organically possible' (CW 8, para. 145).

Symbols are designed by the universal movements of the brush executed by the unique style of an individual (or group, organization, culture, nation or entire Zeitgeist). By observing the symbols expressed, whether through dreams, narratives, somatic occurrences, life events or organizational patterns, we soon notice a deep underlying pattern (and also very soon reach the understanding that we have no idea what it means!). Learning the particular symbolic language of the client requires humility. Together with the client, gradual elucidation of the universal grammar of the archetypal patterns takes place, yet the meaning remains evasive. However, the understandings and interpretations which are organically acquired during the process of deeper discovery aid transformation and the maturation of personality.

Theory of complexes

Pure or direct manifestations of archetypes are rare and they happen in particular circumstances in the energy transformation process. Given that energy from the deepest layers of the unconscious carries the most potent charge, its impact on personality is immense. Loss of a sense of reality, strong somatic reactions, outbursts of uncontrolled behaviour, predictive visions, illness and even death can occur. As stated, for these reasons, professional training and extensive clinical experience is required to consult in this realm. On the other side, we are normally exposed to the impacts of *complexes* on an everyday basis. In our relationship with them can be discerned the warp and weft of our inner worlds. They give us a sense of being alive. 'Complexes are focal or nodal points of psychic life which we would not wish to do without; (…) otherwise psychic activity would come to a fatal standstill' (CW 6, para. 925). Jung discovered complexes quite early on in his career, and through the Word Association Experiment, empirically substantiated his findings (CW 2). This discovery became so important for his research and analytical psychology as such that he considered complexes to be the 'via regia' to the unconscious:

> The *via regia* to the unconscious, however, is not the dream, as [Freud] thought, but the complex, which is the architect of dreams and symptoms. Nor is this *via* so very 'royal', either, since the way pointed out by the complex is more like a rough and uncommonly devious footpath that often loses itself in the undergrowth and generally leads not into the heart of the unconscious but past it.
>
> (CW 8, para. 210)

Complexes are clusters of psychic energy. They are formed around the archetypes and they carry the particular energy related to the given source activated in the collective unconscious. Given that the ego is a complex itself, complexes are connectors between the collective unconscious and the conscious, provided that the ego can develop a relationship with them. In this way our consciousness has the potential to engage and 'deal' with the forces of the collective unconscious which are of the greatest power but only via the mediating energy entities that are of the same make as consciousness itself. The energy charge in each complex is determined by a particular archetype in its core or by a particular interaction of archetypes. As with the archetypes which are 'empty' and are inherited formulae of movement of energy (CW 9i, para. 155), complexes affect the flow of our psychic energy, or how we 'move'. In other words, that inner movement will determine our behaviour in a given situation and we will be moved, both somatically and emotionally. Each complex carries a particular pattern of energy movement. Most importantly, this entire process takes place below our conscious radar so we find ourselves 'moving' or behaving in a determined manner.

Complexes are 'incompatible with the habitual attitude of consciousness' (CW 8, para. 201).

> Complexes interfere with the intentions of the will and disturb the conscious performance; they produce disturbances of memory and blockages in the flow of associations; they appear and disappear according to their own laws; they can temporarily obsess consciousness, or influence speech and action in an unconscious way. In a word, complexes behave like independent beings.
>
> (CW 8, para. 253)

Otherwise astute reality checks are heavily coloured by an altered state in which we both perceive and behave differently. Our ability to reflect, sense of timeliness and capacity to consider different choices are reduced by an inner push to react in a determined way based on the formula of movement encapsulated in the activated complexes. Jung's statement that we all possess complexes but that in actual fact complexes *have us* can reach such a degree that it can be seen as 'the judicial concept of diminished responsibility' (CW 8, para. 200). 'Possession' by a complex has a hugely potent energy impact to the environment and can lead to grave developments, illustrated by WWII:

> We know today that in the unconscious of every individual there are instinctive propensities or psychic systems charged with considerable tension. When they are helped in one way or another to break through into consciousness, and the latter has no opportunity to intercept them in higher forms, they sweep everything before them like a torrent and turn men into creatures for whom the word 'beast' is still too good

a name. They can then only be called 'devils'. To evoke such phenomena in the masses, all that is needed is a few possessed persons, or only
one. Possession, though old-fashioned, has by no means become obso-
lete; only the name has changed.

(CW 18, para. 1374)

Jung draws an analogy to the possession and exorcism of evil spirits and
demons. But applying the teleological view, complexes carry a potent
energy for development if they are made conscious and if we can develop
and maintain a conscious standpoint in relation to them. Otherwise, if they
remain unconscious, they act as split entities, autonomous personalities
which consume our energy and cause an endless automatic repetition of
cognition and behaviour. It is worthwhile emphasising that complexes are
experienced both as 'positive' and 'negative'. They can create an effect of
inspiration, motivation and stamina for carrying out demanding tasks, as well
as insurmountable obstacles which cause abrupt terminations of relationships
and enterprises or irrational persistence in negative endeavours. In any case,
they are tokens of imprisoned energy in the unconscious which, if liberated,
can aid the process of development. The key, therefore, is finding away to
engage with complexes. Given that they reside in the unconscious but that
they manifest to our consciousness and body, analytical psychology provides
many ways of engaging with them and facilitating their integration with
consciousness. This process enriches the personality and energy integrated
from the complexes enables changes from unbearable repetitive experiences
to more realistic views and behaviour towards people and situations. Jung's
complex theory provided a wide and rich scientific foundation for a deeper
understanding of both human inner makeup and patterns of behaviour of
individuals, groups and cultures. It continues to illuminate a wide spectrum
of scientific research including infant research, developmental psychology,
neuroscience, organizational psychology, culture and the social sciences.

Projection

Impactful life situations and significant relationships with others bring us into
contact with vital aspects of our personality and energies from the unconscious. This is especially the case with the psychic energies from the unconscious, which cannot find a path of integration to consciousness. If they
remain unacknowledged in the inner world, engagement with them will fall
upon us externally. This is called *projection*. Projection can find a 'hook' on
anybody and anything which carries some features of our own energy of
which we are unconscious, and which needs integrating for the purpose of
individuation. This is typical for intense experiences in our emotional relationships as well as dramatic events in life with significant others. Fascination, jealousy, severe frustration, hatred, addictive 'love', anxiety, to name

just a few, are known grips of projection mechanisms, which draw the attention of consciousness. In the case of projection, we live it through the relationship in order to become conscious of it as a vital facet of our psyche. 'Projections change the world into the replica of one's own unknown face' (CW 9ii, para. 17). To the extent that consciousness is achieved in the integration process, the projection withdraws and the grip of the projection is released. Therefore, events and people which move us more than usual, are not just isolated occurrences, but they carry a deep meaning for our individuation process and inform us about the underlying issues constellated for our development. Furthermore, projection phenomena carry the essence of the issue of 'I' and 'not I', boundaries of personality, liminality and reality.

Type psychology

It is remarkable that we learn about the unconscious through our consciousness, and that consciousness itself arose from the unconscious. Beebe (2004) beautifully illustrates this most peculiar relationship: 'Jung had grasped that psychological consciousness was not just a knowing about, or a construction or reconstruction of, but (...) "a knowing with" unconscious reality' (p. 86). He further deepens the understanding by citing Edinger's etymology of consciousness:

> Conscious derives from *con* or *cum*, meaning with or together, and *scire* 'to know' or 'to see'. It has the same derivation as conscience. Thus the root meaning of both consciousness and conscience is 'knowing with' or 'seeing with' an 'other'. In contrast, the word 'science', which also derives from *scire*, means simple knowing, i.e. knowing without 'withness'. So etymology indicates that (...) the experience of consciousness is made up of two factors – 'knowing' and 'withness'. In other words, consciousness is the experience of knowing together with an other, that is, in a setting of two.
>
> (Beebe 2017, p. 22)

So how does consciousness work? How does it orient in the vast universe of multidimensional stimuli? What sensors and faculties does it have at its disposal for this purpose and how do they develop?

Jung observed the development of consciousness with its innate predispositions and habitual styles, noting their respective roles in the individuation process. He developed a unique type of psychology based on the movement of energy and principle of opposites. Considering the main direction of the psychic energy towards the inner or outer world, Jung identified the basic attitudes of *introversion* and *extraversion*. Introversion or introverts draw the source of energy from the inner world or subject, while the extroversion or extroverts are drawn to the object or the outer world. Jung explains these concepts vividly in an interview with Dr Evans (1964):

> The psyche has two conditions (…) The one is environmental influence and the other is the given fact of the psyche as it is born. (…) the psyche is by no means tabula rasa here, but a definite mixture and combination of genes, which are there from the very first moment of our life; and they give a definite character, even to the little child. That is a subjective factor, looked at from the outside. Now if you look at it from the inside, then it is just so as if you would observe the world. When you observe the world, you see people (…) you see tangible objects. But when you observe yourself within, you see moving images, a world of images generally known as fantasies. Yet these fantasies are facts. (…) Fantasy is, you see, a form of energy, despite the fact that we can't measure it. (…) And so psychical events are facts, are realities. And when you observe the stream of images within, you observe an aspect of the world, of the world within, because the psyche, if you understand it as a phenomenon that takes place in so-called living bodies, is a quality of matter, as our bodies consist of matter. We discover that this matter has another aspect, namely, a psychic aspect. And so it is simply the world from within, seen from within. It is just as though you were seeing into another aspect of matter.
>
> (Evans 1964, p. 22)

The main faculties of consciousness, which Jung articulated as functions, are organized of pairs of opposites. On the axis of the evaluative or rational function, Jung positions thinking and feeling. The thinking function employs cognition, grasping what things are and their logical order, while the feeling function is directed towards the things' value, and involves subjective judgement. The other irrational, perceiving axis carries the sensation function which informs about things registered by our senses and intuition, which through the unconscious implies the possibilities of things and potential further developments. For optimal orientation of consciousness, participation of all four functions is required in the scope and relation required by a given situation. However, the four functions form habitual combinations of those which are greater and lesser used. Individuation demands a greater degree of balance and wholeness and in this regard inner and outer world challenges stimulate progress. Jung discovered that one of the four functions is most developed and differentiated and acts as dominant or superior function in comparison to the other three. It automatically determines our main predispositions. The least developed and differentiated 'inferior' function reveals aspects of the psyche which stand as inferior to the conscious personality. The inferior function being the most unconscious of four is the most precious source of development. However, as with the shadow, the content of the inferior function is the least desirable and most disturbing, and when activated, it tends to move a person to function in rather inept ways.

Taking into consideration the four functions and the two attitudes of introversion and extraversion, there are sixteen basic types. They illustrate our basic conscious orientation towards life, reality, ourselves and others. In the analytical setting, we consider our own predispositions towards the given situation with the client, their ways of functioning and our automatic preferences and how we relate and act from the position of our conscious orientation.

Jung's typology initiated a number of different classifications and tests which are used in the widest scope of professions and industries across the globe. Jung's original work and post Jungian further developments in this area remain a profound source for research and creative application (see chapters: 'Neuroscience and Jung,' and 'Background to Jungian coaching and consulting in business' of this volume).

Re-ligare

The purpose of Homo Sapiens is to make the unconscious conscious and by so doing, to release the vital, creative energy inscribing a unique inscription into the repository of existence. Consciousness, with the ego in its centre, is a child of the unconscious. At the same time, it is the opposite pole to the unconscious. The choreography of life is designed according to the ego–Self relationship. There are times when the ego is alienated from the Self. There are times when the ego suffers inflation or identification with the Self, and there are times of re-connection. Life brings cycles of forceful interactions with the unconscious, which cause neurotic states, marking the nodal points of life. Jung considered neurosis as a normal occurrence with the potential of strengthening the ego structure and always bringing clues to the way forward. Jung shifted focus from the cause of the problem (psychoanalytic reductionism) to where the energy 'wants' to go, i.e. towards the goal of the individuation process (teleological and constructive point of view). However, if out of some reason, the ego structure is not solid enough and the disintegration takes place under the impacts of the unconscious forces, then there is a loss of the sense of reality (so called psychotic state) and the ability to live in everyday reality is impaired. In this way, there is an innate attraction to the unconscious as a source of vitality and a healthy fear of it. The ego has mechanisms of defending itself from threatening forces of the unconscious (so called 'ego defences') and they also operate unconsciously. If the conscious personality does not develop a stand towards the impact of the unconscious forces and is not able to differentiate and discriminate, and at the same time communicate, the more potent unconscious forces (archetypes or complexes) inflate the ego entity (connoting identification) with the unconscious. The ego acts out the unconscious identity which took it over.

This can be illustrated with depressive or manic states, for example, 'loss of free will, delusion, and enthusiasm in good or evil alike' (CW 7, para. 110). With great peril, an inflated person or group can feel godlike. To dance the music of life, to fall and rise again, to become one self over and over again, puts the toughest demand in front of us: to remain human.

References

Beebe, J 2004, 'Understanding consciousness through the theory of psychological types', in J Cambray & L Carter (eds), *Analytical psychology*, Brunner Routledge, New York, p. 27.

Evans, RI 1964, *Conversations with Carl Jung and reactions from Ernest Jones*, Van Nostrand Reinhold Insight Books, Princeton.

Hillman, J 1961, *Emotion: a comprehensive phenomenology of theories and their meanings for therapy*, Northwestern University Press, Evanston.

Hillman, J 1990, *The essential James Hillman: a blue fire*, Routledge, Hove.

Jensen, F & Mullen, S (eds) 1982, *CG Jung, Emma Jung and Toni Wolff – a collection of remembrances*, The analytical psychology club of San Francisco, San Francisco.

Jung, CG 1904/1990, 'Studies in word association', in *Experimental researches*, CW 2.

————— 1921/1990, 'Definitions', in *Psychological types*, CW 6.

————— 1921/1990, 'The type problem in modern philosophy', in *Psychological types*, CW 6.

————— 1928/1977, 'The personal and the collective unconscious', in *Two essays on analytical psychology*, CW 7.

————— 1931/1990, 'Appendix', in *Psychological types*, CW 6.

————— 1934/1981, 'A review of the complex theory', in *The structure and dynamics of the psyche*, CW 8.

————— 1937/1981, 'Psychological factors determining human behaviour', in *The structure and dynamics of the psyche*, CW 8.

————— 1945/1989, 'Marginalia on contemporary events', in *The symbolic life*, CW 18.

————— 1951/1978, 'The ego', in *Aion*, CW 9ii.

————— 1952/1993, 'Introduction', in *Psychology and alchemy*, CW 12.

————— 1954/1990, 'Archetypes of the collective unconscious', in *Archetypes of the collective unconscious*, CW 9i.

————— 1954/1990, 'Psychological aspects of the mother archetype', in *The archetypes of the collective unconscious*, CW 9i.

————— 1956/1989, 'The personification of the opposites', in *Mysterium coniunctionis*, CW 14.

————— 1957/1978, 'The Shadow', in *Aion*, CW 9ii.

————— 1957/1981, 'The transcendent function', in *The structure and dynamics of the psyche*, CW 8.

————— 1981/1948, 'On psychic energy', in *The structure and dynamics of the psyche*, CW 8.

————— 2000, *The collected works of C. G. Jung* (CW), eds. H Read, M Fordham, G Adler & W McGuire, trans. RFC Hull, Princeton University Press, Princeton.

———— 2018, 'Lecture VI 2 June 1934', in E Falzeder (ed), *History of modern psychology: lectures delivered at ETH Zurich. Volume 1, 1933–1934*, Philemon Foundation Series, Princeton University Press, Princeton, p. 113.

Meier, CA (ed) 2014, *Atom and archetype: the Pauli/Jung letters, 1932–1958 – updated edition*, Princeton University Press, Princeton.

Morariu, VV & Card, CR 1998, 'The archetypal hypothesis of CG Jung and W. Pauli and the number archetypes: an extension of the concept to the Golden Number', *Paideusis – Journal for Interdisciplinary and Cross-Cultural Studies*, vol. 1, viewed 18 November 2019, http://smu-facweb.smu.ca/~paideusis/volume1/n1mc.pdf.

Samuels, A, Shorter, B & Plaut, F 1986, *A critical dictionary of Jungian analysis*, Routledge, Hove.

Sharp, D 1991, *CG Jung Lexicon. A primer of terms and concepts*, Inner City Books, Toronto.

Suzuki, S & Suzuki, W 1969, *Nurtured by love. A new approach to talent education*, Warner Bros Publications, Miami.

Szegedy-Maszak, M 2005, 'Mysteries of the mind', *US News & World Report*, 28 February, viewed 13 November 2019, http://webhome.auburn.edu/~mitrege/ENGL2210/USNWR-mind.html.

Wertheimer, M 1945, *Productive thinking*, Harper, New York.

Chapter 5

Neuroscience and Jung

Michael Escamilla

At the beginning of Marcel Proust's masterpiece *A la recherche du temps perdu* (1922–1931), the narrator tells of tasting a pastry, a *madeleine*, and subsequently remembering (and re-experiencing!) an earlier time of his life in great and extended detail. This is perhaps the most exquisite literary representation of how a particular sensation (in this case, the taste of a cookie) can trigger a set of emotions, memories and thoughts, all interconnected at some intricate level in our psyche. A few years before Proust began writing his book, Carl Jung had made a similar discovery. Working at the Burghölzli psychiatric hospital near Zurich, in the first decade of the 20th century, Jung and his colleagues had been performing a series of experiments using word associations. In the course of these experiments, Jung noticed what he called 'complexes' of words, memories and emotions. According to Jung, these webs of emotion, meaning and ideas constituted key building blocks of experience and were present in every human being. Complexes were behavioural reactions to environmental stimuli. In Jung's case, the stimuli were particular words conveyed through hearing. In Proust's case, memories and emotions (what Jung would call 'a complex') were stimulated through the sense of taste. From a psychological perspective, Jung and his colleague Franz Riklin were building upon the work of previous scientists, including Francis Galton, a cousin of Charles Darwin, and German psychiatrist Theodor Ziehen, who originally coined the term 'complex' to describe emotions and thoughts evoked in the Word Association Test. (Jones 1955, p. 127). Jung furthered the ideas of Ziehen and others who were using Galton's experiment, to construct a psychological theory of the unconscious in which the mind (the psyche) is actually formed, uniquely in each person, by these webs or nets of associations. The idea of complexes, and how the human psyche in each individual is composed of large numbers of complexes became quite central to Jung's later psychological system. In fact, when he was asked to come up with a name to describe his type of psychology, Jung initially considered calling it 'complex psychology', so key did he feel complexes were in describing the economy and biology of human psychology.

He would later settle on the term 'Analytic psychology', to contrast it with Freud's 'psychoanalysis'.

One hundred years after Jung first wrote of complexes and began to develop his psychological construct of the mind, modern neuroscience is just catching up to Jung's ideas. In this chapter, I will outline some of the key neuroscience research that supports and sheds light on many of Jung's key concepts. The scientific study of complexes and how affect, ideas and concepts come together in the brain, is one of these areas of current interest. Other concepts of Jung that are being validated or studied in current neuroscience (usually without the scientist realising how their research fits in with Jung's concepts) include research on personality types, schizophrenia, levels of consciousness and how experiences are passed on biologically and genetically across generations.

The neuroscience of complexes

In the word association studies conducted by Jung and Riklin, which they published in 1904 (CW 2), Jung noted that when subjects were responding to a set of 400 words (subjects were asked to respond with the first word that came to mind after hearing each word), certain words caused 'reactions' or triggers, leading to delays in responding, flushing, stammering or other subtle displays of emotion. For Jung, such words were postulated to be causing 'emotionally charged complexes' in the research subjects. Notably, this first set of studies done by Jung and Riklin were conducted in control subjects, persons without mental disorders. Jung's original intent was to gather information on the words used by the subjects (their associations to the 400 experimental words) but instead he focused on complexes which he tied into the work of Sigmund Freud. Freud was postulating unconscious processes which could, unknown to patients, control their behaviours and emotions.

By 1906, Jung had edited a book pulling together several of the word association papers from the Burghölzli group, while also publishing an in-depth tome on the psychology of *Dementia praecox* (CW 3), which also used the theory of complexes to explain the phenomena found in patients with that diagnosis. He sent the latter book to Freud, who was excited to see an academic psychiatric hospital group taking seriously his theories of the unconscious, and Freud in turn extended an invitation for Jung to visit him in Vienna. For the next four years, Jung and Freud collaborated extensively in forming an association of psychoanalysis and sponsoring the first few international meetings of psychoanalysis, as well as a journal to further develop the field.

While Jung's and Freud's respective schools of thought have developed significantly over the last 100 years, in many respects, since their collaboration in the first decade of the 20th century, psychoanalytic and analytical psychology schools have largely developed outside of the realm of academia and experimental psychology. In some senses, this has been justified and supported by Jung and his followers, who have stressed that psychology can be studied empirically through the analysis of dreams and the amplification of symbols and archetypes, and that this work does not need a grounding in experimental and biological research in order to proceed as a field of practice. The negative consequence of this approach has been the gradual erosion of both psychoanalysis and analytical psychology from the modern university, including departments of psychology and (in medical schools) psychiatry and neurology. Other theories of psychological treatment have been developed (for example, cognitive behavioural therapy) which are well studied in terms of efficacy and the components which contribute to the therapeutic outcome, and which have also used modern neuroscience to further validate and provide guidance to these therapies for the treatment of a myriad of psychological and psychiatric problems. The very word 'unconscious', so revered and motivating for both Freud and Jung, is virtually non-existent in current experimental psychology and psychiatric publications, where seemingly more specific words such as 'implicit memory' are used to describe neurological and psychological processes that occur below the level of our own awareness. Although in my view, we have lost valuable ground over the last 100 years, in terms of validating our approaches and keeping them in the academies and universities, there are now possibilities to use modern neuroscience techniques to validate Jung's theory of complexes, and to give us further insight into what is happening in detail at the level of the brain and the body when complexes are triggered.

In the last few years, two research groups, one working in Australia and the other in the United States, have used functional magnetic resonance imaging (fMRI) and electroencephalogram tracings (EEGs) to study the brain in detail when subjects are responding to neutral words and to words which cause complexes. In each individual tested, specific words can be seen to cause complexes. These vary from person to person, and can be scientifically studied using observations such as response time, facial or body changes, voice changes and failures to recall words during the test. fMRI uses an MRI scanner, and measures in detail all brain regions, defining them structurally, but also recording the level of blood flow in each region over short periods of time. fMRI readings can be used to study brain activation during particular conditions, for example, when the brain is responding to a 'neutral' word or a 'complex generating' word during the Word Association Test. In studies by the Australian group, led by L. Petchkovsky, studying twelve normal (non-psychiatric) subjects, fMRI was able to detect significant differences in areas of the brain when comparing activation patterns after complex generating words were compared to 'neutral' words. The Petchkovsky studies highlighted brain areas on both the right and left side of the brain, and noted that areas of the brain involved in empathic monitoring, self-awareness and conflict monitoring all showed increased activation when 'complex' generating words were triggered (Petchkovsky et al. 2013). More recently, Petchkovsky has suggested that quantitative electroencepholograms (qEEGs), which measure brain waves using electric leads, might yield additional information on cortical areas involved in the brain when complexes are activated (Petchkovsky et al. 2013).

In addition to the work by Petchkovsky and colleagues in Australia, we have conducted a parallel set of experiments in the United States (Escamilla et al. 2018). As, to our knowledge when we began this work, there had been no previous research on visualising complexes with fMRI, we took the approach Riklin and Jung did back in 1903. Rather than study these processes in a patient sample, we decided to use a control sample, in our case, of students from a university in El Paso, Texas. Our questions were simple: 1. Could we find differences in brain activity when a complex is activated, compared to normal brain activity, and 2. If these differences could be found, could they help us understand the neurological circuits which are involved?

Our subjects consisted of twenty persons, ten female and ten male. We used a research protocol modelled after the protocol for the Word Association Test as described by Dr Verena Kast (1980) in Zurich. This involved reading a sequence of 100 words to a research subject and having them respond with the first word that came to their mind. A recorded voice was used to read each word, to preserve consistency across cases. Videos of facial and body movements were recorded. Each case was scored, word by word, for the number of complex indicators the subject showed when responding. We also recorded electroencephalography (EEG) during the test. We selected, for each subject, five words which had the most complex indicators, and five neutral words (words with no complex indicators). fMRI readings were done for each subject, within a week of their having performed the Word Association Test. As it was difficult to hear words while in the scanner, we presented words visually, and asked the subject to respond with the first word that came to mind. fMRI readings were recorded in blocks, alternating between no activity, responding to complex words, no activity, and responding to neutral words. Words were specific for each subject. The brain was imaged using a subdivision into 180 volumes across all sections of the brain. All images were combined for the twenty subjects.

Fifty brain circuits were identified, without a priori information, based on subdivisions which correlated highly with each other. We then used statistical analyses to determine which of these circuits showed the greatest difference between the three blocks: no activity, response to neutral words and response to complex words. In order to determine brain activation specific to when complexes were being triggered, we looked at differences in activation when responding to neutral words and when responding to complex words.

Two circuits were statistically associated with responding to complex words compared to when responding to neutral words. Circuit 1 we called 'memory, body and action'. This circuit involved the parietal cortex (epi-sodic memory, body and sensory information), frontal cortex (feelings of uncertainty and body movement planning) and motor cortex (movement). This circuit, interestingly, does not utilise parts of the brain used in language or sense-making, but operates independently through non-verbal memory (or memories) which cause uncertainty and initiate bodily reactions. Circuit 2, also activated by complexes, we call the 'memory, emotion, language, meaning' circuit. Memories are again triggered but here in the temporal lobes (episodic, semantic, visual), as is the part of the brain active in learning and approach/avoidance behaviour (caudate), deeper structures in the thal-amus and cingulate area (emotions, fear, anger, sexual pleasure, motivation, behaviour) and areas of the temporal lobe involved in the comprehension of language and assigning meaning to words. This second circuit makes use of language memories, meaning and motivation, which the other circuit does not. Both circuits perform extra 'work' when complexes are triggered by words, and the one area they have in common is an activation of parts of the brain that deal with memory. It is important to note that there are sev-eral forms in which memory can be encoded (episodic, semantic, visual), and they use different areas of the brain. One type of memory (episodic), in the context of complex generating words, links directly to body movement.

As mentioned above, while performing the Word Association Test, sub-jects were wearing a cap with sixty-eight electrodes. EEG tracings, using a software program called sLORETA, were filtered to look at slow cortical potentials. There are slower moving waveforms that have been shown to highly correlate with blood flow in the brain (blood flow is what is meas-ured in fMRI). Advantages of using EEG are that it is less expensive than fMRI, can be done in an office setting and can measure changes over time in great detail. Disadvantages of EEG are that it is less spatially detailed than fMRI and also that it really only measures cortical activity (and not the deeper brain structures one can see in fMRI). We analysed ten subjects who had valid tracings, looking at differences in cortical slow-wave activation after the subjects heard complex generating words, compared to after hearing neutral words. The EEG reading showed large activations in the frontal and temporal areas of the brain upon hearing complex words (versus neutral words), and a decrease in the parietal area of the brain. This can be considered as showing increases in motivational planning and executive functioning (frontal area), memory and word association (temporal) and an inhibition of the right parietal area (the more logical, mathematical part of the brain).

In summary, both the studies in Australia by Petchkovsky et al. and in the United States by Escamilla et al. utilised the Word Association Test to define complexes in control subjects, and then used fMRI (or EEG) to dem-onstrate that there is increased brain activation in specific areas of the brain when a complex is triggered by particular words. (Again, each subject will have certain words which trigger complexes within them, based on their personal psychological experiences and histories.) These reactions at the level of the brain are instantaneous, strong enough to be visualised by fMRI and EEG and involve two brain systems that are quite complex, and which work by using different types of memory. They signal at an unconscious level that a conflict has been triggered, and put a number of neural circuits into motion. Since the neuroscientific study of complexes is in its infancy, there is much research to be done with regard to how complexes may respond to treatment or environmental alterations, and to how fixed they are over time. The neuroscience studies confirm the biological basis of the complexes that Jung identified over a hundred years ago, and which he built his entire psychological system upon.

The science of personality types

C. G. Jung was not the first person to suggest that people can be said to have different personality types. For instance, an older classification of mental maladies made by Hippocrates and developed by Galen defined patients according to the four humours or temperaments; melancholic, choleric, sanguine and phlegmatic (Jouanna & Allies 2012). Nevertheless, Jung is also well known for having written extensively about inborn differences of personality, which he explained in great detail in his book *Psychological types*, originally published in German in 1921 (CW 6), and now comprising volume 6 in the English translation of his collected works. He found himself compelled to study this subject as a way of explaining differences in the psychological theories and virtually insurmountable viewpoints of Freud, Adler, and himself. In brief, Jung postulated two distinct types of personality, an introverted and extraverted type. He further postulated four additional functions, which consisted of opposing polarities; sensation versus intuition based, and thinking versus feeling based modes of functioning. In Jung's view, people tended to have either a more introverted or extraverted focus in their attention and interests, although all gradations of this could be seen. Similarly, he felt that people tended to have one of the four functions (sensation, intuition, feeling and thinking) which they were most adept at and most likely to use when interacting in the world or when solving problems. Importantly for Jung, the facility that a person has with any particular function can change over time, and for him, the purpose of therapy might include the goal of developing 'inferior' or less used functions.

Later in the 20th century, the Myers-Briggs test (Myers 1962) was developed as a way of categorising people based largely on Jung's ideas of introversion/extraversion, and the four functions, with an added dyad of functions which Myers-Briggs called judging and perceiving. Although widely used in both business and educational settings, at the level of neuroscience this specific scale or test has been criticised. The main shortcomings of the Myers-Briggs as a psychological test is that it categorises subjects in different typologies (for instance extraverted, thinking, sensation, perceiving) and that it does not allow for good quantitation of the different domains.

A much more validated scale for measuring variants of personality is called the 'Five Factor Model' (FFM), developed by Costa and McCrae (1992). This scale measures five domains of personality, which they describe as Neuroticism (N), Extraversion (E), Openness to Experience (O), Agreeableness (A) and Conscientiousness (C). There are other models of personality, and additional scales, that have been researched, and there are ongoing debates about whether additional domains (beyond the five noted by Costa and McCrae) should be captured, but the five-factor model has, at this point, the most validated scientific literature published on personality thus far. Of note, the FFM does incorporate Jung's key concept of extraversion (a low score on this scale correlates with what Jung would have called an introverted type) and, unlike in the Myers-Briggs tests, allows for quantitative measurement across a spectrum from very introverted to very extraverted. Jung's other functions (thinking, feeling, sensation and intuition) are, unfortunately, missing from the FFM and, therefore, there is little scientific data for studying these proposed functions, which Jung felt were critical to understanding personality.

An alternate, quantitative questionnaire has been developed to test functions originally postulated by Jung (King et al. 1999), called the 'Personal Preferences Self-Description Questionnaire' (PPSDQ), but it has been used in relatively few studies, especially compared to studies of the FFM.

Research on personality measures, using the FFM, have provided much information about how personality measures vary among individuals, validating Jung's strong belief that personality traits are varied among human beings and influence any number of behaviours. Although there are large scale perceptions, or stereotypes that people have about personality differences between cultures, most rigorous scientific research has shown that in every country or culture studied, there is significant variation across the spectrum within each country, and this is far greater (within country variation) than any subtle differences in average scores of persons from different cultures (i.e. the difference in average scores between countries) (Terracciano et al. 2005).

In studies conducted by my own research team, using the FFM, we have shown that the five factors (including Jung's extraversion trait) are under a combination of genetic and environmental control (Hare et al. 2012). In that study we also showed that a psychiatric illness (bipolar disorder) was associated with lower scores on extraversion (i.e. this mood disorder was associated with introverted personality scores). Most recently, our team has begun to identify particular genetic variants associated with personality traits (Lee et al. 2017).

In summary, Jung's important insight that there were differences in personality types, which seemed to be at least in part inborn (inherited genetically), have been supported by scientific research in personality disorders conducted in the last few decades. Jung's main focus on introversion and extraversion has been shown to be measurable as a quantitative trait that does not cluster automatically into introverted or extraverted types but rather falls out in more of a bell curve state. Individuals can be found that score remarkably high in extraversion or introversion, though. And perhaps most importantly, we can now show that the introversion/extraversion trait is under some genetic control. The fact that there is an environmental component speaks to Jung's hypothesis that therapy could help develop the less utilised parts of the personality.

The neuroscience of schizophrenia

Much of Jung's early work involved the study of a psychiatric condition which he and his mentor, Eugen Bleuler (a fellow psychiatrist at the Burghölzli clinic in Zurich), would call 'schizophrenia'. A more thorough study of Jung's theories about schizophrenia and modern neuroscience findings regarding this condition can be found in 'Bleuler, Jung and the creation of the schizophrenias' (2016). Bleuler and Jung postulated that a core component of this psychiatric condition was a disconnect between affect (emotions) and cognition and that other phenomena such as hallucinations and delusions were secondary phenomena and not characteristic of the core illness. Bleuler also postulated that there were many forms of schizophrenia and that these were largely due to genetic causes and that the genetic component causing schizophrenia was also correlated somehow with creative and artistic tasks. Jung, for his part, noted that apart from people hospitalised for severe forms of schizophrenia, there was a large proportion of the population that carried traits of schizophrenia. Jung also postulated that schizophrenia correlated with introversion and might be an extreme version of introversion.

Modern neuroscientific studies of schizophrenia have supported many of Jung's and Bleuler's insights. For instance, over the last twenty years, over 100 genes have been identified which are associated with schizophrenia, supporting Bleuler's theory that the disease was largely genetic, and that there are many types of schizophrenia. It is also evident from recent neuroscience findings that these gene variants are in a substantial portion of the population, and perhaps the majority of people with these risk variants do not manifest the severe form of schizophrenia found in hospitals or institutions. Many of the genes discovered thus far do involve neural connections within the brain, and thus support Bleuler and Jung's conceptualisation that schizophrenia at its core involved poorly integrated functions within the brain. Studies of schizophrenia and psychosis have supported Jung's intuition that the illness is associated with increased introversion. Finally, recent studies have shown that the variants associated with schizophrenia are also associated with creativity. Details and references for these studies can all be found in *Bleuler, Jung and the creation of the schizophrenia* (Escamilla 2016).

The neuroscience of levels of consciousness

In Jung's book *Wandlugen und Symbole der Libido* (1912/1952) (translated as 'Symbols of transformation', 1956) Jung described two types of thinking. He developed these theories in response to his interest in the mechanisms of thought processes found in dreams and often seen in patients with schizophrenia, both of which differed from the thought processes used in the 'directed' thinking used in usual conversation, logical thinking and the language of science and philosophy. Jung makes the case that these are two different forms of thought, each with its own set of processes and functions, and makes the case that each of these are active within every human being. For Jung, the 'directed' type of thinking uses the logic of mathematical and linguistic structure, requires an additional expenditure of energy and concentration, and is responsible for many of the successes of what Jung considered the modern world. This level of thought and discourse can be said to have been crucial in developing laws, governments, businesses, economies and scientific discovery. In Jung's view, he postulates this type of thinking as a later development in humankind, which gradually became more important than an earlier type of thinking which was 'undirected', non-verbal, visual, symbolic and associative in nature. This other type of 'undirected' thinking, for Jung, is fundamentally different than directed thinking, and he makes the case that, in modern man, this type of thinking acts as a complementary and often as a compensatory mechanism, bringing new information to consciousness that is not arrived at through the 'directed' type of thinking.

From the perspective of neuroscience, these ideas of Jung's are supported by analyses of brain function, in particular made possible by functional MRI studies and the analysis of neural networks (how different parts of the brain are activated when a research subject is doing different tasks). fMRI studies have shown that different brain circuits are activated when the brain is at a resting state (not engaged in a particular, directed activity) and that, when engaged in a task, different regions of the brain show increased blood flow and activation (Elton & Gao 2014). The study of neural networks and how different networks become activated in different states of consciousness and when doing different tasks is a topic of great interest in the current decade. As we now know particular areas of the brain involved in symbol formation, non-verbal and verbal pathways, it should be possible to further test Jung's ideas about these two types of thinking. Preliminary findings, although not set up to directly test Jung's theories, do support quite significant differences in circuits activated and energy expended depending on what type of thinking the person is doing (resting, non-directed versus directed, task oriented).

Imprinting and genetic mechanisms of transmitting memories of the environment

Although widely accepted within analytical psychology, as well as in the popular culture, Jung's concept of 'archetypes' remains a controversial one from the perspective of the biological sciences and from neuroscience in particular. Jung's concept of archetypes requires that there are inherited capacities in the psyche (or psychologic structure) of human beings, which ensure that all humans, regardless of culture, will experience certain symbolic internal images, and respond to them in similar ways. Jung also postulated that our psychology has carried over psychological structures from previous historic eras, which we experience again, and that the evolutionary experiences of our human and pre-human ancestors are somehow transmitted to us through a biological mechanism. As the study of DNA evolved in the 20th century, Jung saw DNA as the natural biological vehicle in which archetypes would need to be transmitted, as DNA codes for all of our brain and body structures, and is inherited from our ancestors.

From a scientific perspective, much work is needed to operationalise Jung's ideas of the archetypes, and this work is complicated by changes in Jung's thinking regarding archetypes at different stages of his career. In Jung's later, more developed conceptualisations of this theory, it is clear that he did not postulate that we inherit particular symbols or images, but rather that we are somehow programmed to react in certain ways, both internally and behaviourally, to particular experiences or structures we encounter in our environment and from our internal images. Jung was greatly influenced by animal studies and the ethologist Konrad Lorenz. Lorenz characterised specific instinctual drives (inbuilt, inherited capacities for specific behaviours in response to specific stimuli) that he could see in his studies of animals, and Jung hypothesised that these same instincts were built into humankind. More recently, child psychologists such as Daniel Stern (2010) have described in greater detail the forms in which infants respond to stimuli and develop particular relationships ('behavioural engrams') and neural scientists have studied the way early experiences are organized neurally ('neurologic engrams'). These patterns do seem to be built-in ways of responding to the environment, with clear psychological and biological building blocks, and are experienced across the human species.

Both Freud and Jung utilised theories of evolution (from Darwin) to underpin their psychological systems. And both were interested in how behaviours and experiences from previous generations of humanity shaped our current behaviours. Freud tended to use Lamarckian explanations, which postulated that experiences of one generation could affect the genetics of that generation and, in this way, the environmental experiences of previous times were somehow then incorporated in our genetic material. Jung, on the other hand, tended to reject Lamarckian explanations and instead tried to tie inheritance of traits into theories of selection for traits which conferred survival value (Hogenson 2001), drawing from current biologic studies of other species.

In the last two decades, researchers have identified another genetic mechanism, called 'imprinting', which does provide a mechanism where environmental experiences can directly affect the DNA of a mother or father, and modify the expression of genes accordingly in the infant; a separate, 'epi-genetic' mechanism to that of evolution and selection. The imprinting mechanism consists of methylation of DNA. It does not change the sequence of nucleotides in the DNA that is inherited, but the methylation patterns can effect transcription of particular genes. Variations in imprinting have been studied to show how traumas experienced by a mother, through methylation patterns in her own genes, can later affect the DNA expression patterns in her children (as the children will inherit not just the DNA from mother and father, but the methylation patterns from the mother).

In a very real sense, the idea of imprinting has 'rescued' Lamarckian ideas and shown that both immediate environmental effects as well as the more long term variation in DNA sequences that can arise through evolution and selection are both operative in the human species. Understanding the scientific mechanisms that would underlie any inheritance of behaviour patterns based on previous time periods gives us new 'tools' with which to test out Jung's theories. Jung's more general theorising that humans inherit particular ways in which they will respond to environmental cues is certainly supported by what we have learned thus far in the neurosciences. How much our behaviours are dictated by the environment that we, our parents or grandparents experienced versus environments our very distant ancestors experienced remains to be unravelled. Jung's theory of archetypes relies more on our very distant human ancestors and proto human groups (DNA variation and traits selected for over many generations) but this theory may need to be adapted to take account of additional effects of recent environmental exposures that are transmitted through imprinting (epi-genetics).

In closing, modern neuroscience has by and large confirmed many of Jung's key concepts, and given us both biological validity and mechanisms for further research. We can finally start to identify the brain circuits involved in complexes, the DNA variations that underpin aspects of personality and behaviour, the brain circuits that are activated according to the type of thinking a person is engaged in, and the biology underneath medical conditions such as schizophrenia and their related behavioural factors (for instance creativity). Although Jung himself grounded his theories in empirical research of psychological experience and behaviour, he did anticipate a future time when the brain and biological research would allow for a more comprehensive understanding of human psychology. In these first decades of the 21st century, we can say that the time where the fields of biology and psychology can work together constructively has finally arrived.

References

Costa, PT & McCrae, RR 1992, *Revised NEO Personality Inventory (NEO-PI-R) and NEO Five-Factor Inventory (NEO-FFI) manual*, Psychological Assessment Resources, Odessa.

Elton, A & Gao, W 2014, 'Divergent task-dependent functional connectivity of executive control and salience networks', *Cortex*, vol. 51, DOI:10.1016/j.cortex.2013.10.012.

Escamilla, M 2016, *Bleuler, Jung and the creation of the schizophrenias*, Daimon Verlag, Einsiedeln.

Escamilla, M, Sandoval, H, Calhoun, V & Ramirez, M 2018, 'Brain activation patterns in response to complex triggers in the Word Association Test: results from a new study in the United States', *Journal of Analytical Psychology*, vol. 63, no. 4, pp. 484–509.

Hare, E, Contreras, J, Raventos, H, Flores, D, Jerez, A, Nicolini, H, Ontiveros, A, Almasy, L & Escamilla, M 2012, 'Genetic structure of personality factors and bipolar disorder in families segregating bipolar disorder', *Journal of Affective Disorders*, vol. 136, no. 3, pp. 1027–1033.

Hogenson, GB 2001, 'The Baldwin effect: a neglected influence on C.G. Jung's evolutionary thinking', *Journal of Analytical Psychology*, vol. 46, no. 4, pp. 591–661.

Jones, E 1955, *Sigmund Freud, life and work*, vol. 2, Basic Books, London.

Jouanna, J & Allies, N 2012, 'The legacy of the Hippocratic treatise the nature of man: the theory of the four humours', in PVan der Eijk (ed), *Greek medicine from Hippocrates to Galen: selected papers*, Leiden, Boston, pp. 335–360.

Jung, CG 2000, 'The collected works of C. G. Jung (CW)', in H Read, M Fordham, G Adler & W McGuire eds., trans. RFC Hull, Princeton University Press, Princeton.

—— 1907/1960, 'The psychology of Dementia praecox', in *The psychogenesis of mental disease*, CW 3.

—— 1912/1952, *Symbols of transformation*, CW 5.

—— 1921/1990, *Psychological types*, CW 6.

Kast, V 1980, *Das Assoziationexperiment in der Therapeutischen Praxis*, Bonz Verlag Fellbach, Oeffingen.

King, JE, Melancon, JG& Thompson, B 1999, 'Score validation and theory elaboration of a Jungian personality measure', poster presented at the annual meeting of the American Psychological Association, Boston.

Lee, BD, Gonzales, S, Villa, E, Camarillo, C, Rodriguez, M, Yao, Y, Guo, W, Flores, D, Jerez, A, Raventos, H, Ontiveros, A, Nicolini, H & Escamilla, M 2017, 'A genome-wide Quantitative Trait Locus (QTL) linkage scan of NEO personality factors in families segregating bipolar disorder', *American Journal of Medical Genetics Part B: Neuropsychiatric Genetics*, vol. 174, no. 7, pp. 683–690.

Myers, IB 1962, *The Myers-Briggs type indicator: manual*, Consulting Psychologists Press, Palo Alto.

Petchkovsky, L, Petchkovsky, M, Morris, P, Dickson, P, Montgomery, D, Dwyer, K & Burnett, P 2013, 'fMRI responses to Jung's Word Association Test: implications for theory, treatment and research', *Journal of Analytical Psychology*, vol. 58, no. 3, pp. 409–431.

Proust, M 1922–1931, *À la recherche du temps perdu*, trans. CKS Moncrieff, S Hudson, T Kilmartin, LDJ Grieve, Grassetand and Gallimard, Paris.

Stern, D 2010, *Forms of vitality: exploring dynamic experience in psychology and the arts*, Oxford University Press, Oxford.

Terracciano, A, Abdel-Khalek, M, Ádám, N, Adamovová, L, Ahn, CK, Ahn, HH, Alansari, BM, Alcalay, L, Allik, J, Angleitner, A, Avia, A, Ayearst, LE, Barbaranelli, C, Beer, A, Borg-Cunen, MA, Bratko, D, Brunner-Sciarra, M, Budzinski, L, Camart, N, Dahourou, D, De Fruyt, F, de Lima, MP, del Pilar, GEH, Diener, E, Falzon, R, Fernando, K, Ficková, E, Fischer, R, Flores-Mendoza, C, Ghayur, MA, Gülgöz, S, Hagberg, B, Halberstadt, J, Halim, MS, Hřebíčková, M, Humrichouse, M, Jensen, HH, Jocic, D, Jónsson, FH, Khoury, B, Klinkosz, W, Knežević, G, Lauri, MA, Leibovich, N, Martin, TAMarušić, I, Mastor, KA, Matsumoto, D, McRorie, M, Meshcheriakov, B, Mortensen, EL, Munyae, M, Nagy, J, Nakazato, K, Nansubuga, F, Oishi, S, Ojedokun, AO, Ostendorf, F, Paulhus, DL, Pelevin, S, Petot, SM, Podobnik, N, Porrata, JL, Pramila, VS, Prentice, G, Realo, A, Reátegui, N, Rolland, JP, Rossier, J, Ruch, W, Rus, VS, Sánchez-Bernardos, ML, Schmidt, V, Sciculna-Calleja, S, Sekowski, A, Shakespeare-Finch, J, Shimonaka, Y, Simonetti, F, Sineshaw, T, Siuta, J, Smith, PB, Trapnell, PD, Trobst, KK, Wang, L, Yik, M, Zupančič, A & McCrae, RR 2005, 'National character does not reflect mean personality trait levels in 49 cultures', *Science*, vol. 310, pp. 96–100.

Chapter 6

Post Jungian research on trauma

John O'Brien

Modern trauma science informs us that all human beings have both suffered personal trauma and have inherited the biological and psychological effects of the individual and collective traumas of our ancestors (Cambray 2018). However strange it might seem, as part of everyday life, our perception, decision making and actions are shaped by these powerful forces, usually without our awareness. Knowledge and integration of them reduce automatic thinking and behaviour, and increases psychological freedom to adapt more effectively to evolutionary demands.

Trauma theory originated as a medical and psychological field of research conducted by Charcot (1877), Breuer and Freud (1895/1955) and Janet (1907). It was thought of as an over excitation of the nervous system, causing a dissociative psychological split. Jung fully acknowledged that his ideas developed in the process of coming to terms his own early traumatic experiences, and his analytical psychology can therefore be regarded as a 'trauma-based psychology' par excellence (Cambray 2018, p. 9). From this perspective, trauma is not only applicable to clinical patients but to us all. It profoundly addresses the very nature of the body, mind and spirit in the individual and the collective.

As is often the case in scientific advancements applicable to the general population, early discoveries emerge from wartime situations. In the UK, the field of trauma research was substantially developed by Crichton-Miller, who founded the Tavistock Clinic (London) in 1920/1922 (Dicks 1970). He developed practices learned from working with 'shell shock' victims of WWI for the treatment of the general public suffering from nervous disorders. His spirituality strongly informed his work and he enjoyed a long and close friendship with Carl Gustav Jung (Crichton 1961). Subsequent clinical research at the Tavistock took a predominantly psychoanalytic route and this was mirrored in the US by Kardiner (1941). Nonetheless, important discoveries were that symptoms described as abnormal are often be considered to be normal reactions to abnormal circumstances. Looked at this way, trauma research yielded insights into the adaptive and self-healing nature of the psyche. At the same time, the seemingly opposite tendency of traumas to repeat themselves became apparent. Actions which had failed to defend against trauma are often automatically repeated by victims in post traumatic stress. These can invite trauma repetition. This phenomenon gives understanding into the very nature of our perception and construction of reality. Inviting consideration of the self-perpetuating nature of conflict, it provides a solid foundation both for the reduction of dysfunction in individual and organizational life and a shift of norms towards increased connectedness and adaptation.

What is trauma?

Traumas can be considered to be emotionally intense experiences which disturb psychic balance. They can vary from falling off a bicycle when learning to ride as a child, to exposure to bombing in a war zone. While traumas are part of the human experience, extreme disturbances can result in post traumatic stress disorder (PTSD), which requires professional clinical expertise. Traumatic experiences set up autonomous psychological and behavioural patterns, or complexes (Wilson 2004). Scientific and medical understanding of individual trauma progressed throughout the 20th and 21st centuries with the advance of neuroscience which explains the basic mechanics of trauma in terms of the inability of the medial prefrontal cortex to inhibit the midbrain amygdala (Bremner 2007).

Post Jungian clinical perspectives

Perspectives on trauma which illuminate the deepest layers of psychological life are represented, for example, byPapadopoulos (2007), Knox (2003) and Kalsched (2013). Papadopoulos emphasises the social contexts which create trauma. His extensive work with refugees is grounded in clinical psychology, systemic family and Jung's analytical psychology and he is an expert adviser to the United Nations. He has noted the beneficial effects of *active* response by trauma victims to external difficulties and this concurs with Knox's agency theory which describes the importance of impact and influence on others (as well as environmental shaping) to the building of unique identity and a sense of self. Her work has its foundations in early attachment theory, psychiatry and analytical psychology. Kalsched has strongly emphasised the philosophical and spiritual aspects of clinical psychology and analytical psychology, which he blended with psychoanalytic object relations theory.

Just as the psychoanalytic work of the Tavistock Clinic formed the basis for the foundation of the Tavistock Institute of Human Relations in 1947, the methods and discoveries of such noteworthy Jungian clinicians are now beginning to find their ways into non-clinical arenas such as leadership coaching and organizational consulting (O'Brien & O'Brien 2019).

Post Jungian neuroscience

Brain network theories

Cambray (2018) gives an account of the significant research into brain network theories and their overlap with analytical psychology. For example, he cites Chan et al. (2014) who demonstrate that as healthy brains age, they segregate associations less and make more global connections. This reflects Jung's ideas about individuation, which suggests progression towards more holistic experience with age. The Chan research also points out that the effect of trauma on brain networks can be to weaken segregation and thereby contribute towards the worsening of functioning. This is especially so in PTSD cases. Healthy individuation demands cognitive functions, the ability to make global connections and the ability to differentiate and this process is supported by the analyst/coach particularly through life and career transitions.

Mirror neuron theory

Based on the mirroring of hand movements of primates, there is some evidence to suggest that the human mirror neuron system is involved in the development of empathy (Keysers 2011) and also in the contagion of violence (Iacoboni 2013). It is possible that neuron mirroring could account for the process of infant identification with domestic parental violence and its subsequent re-enactment by the child, even some years later (Gaensbauer 2011). Mirroring occurs not only through observed behaviour but also through neural resonance with the intentions of the other (Iacoboni & Mazziotta 2007).

There are some clear implications for the analyst/coach in authentically holding in mind the full potential of the client, quietly noticing and guarding the client's highest vision. This requires self-management of the full range of feelings evoked by the client, so as to notice and understand the neural resonance without reacting automatically, one of the toughest challenges for busy line managers and HR Directors. Professional clinical organizational supervision/consultancy can be helpful in this regard.

Resilience

Post Jungians such as Stein (2011) and Stein working with Choi et al. (2019) have engaged in significant medical research addressing the molecular biological issues relating to trauma. A present area of interest is resilience, which aims to improve adaptation to stress, prevention through targeted early intervention and mitigation of negative outcomes in cases of high genetic risk. Not only post traumatic recovery applications, but also military uses are quite evident in that it might be possible to enhance soldier resilience to trauma (Nindle et al. 2018) through molecular biology and that the science can be used for soldier selection and treatment. Both new pharmacological and psychological interventions are advocated by Wu et al. (2013) and bioethics, such as the implications of treating trauma through memory erasure is becoming increasingly relevant.

Perhaps the natural flow through of such scientific advances to corporate leadership and workforces is to be expected. In addition to the important bioethical questions in these cases, the pragmatic question remains as to how the individual and collective psyche would react to such interventions. From the analytical psychology perspective, the answer might be found in the images of the unconscious from individuals and groups indicating the extent to which consciousness is raised and progression in individuation is made towards that sense of wholeness which inspired Crichton-Miller a century ago.

Post Jungian perspectives on collective trauma

Perhaps the most significant development of analytical psychology into groups and culture was heralded by Joe Henderson (1984), one of Jung's contemporaries. His work on cultural attitudes was taken forward by Singer and Kimbles (2004) and by Singer (2006) in the form of 'the cultural complex'. From a group perspective, where traumatic themes repeat, the players might change roles (Karpman 1968). The typical roles are those of persecutor, rescuer and victim. According to Neimeyer (2001) recovery requires a process of integration and mourning and the making of meaning through which the past and present can be linked symbolically. It requires a personal process of truth and reconciliation effected through collective means.

Transgenerational trauma in individuals and groups

Related themes in individual psychotherapy can frequently be traced to traumatic occurrences in previous generations. It is as though the trauma has its own life which carries on regardless down the family chain, making its appearance in various problematic forms until the core feelings have been recognised and integrated. The nature of the present problem carries symbolic reference to key points of disturbance in the family history. These become apparent during the course of the therapy through dreams, recollections, family research data and present circumstances and experience constellated in the client's life. Disturbances can range from relationship problems and delinquency to physical and mental illness. While Kirkmeyer et al. (2007, p. 10) emphasise the role that parent–child relationships play in the transmission process, more recent epigenetic research at ETH Zurich (Gapp et al. 2016) appears to show that DNA structure is affected by trauma and is a significant factor in transmission. However, the research also suggests that recovery from transgenerational trauma can occur if a benign environment is provided for present carriers. In the UK, Jungian analyst and psychiatrist, Pitt-Aikens (Ellis & Pitt-Aikens 1986) successfully pioneered family group and institutional approaches on this basis, noting that traumas could skip generations or appear elsewhere in the geological matrix before the current scientific DNA discoveries.

The implications are that each trauma has significant downstream reverberations, as it is in their nature to slip out of conscious awareness over time and then to be re-enacted. Traumas with their roots in history might seem remote from current, but when understood, they can explain and free up otherwise intractable problems.

As noted by the author (O'Brien 2017) traumatic incidents in a nation at a given point in history are likely to impact groups and individuals alike for several generations. There seems to be no time in the unconscious. Intense collective experiences felt by the group, significantly include traumas. The most intense traumas can be considered as 'nodal' (O'Brien 2019) in that they become significant reference points which gather similar memories to them and drive unconscious re-enactment, diverting available energy from creative and productive activity. These group phenomena appear at the level of families, business corporations and nations. Examples of these traumas in groups and organizations and the analytical psychology transformation approaches used to deal with them are described in the following chapters of the book. Collective trauma can result from the shock of unforeseen or rapid change in the environment (political, economic, environmental, sociodemographic, technological, ecological, legal or competitive landscape).

Trauma repetition occurs in nations with the profound consequences of repeated warfare characterised by atrocities. The prize of the analytical psychology effort at the national level is therefore great and worthy. At best, improved consciousness can result in the reduction of automatic cycles of warfare.

Dealing with trauma

Post Jungian principles of dealing with trauma derive from the fundamental concepts of the unconscious, individuation, complexes and archetypes and involve some form of intersubjectivity, most commonly transference counter-transference. Given the full history of the human race, trauma is a basic characteristic of the psyche. It affects everyone, to some extent and is by its nature, unconscious. Integration reduces the risk of repetition and awareness reduces bias. The process of integration is a natural one, a Self-healing force of the psyche which involves the processes of differentiation and union described by Jung as individuation. Inevitably, this means facing dealing with complexes, groups of feeling toned memories, at the heart of which are found universal organizing patterns, or archetypes. In the process of this work, both the analyst/coach and client are transformed. This work extrapolated to the organization and culture is the art of leadership and change agency and usefully complements the systemic approach proposed by Shamai (2003).

References

Bremner, JD 2007, 'Does stress damage the brain?', in L Kirkmayer, R Lemelson & M Mrada (eds), *Understanding trauma*, Cambridge University Press, Cambridge, pp. 118–141.

Breuer, J & Freud, S 1895/1955, 'Studies on hysteria', in J Strachey (ed), *The standard edition of the complete psychological works of Sigmund Freud*, vol. 2, Hogarth Press, London.

Cambray, J 2018, 'Neuroscientific studies of trauma applied to Jungian psychology', in C Roesler (ed), *Research in analytical psychology. Empirical research*, Routledge, London.

Chan, MY, Park, DC, Savalia, NK, Petersen, SE & Wig, GS 2014, 'Decreased segregation of brain systems across the healthy adult lifespan', *Proceedings of the National Academy of Sciences of the United States of America*, 111(46), E4997–E5006. DOI:10.1073/pnas.1415122111

Charcot, JM 1877, *Lectures on the diseases of the nervous system, delivered at La Salpêtrière*, The New Sydenham Society, London.

Choi, KW, Stein, MB, Dunn, EC, Koenen, KC & Smoller, JW 2019, 'Genomics and psychological resilience: a research agenda', *Molecular Psychiatry*, DOI:10.1038/s41380-019-0457-6.

Crichton, MH 1961, *Hugh Crichton-Miller, 1877–1959: a personal memoir by his friends and family*, Friary Press Longmans, Dorchester.

Dicks, HV 1970, *50 years of the Tavistock Clinic*, Routledge and Kegan Paul, London.

Ellis, A & Pitt-Aikens, T 1986, *Secrets of strangers*, Duckworth, London.

Gaensbauer, TJ 2011, 'Embodied simulation, mirror neurons, and the re-enactment of trauma in early childhood', *Neuropsychoanalysis*, vol. 13, no. 1, pp. 91–107, DOI:10.1080/15294145.2011.10773665.

Gapp, K, Bohacek, J, Grossmann, J, Brunner, AM, Manuella, F, Nanni, P & Mansuy, IM 2016, 'Potential of environmental enrichment to prevent transgenerational effects of paternal trauma', *Neuropsychopharmacology: Official Publication of the American College of Neuropsychopharmacology*, vol. 41, no. 11, pp. 2749–2758, DOI:10.1038/npp.2016.87.

Henderson, J 1984, *Cultural attitudes in psychological perspective*, Inner City Books, Toronto.

Iacoboni, M. 2013, 'Contagion of Violence: Workshop Summary', Forum on Global Violence Prevention, Board on Global Health, Institute of Medicine, National Research Council, National Academies Press, Washington. https://www.ncbi.nlm.nih.gov/books/NBK207238.

Iacoboni, M & Mazziotta, J 2007, 'Mirror neuron system: basic findings and clinical applications', *Annals of Neurology*, vol. 62, no. 3, pp. 213–218.

Janet, P 1907, *The major symptoms of hysteria: fifteen lectures given in the Medical School of Harvard University*, The Macmillan Company, New York.

Kalsched, D 2013, *Trauma and the soul: a psycho-spiritual approach to human development and its interruption*, Routledge, Hove.

Kardiner, A 1941, *The traumatic neuroses of war*, Martino fine books, Washington.

Karpman, S 1968, 'Fairy tales and script drama analysis', *Transactional Analysis Bulletin*, vol. 7, no. 26, pp. 39–43, viewed on 18 December 2019, www.karpmandramatrian gle.com/pdf/DramaTriangle.pdf..

Keysers, C 2011, *The empathic brain: how the discovery of mirror neurons changes our understanding of human nature*, Social Brain Press, n.p.

Knox, J 2003, 'Trauma and defences: their roots in relationship – an overview', *The Journal of Analytical Psychology*, vol. 48, no. 2, pp. 207–233.

Neimeyer, RA 2001, 'The language of loss: grief therapy as a process of meaning reconstruction', in RA Neimeyer (ed), *Meaning reconstruction & the experience of loss*, American Psychological Association, Washington.

Nindle, BC, Billing, DC, Drain, JR, Beckner, ME, Greeves, J, Groeller, H, Teien, HK, Marcora, S, Moffitt, A, Reilly, T, Taylor, NAS, Young, AJ & Friedl, KE 2018, 'Perspectives on resilience for military readiness and preparedness: report of an international military physiology roundtable', *Journal of Science and Medicine in Sport*, vol. 21, no. 11, pp. 1116–1124, DOI:10.1016/j.jsams.2018.05.005.

O'Brien, J 2017, 'The healing of nations', *Psychological Perspectives*, vol. 60, no. 2, pp. 207–214.

O'Brien, J & O'Brien, N 2019, *Introduction to corporate analytical psychology*, Dosije Studio, Belgrade.

Papadopoulos, RK 2007, 'Refugees, trauma and adversity-activated development', *European Journal of Psychotherapy and Counselling*, vol. 9, no. 3, pp. 301–312.

Shamai, M 2003, *Systemic interventions for collective and national traumatheory, practice, and evaluation*, Routledge, New York.

Singer, T 2006, 'The cultural complex: a statement of the theory and its application', *Psychotherapy and Politics International*, vol. 4, pp. 197–212.

Singer, T & Kimbles, SL 2004, *The cultural complex*, Brunner-Routledge, New York.

Stein, M 2011, 'A molecular shield from trauma', *Nature*, Macmillan, Vol. 470, p 468.

Wilson, JP 2004, 'The abyss experience and the trauma complex: a Jungian perspective of posttraumatic stress disorder and dissociation', *Journal of Trauma & Dissociation*, vol. 5, no. 3, pp. 43–68.

Wu, G, Feder, A, Cohen, H, Kim, JJ, Calderon, S, Charney, DS & Mathé, AA 2013, 'Understanding resilience', *Frontiers in Behavioral Neuroscience*, vol. 7, no. 10, DOI:10.3389/fnbeh.2013.00010.

Chapter 7

The cultural complex

John O'Brien

In 1939, World War II began. Poland was invaded by Germany supported by the assured neutrality of the Soviet Union. Great Britain declared war and the US began its nuclear programme. The same year, in the United States, in a study of farming practices, Hornell Hart published his work *Culture-complex as a concept as research tool*. The cultural complex as we now know it, of 2020, is an essential analytic concept for Jungian analyst/coach involved in national, institutional and organizational transformation work as well as traditional work with individuals.

Definitions of the cultural complex

Hart (1939, p. 10) defined the culture complex as 'identifiable through certain psychological uniformities, desires, attitudes, skills, symbols and ideas' which amount to anthropological traits in specific groups of people. The term, 'cultural complex', however, has a special meaning in analytical psychology, one defined by Singer and Kaplinsky (2010) as follows:

> Cultural complexes are based on frequently repeated historical experiences that have taken root in the collective psyche of a group and in the psyches of the individual members of a group, and they express archetypal values for the group.
>
> (p. 22)

The definition builds on the seminal work of Carl Jung (CW 9i) in *The archetypes and the collective unconscious* and on the contemporaneous and subsequent work of Joe Henderson on the cultural unconscious (1988). Henderson argues that an understanding of unconscious cultural conditions helps to understand the nature of projections made by individuals on each other. Singer and Kaplinsky 2010) cite a letter written in 1947 by Henderson to Jung in which he uses the term 'cultural complex'. The substantive modern work on cultural complexes was published by Singer and Kimbles in 2004, and the clinical view is usefully explored by John Beebe in that publication.

Angels and demons

Singer's (2002) formulation of the cultural complex draws heavily upon Kalsched's (1996) work with individuals. In his description of how the psyche deals with trauma Kalsched suggests that at the centre, or archetypal core of personality is the spirit of the individual 'the Divine Child', the source of life. When threatened by trauma, archetypal (unconscious) defences appear in the form of daemons (such as a guardian angel). These forces turned inwards protect the ego by providing shelter and comfort (angels) or attack it (demons) to cause enough splitting to avoid the destruction of the ego. This bipolar dynamic protects the Divine Child at the centre and protects the ego from annihilation by the trauma (Kalsched 2003). The daemons might be identified with or projected out. According to Kalsched, reintegration occurs during the process of working through with a trained analyst.

Singer suggests that group and cultural complexes work in the same way, and he differentiates them from individual complexes by describing them from the perspective of the 'group as a whole', a systems perspective coined by Agazarian and Peters (1995). In this sense, the collective spirit is defended in a similar bipolar fashion: Inward attacks take the form of self-loathing and outward attacks that of hostility and torture. However, if we extend the approach further an explanation appears which accounts for the appearance of angels and demons both within the group and outside it. The rescuing angels of an injured group are often seen as devils by the other group, which is attacked by them. The same 'angels' might also rescue those inside the group who share the trauma at a personal or transgenerational level, and have similar defence mechanisms while being impenetrable and aggressive towards others in the same community.

Singer's ideas are based on the idea that groups and cultures behave in a similar manner to individuals. While there are clear differences between individuals and culture, as demonstrated by Kalsched and Singer, they share common archetypal images.

Recent Jungian publications show a growing interest in theories of cultural complexes, at the national level. For example, Gudait and Stein (2014) gathered contributions from Jungian analysts describing different approaches to cultural trauma in a number of countries, including Russia, Eastern Europe, Israel, Africa, and Asia. The *Jung Journal* has recently (2019) carried articles concerning national cultures in China (Meili 2019) and Japan (Megumi 2019).

Bridging business and analytical psychology

Jungian cultural complex theory finds resonance with the science of organizational development. According to Groysberg et al. (2018), there are four accepted attributes which definite corporate culture. First, it is found in shared behaviours, values and assumptions, and can be discerned in the unwritten rules. Second, it is pervasive in that it applies to many levels of the organization and in different ways. This view accords with corporate analytical psychology (O'Brien & O'Brien 2019) which explains the universality of the phenomenon in Jungian terms. Third, it is enduring. One explanation of this factor is that like attracts like. This social reinforcement model is especially valid for type psychology and its later applications where teams may become less functional owing to one sidedness. Fourth and perhaps most significantly, culture is an implicit factor which affects all the others. We suggest that universal themes relating to cultural complex are discernible across the various disciplines addressing culture be it experienced by the individual in a one-to-one encounter, by the organization or by the nation. Yakushko et al. (2016) emphasise the relevance of taking into account unconscious factors when considering multicultural situations, and note that the process of such research can be therapeutic to the community study and to the researcher.

This is further testament to the post Jungian view of archetypal patterns in corporates, and it appears to support the Singer and Kimbles definition. The implicit nature of the corporate complex invites us to proceed beyond standard coaching and consulting approaches into the world of applied analytical psychology.

In 2020, we might reflect on the knowledge of cultural complexes made available to us since the start of World War II, and wonder what the reflections of our descendants will be in 2079. As we engage with the issues of our times, Jungian analyst/coaches enter the field of the cultural complex, a field where universal themes are played out. These themes characterise the past, colours the present and the manner of our engagement just might create the future.

References

Agazarian, Y & Peters, R 1995, *The visible and invisible group: two perspectives on group psychotherapy and group process*, Karnac Books, London.

Beebe, J 2004, 'A clinical encounter with a cultural complex', in T Singer & S Kimbles (eds), *The cultural complex: contemporary Jungian perspectives on psyche and society*, Brunner-Routledge, London, pp. 223–236.

Groysberg, B, Lee, J, Price, J & Cheng, J Yo-Jud 2018, 'The culture factor: the leader's guide to corporate culture', *Harvard Business Review*. January–February 2018.

Gudait, G & Stein, M (eds) 2014, *Confronting cultural trauma: Jungian approaches to understanding and healing*, Spring Journal Inc, Los Angeles.

Hart, H 1939, 'The culture-complex concept as a research tool', *Social Forces*, vol. 18, no. 1, pp. 1017.

Henderson, JL 1988, 'The cultural unconscious', *Quadrant: Journal of the C. G. Jung Foundation for Analytical Psychology*, vol. 21, no. 2, pp. 7–16.

Kalsched, D 1996, *The inner world of trauma: archetypal defences of the personal spirit*, Routledge, London.

Kalsched, D 2003, 'Daimonic elements in early trauma', *Journal of Analytical Psychology*, vol. 48, pp. 145–169.

Megumi, Y 2019, 'The meaning of mystical experiences on the boundary between life and death', *Jung Journal*, vol. 13, no. 2, pp. 21–34.

Meili, MLP 2019, 'Confucius's hero's journey', *Jung Journal*, vol. 13, no. 2, pp. 35–45.

O'Brien, J & O'Brien, N 2019, *Introduction to Corporate Analytical Psychology*, Dosije, Belgrade.

Singer, T 2002, 'The cultural complex and archetypal defenses of the collective spirit', *The San Francisco Jung Institute Library Journal*, vol. 20, no. 4, pp. 5–28.

Singer, T & Kaplinsky, C 2010, 'Cultural complexes in analysis', in M Stein (ed), *Jungian psychoanalysis: working in the spirit of C.G. Jung*, Open Court Publishing Company, Chicago.

Singer, T & Kimbles, S 2004, *The cultural complex: contemporary Jungian perspectives on psyche and society*, Brunner-Routledge, Hove.

Yakushko, O, Miles, P, Rajan, I, Bujko, B & Thomas, D 2016, 'Cultural unconscious in research: integrating multicultural and depth paradigms in qualitative research', *Journal of Analytical Psychology*, vol. 61, no. 5, pp. 656–675.

Chapter 8

Infant research and analytical work with adults

Nada O'Brien

Human encounters are based on the primary relational experiences we had as infants. The ways in which we interacted with our parents, caregivers and significant others model the patterns of our relationships with others as adults. Early experiences reside in our unconscious and to different extents they are triggered with each interaction with a new stimulus. The patterns of relationship quality, satisfaction as well as deepest frustration, distress and wounding are modelled in these primal infant experiences. How we interpret the reactions of others in relation to us is based on these formative experiences. Therefore, getting to grips with the realities of relationships is a complex process.

Infant research provides the basis for understanding fundamental relationship patterns between the analyst/coach and the client. It is this which can serve as a vessel for transformation. The transformation of old patterns is directed by and towards the archetypal potential of the client. We might ask what is the client's finest vision? How can we keep this mind during the progress of our work?

The psychological setup and life of the analyst coach is critical to the outcome. Therefore, a high level of self-awareness of underlying patterns formed in infancy is necessary. It informs the unconscious 'match' with the client. In Jungian practice, as part of the process of deciding if the analyst is right for the client's needs, we usually encourage our clients to have a first exploratory session to 'check the chemistry'. The underlying patterns of being nourished during infancy, affect how we obtain nourishment; emotionally, socially and intellectually as adults in all arenas of life. This connotes the ways in which, in adult life, we choose partners and make demands upon them. In the corporate context, early relational patterns affect leadership and governance styles, as well as all other relationship based functions.

The post Jungian research presented here is narrowed down to the main categories relevant for coaching and consulting work with organizations. These comprise communication patterns, affect attunement, stages of development of the sense of self, transference and countertransference and intersubjective field.

Communication patterns and styles

Coenesthetic communication

Infant research provides insight into the unconscious world of shared relationship between analyst and client. The concept of an earliest interactional world was a result of the infant observation and was usefully explained by René Spitz (1965). Spitz inferred early communication patterns modelled both by the interaction of the archetypal foundation of the infant and the specific environment. He termed the primal and non-verbal mode of relating *coenesthetic communication*. The coenesthetic communication between an infant and a caregiver in the first six months of life involves a 'total sensing system' of the body (Spitz 1965, p. 134).

> In the first months of life infants are exposed to changes in equilibrium, tension, vibration, rhythm, intensity, contact, time duration, voice timbre and tone, etc. They register impressions, not through separate sensory channels, but by the coenesthetic organisation of their bodies. It is interesting that the medical meaning of 'visceral' refers to the vital internal organs of the body, such as those within the chest, including the heart or lungs, or abdomen, including the kidneys, liver or intestines. Language reflects these impressions in sayings that seem to exist universally, such as 'the gut feeling', 'heartache', 'get something off one's chest'.
>
> (O'Brien 2019, p. 137)

According to Spitz, the involved adults are not aware of this highly complex and 'total sensing system' because it is replaced by a diacritic (signified), conscious mode. However, the coenesthetic mode of perception and interaction remains our deepest and most immediate mode of experience and exists simultaneously with all other modes closer to consciousness. It is a source of so called 'non-directed thinking' (see the chapter 'Neuroscience and Jung' from this volume). According to later research, this archaic mode of experience does not actually 'disappear'. It instead exists alongside our other modes of comprehension that are just closer to our consciousness.

> We constantly experience these as modal inputs through our deepest, immediate reactions and perceptions. We continuously encounter the evidence for this. For example, we experience a person as 'cold' or 'warm'; something is 'dry', 'fulsome' or 'empty'. People could be 'sharp' or 'soft'. We feel them 'distant' or 'close' and a mind could be 'open' or 'closed'. It is from this form of an archaic mode of experience, of the undifferentiated mode of infant relating experience, that our adult comprehension and relating predispositions evolve. These kinds of

impressions regarding the person or situation that we receive are automatic; they precede our cognition and are based on our innate ability to assess in a natural, primal way.

(O'Brien 2019, pp. 136–138)

These phenomena bring the wide spectrum of topics related to body into the analytic process, especially in Jung's concept of 'the physical materiality of the psyche' (CW 9i, para. 392).

Evoked other

Precisely how early experiences lay the foundations for complexes and relational expectations is explained by Daniel Stern (1985). For Stern, the building blocks are 'Representations of Interactions that have been Generalised' (RIGs). He considered RIGs as fundamental units of the organizing principles of infant life experience and, subsequently, reactional patterns in adults. RIGs are based on episodes:

> An episode is made of smaller elements or attributes. These attributes are sensations, perceptions, actions, thoughts, affects, and goals, which occur in some temporal, physical, and causal relationship so that they constitute a coherent episode of experience.
>
> (Stern 1985, p. 29)

RIGs are conceptualised as generalised summaries of experience, not exact activated memories. As such, they are the building blocks of complexes (Jacoby 1999). An infant lives with the regulating 'other'. Therefore, an infant, a child and eventually an adult will always live internally with the historical other, or the *evoked companion*. 'The evoked companion functions to evaluate the specific ongoing interactive episode' (Stern 1985, p. 113) and in the same vein as RIGs, the evoked companion is the main factor of the unconscious expectations of the quality and likelihood of our experience. These expectations are coenesthetic in nature, and comprise the expectations of both somatic, affective and behavioural states and situations. Interestingly, even if the actual other is present, the evoked other with all the complex history will be internally present as well. This has a multidimensional time and reality implication in the sense that an infant (and subsequently an adult) deals with the past, present and future internal and external experiences. In this context we are never alone and we are always interacting with an internal historical other and at the same time with people in the external world. This is especially obvious in the analytical session as well as in the social system of the workplace, particularly when people are under stress to perform.

Affect attunement

Relational match and 'chemistry' between the analyst and client are informed by infant research through the concepts of affect attunement (Stern 1985). Affect attunement signifies the quality of emotional resonance and serves as a base for interaffectivity. Via selective attunement, it ranges from non-attunement, mis-attunement and authentic attunement to over-attunement. The patterns of primal emotional exchanges form the underlying patterns of relational 'matching' in adults, which furthermore raises the question of the role of the analyst. Given that affect attunement is the core of the deep mirroring process, for a good working alliance, the analyst should meet the criteria for 'good enough' affect attunement with the client (Jacoby 1999, p. 183). The internalised patterns of emotional relationships have also been studied from the perspective of attachment theory which sheds new light on the working of complexes (Knox 2002). Recent research also includes a neuro-archetypal perspective given by Alcaro, Carta & Panksepp (2017) who describe the formation of prototypical affective states in animals. This is closely linked to innate motivational systems (Lichtenberg, Lachmann & Fosshage 1992) which in Jungian work provide diagnostic orientation and information about the analytic field (Jacoby 1999).

Development of the sense of self

The body of research informs diagnosis of developmental stages, disbalance and the analyst–client relationship. Daniel Stern's research (1985) provides an overview of the development of the deepest preverbal sense of self to a cultural self, with the ability of linguistic expression. It also provides insight into the split which occurs when the deepest experiences cannot be expressed linguistically, not because of the limitations of language, but because of challenging formative experiences. *The emergent self* in the first two months of an infant's life is an early organization of the various experiences out of which basic patterns will take form. 'This is the primal form of what in later life is called the emerging of contents from the unconscious' (Jacoby 1999, p. 50). Around the second month, the sense of the togetherness with the regulating other based on RIGs is formed. Expectations of responses mark the development of *the core self*. The sense of the *subjective self* emerges from shared, common experiences with the other, and supports the development of interpersonal relatedness. By the fifteenth month, the verbal self, with its ability of linguistic expression, comes together with the split between the previous subjective self and objective self. 'The infant is aware that there are levels and layers of self-experience that are to some extent estranged from the official experiences ratified by language. The previous harmony is broken' (Stern 1985, p. 272). In analytical work with adults, the lack of development or over development of different senses of the self is highly relevant as well as the multilayered *motif* of the split.

The opus of Jungian work is bridging the split in the analytical intersubjective field. The transformational and healing power of symbols can retrieve the bond between the unspeakable and that which can be expressed.

Transference and countertransference

Transference and countertransference are some of the key features of the relationship between the analyst/coach and client. Transference signifies the projection of the unconscious content relevant for the client's development onto the analyst. This informs about the primal relational models and basic patterns of the client's formative period which are activated in order to be further developed within the framework of the individuation process. The content which is projected on the analyst is from both the personal and collective unconscious worlds of the client. It informs the analysis with the root issues, the stage of the process and potential ways forward. Countertransference is constellated in an analyst as a reaction to transference. It is equally informative of the relationship and is a precious source for transformation. However, if the analyst is not doing the personal work of making the unconscious conscious, Jung warns about 'psychic infections' which bring the process to a standstill. 'This state of unconscious identity is also a reason why an analyst can help his patient just so far as he himself has gone and not a step further' (CW 16, para. 545).

The field

Infant research sheds new light on the phenomena of transference and countertransference in terms of the mutual relational field which comprises more than individual contributions of the analytic dyad. Studies of the field provide insight into the activation of the multiple selves 'within the multitiered analytic system (brain, mind and culture)' (Carter 2010, p. 202). The relationship between the analyst and the analysand starts from the original intersubjective field and then transforms towards its natural potential (entelechy) contained in archetypes. The phenomena of the intersubjective field open a wide spectrum of perspectives, starting from infant research, neuroscience to quantum physics and are looked at more closely in Part III of the book.

Symbolising

One of the most relevant aspects of infant research for Jungian work is the insight it provides into the symbolising capacity. This feature is of pivotal importance for development, the transformation of trauma and individuation process itself. It is a prerequisite for the ability *to play*. Infant research illuminates the early formative conditions responsible for the development of symbolisation and its potential indications for the way forward (Bovensiepen 2002; Feldman 2012). The state of affairs of the symbolising capacity and styles is of special interest for our work in organizations.

References

Alcaro, A, Carta, S & Panksepp, J 2017, 'The affective core of the self: a neuro-archetypical perspective on the foundations of human (and animal) subjectivity', *Frontiers in Psychology*, vol. 8, DOI:10.3389%2Ffpsyg.2017.01424.

Bovensiepen, G 2002, 'Symbolic attitude and reverie: problems of symbolization in children and adolescents', *Journal of Analytical Psychology*, vol. 47, no. 2, DOI:10.1111/1465-5922.00309.

Carter, L 2010, 'Countertransference and intersubjectivity', in M Stein (ed), *Jungian psychoanalysis: working in the spirit of Carl Jung*, Open Court Publishing Company, Chicago, pp. 201212.

Feldman, B 2012, 'Working with infantile states of mind in Jungian analysis', in P Bennett (ed), *Montreal 2010: facing multiplicity: psyche, nature, culture*, Deimon Verlag, Einsiedeln, pp. 10661071.

Jacoby, M 1999, *Jungian psychotherapy and contemporary infant research: basic patterns of emotional exchange*, Routledge, Hove.

Jung, CG 1937/1985, 'Appendix', in *The practice of psychotherapy*, CW 16.

——— 1948/1990, 'The phenomenology of the spirit in fairy-tales', in *The archetypes and the collective unconscious*, CW 9i.

——— 2000, *The collected works of C. G. Jung* (CW), eds. H Read, M Fordham, G Adler and W McGuire, trans. RFC Hull, Princeton University Press, Princeton.

Knox, J 2002, 'The relevance of attachment theory to a contemporary Jungian view of the internal world: internal working models, implicit memory and internal objects', *The Journal of Analytical Psychology*, vol. 44, no. 4, DOI:10.1111/1465-5922.00117.

Lichtenberg, JD, Lachmann, FM & Fosshage, JL 1992, *Self and motivational systems*, The Analytic Press, Hillsdale.

O'Brien, N 2019, 'Who is listening? a psychoanalytic view on listening phenomena', *New Sound*, vol. 52, pp. 131–147.

Spitz, R 1965, *The first year of life: a psychoanalytic study of normal and deviant development of object relations*, International Universities Press, New York.

Stern, D 1985, *The interpersonal world of the infant*, Basic Books, New York.

Chapter 9

Post Jungian quantum theory approaches

John O'Brien

Why should a section on quantum physics be included in a book on Jungian coaching and consulting? A compelling pragmatic argument is that it helps clients make money. It can be used not only directly in trading decisions but also in general executive decision making. It informs the most profound aspects of individual, organizational and social psychology, and as a developing science it stands at the forefront of human enquiry into the mysteries of our own natures.

The relationship between quantum physics and analytical psychology has been one of fruitful mutual challenge and collaborative research, yielding profound discoveries which have affected both disciplines while opening areas for research currently being explored. At best, it holds promise for expanding, understanding and insight into human consciousness, the material world and the relationship between them. Learning from this field has been applied not only in the clinical practice of Jungian analysis but also in analytical coaching in the corporate setting.

What is quantum physics?

Quantum theory is defined as:

> A theory in physics based on the concept of the subdivision of radiant energy into finite quanta and applied to numerous processes involving transference or transformation of energy in an atomic or molecular scale.
> (Merriam-Webster dictionary 2019)

It includes quantum mechanics:

> A theory of matter that is based on the concept of the possession of wave properties by elementary particles, that affords a mathematical interpretation of the structure and interactions of matter on the basis of these properties, and that incorporates within it quantum theory and the uncertainty principle.
> (Merriam-Webster dictionary 2019)

In 1802, Thomas Young published the results of his famous double slit experiment. The passing of light through two slits resulted in an interference pattern demonstrating that light can not only be considered as particles, as imagined classically (by Newton) but also as waves. With the advance of scientific knowledge and methods, the experiment has been developed to include the study of molecules, atoms and electrons (Young 1802).

The study of quantum mechanics led to the discovery of the uncertainty principle and the observer effect. The uncertainty principle, introduced by Heisenberg (1930), states that it is not mathematically possible to precisely define the particular paired property variables of particles. For example, the greater the precision is of measuring the position of a particle, the lesser is the precision of measuring the momentum. The uncertainty principle applies to all matter/wave-like phenomena. The related observer effect is that when something is measured, its measurement is affected by the observation. Strictly speaking, observation in the sense of physics is defined as measurement, not as perception involving human consciousness.

Nonetheless, these physics phenomena have their analogies in modern analytical psychology, and the same terms are used to describe psychological processes.

Beginnings

The dialogue between quantum physics and analytical psychology started to take form in the correspondence (1932–1958) between Carl Gustav Jung and one of his patients and colleagues, the Nobel Prize winning physicist, Wolfgang Pauli (Meier 2001). Pondering the unusual phenomenon of synchronicity, Jung arrived at the explanatory idea of a potential unified world underlying the conventional divisions of mind and body, time and space. He termed this the 'unus mundus', or one world.

> Undoubtedly the idea of the unus mundus is founded on the assumption that the multiplicity of the empirical world rests on an underlying unity. (...) everything divided and different belongs to one and the same world.
>
> (CW 14, para. 767)

Pauli seemed to agree with this idea. Referring to quantum physics, in his correspondence with Jung in 1953 he stated, 'since matter has now become an abstract *invisible reality* for the modern physicist, the prospects for a psychophysical monism have become much more favorable' (Pauli 2001, p. 87). By 'psychophysical monism' he meant a unified world of body and psyche, in other words, one world. In the same letter he proceeded to make the link between quantum physics and humans develop more explicit:

This wholeness of man's seems to be placed in two aspects of reality: the symbolic 'things in themselves', which correspond to 'potential being', and concrete manifestations, which correspond to the actuality of 'being'. The first aspect is the rational one, the second the irrational one. (...) The interplay of the two creates the process of becoming.

(2001, pp. 95–96)

This unified world or 'unus mundus' approach was a philosophical and religious perspective which had been substantially developed by Duns Scotus in the 13th century (Williams 2016). Jung's analytical psychology and Pauli's quantum physics can be regarded as analogous to it, if not as possibly in Jung's case, founded upon it.

Developments in quantum physics

Introducing quantum mechanics, the luminary physicist, Richard Feynman, in his *Lectures on physics* (1965), described the double slit experiment thus:

We choose to examine a phenomenon which is impossible, *absolutely* impossible, to explain in any classical way, and which has in it the heart of quantum mechanics. In reality, it contains the *only* mystery. We cannot make the mystery go away by 'explaining' how it works. We will just *tell* you how it works. In telling you how it works we will have told you about the basic peculiarities of all quantum mechanics.

(p. 1)

The double slit experiment was introduced to analysts in training at the C. G. Jung Institute by Dr Jeffrey Satinover (2001). It is a useful window into the world of quantum physics for non-specialists and its some recent developments seem to support the one world hypothesis.

Double slit experiments

Two broad explanations of the wave/particle dilemma are the 'Copenhagen' and 'Many Worlds Interpretation' (MWI). In the mid-1920s, in Copenhagen, Neils Bohr and Werner Heisenberg agreed that the paradox could be understood as wave function collapse. By this they meant that probabilities of different states were reduced immediately after measurement. The MWI (Everett 1957) suggests that there are many possible worlds which exist in parallel to the space and time with which we are familiar. In 1952, Bohm had provided a 'hidden variable' solution which 'provides a broader conceptual framework than the usual interpretation' (p. 166), and in 1987 Bohm, Hiley and Kaloyerou published a ground-breaking paper, proposing a holistic perspective introducing non-local causality. According to 'local theory', particles are only affected by their immediate surroundings. In this context, Einstein had regarded particles as separate entities of reality with no demonstrable 'local' effect. Bohm's idea of non-local causality seemed to solve the problem:

> Einstein found it natural to assume that the particles were not connected in any way at all. However, in the causal interpretation they are connected by quantum potential; and therefore they are not separate 'elements of reality' (…) all these are participating in an undivided whole.
>
> (Bohm, Hiley & Kaloyerou 1987, p. 373)

Bohm's theory faced strong critical examination in 1992 by Englert et al. in the form of the ESSW experiment (ESSW is an acronym named after the initials of the researchers). However, according to Ananthaswamy (2016) later experiments conducted by Steinberg appear to vindicate Bohm's ideas and open the door for serious reconsideration of his work.

Quantum physics and consciousness

Perhaps one of the most interesting areas of post Jungian research is emerging from the dialogue between quantum physics, neuroscience and human consciousness (Jedlicka 2017). The literature relating to quantum physics and consciousness has been comprehensively reviewed and explored by Atmanspacher and Primas (2009) and Atmanspacher (2004, 2015). Hameroff and Penrose (1996) attempted to bring together microbiology, quantum physics and consciousness, observing not only the brain as a networked system of neurons but also the quantum effects of proteins within the neuron. They propose that this neural activity behaves analogously to both human consciousness and to wave collapse theory.

Most recently, Narasimhan & Kafatos (2017) have conducted 'quantum eraser' double slit experiments which they argue imply the existence of an invisible non-local conscious observer, outside space/time. Their research includes discoveries from information theory.

Quantum physics and information

Quantum information processing seems to be advancing dramatically. Rieffel et al. (2019)have suggested that a new quantum computer will be able to process in 200 seconds a task which it would take 10,000 years for a 'state of the art' supercomputer to perform. There are many applications of rapid computer processing ranging from enhanced security for computer systems and super competitive trading to a unified world with the meaning of information at its core.

Synchronicity

In relation to his postulate of a unified world of psyche and matter, and in collaboration with Pauli, Jung developed the idea of the acausal connecting principle of synchronicity (Jung 1989 CW 8). Synchronicities are defined as meaningful coincidences. As such they involve both objective events and subjective experience and attribution of significance. They make sense but there is no immediately apparent empirical causal relationship between the occurrences. With reference to this, he suggests that there is an interconnection between and a unity of causally unrelated events. Jung refers to this as the *philosopher's stone*, the central point of potential becoming. It appears through synchronistic phenomena, or meaningful coincidences unconstrained by time or space. Later, in 1972, Jung emphasised the importance of making real and applying the insights gained from the awareness of this paradoxical wholeness. 'An insight might just as well remain in abeyance if it is not used' (CW 8, para. 679). It precisely that concern with pragmatism which leads us to the observations of synchronicity in analytic/coaching practice.

Research into synchronicity in the practice of analytical psychology has been extensively developed by Spiegleman (2003). Related speculative work in microbiology includes Limar's postulate (2011) that DNA carries consciousness. Cambray (2009) addresses the idea of 'cultural synchronicities', an area described in tribal terms from the perspective of Castleman's tribal field theory (2004). Field theory examines the relation between the system and its environment. Its relevance to the interaction between analyst and patient was researched by the communicative psychoanalyst Robert Langs (1976), and was further clarified by the interdisciplinary perspective of physics and analytical psychology by Mansfield and Spiegelman (1996), who describe the historical development of the therapeutic relationship from early reductive and causal psychoanalytic approaches to modern synchronistic acausal expressions of meaning in the interactive field.

The heart of the matter

In a paper, which can only be described as beautiful, Hiley (2019) wrote, 'There is no Cartesian dualism. We have a thoroughgoing wholeness in which the mental and physical sides participate' (1995, p. 335). Hiley (2019) has stated that the quote 'captures nicely the idea I was trying to convey. No doubt you are well aware of the Pauli-Jung discussions, topics that I have found extremely interesting and informative'. In our opinion, Hiley's physics based argument gives a good account of the fundamental unity noted with scientific caution by Jung and Pauli, and adds clarification, taking into account research up to the 1990s. Hiley's view is that mind and matter are aspects of the same reality, a view which is fundamental to the theory and practice of analytical psychology. As already noted, Feynman, with similar poetic expression wrote of 'the *only* mystery' at 'the heart of quantum mechanics'.

From the perspective of Jungian analytical psychology, it is axiomatic that the dual relationship of the ego and Self is contained within the Self. To the ego this appears as a mystery. It can be argued that duality arises as a result of the human necessity of the binary thinking necessary for orientation. We need coordinates and maps to find our way around. However, where this map-making function is mistaken for the territory, we can lose awareness of unity. The interplay between these two modes of perception is analogous to the processes of differentiation and unity found in Jung's concept of individuation. The rediscovery of unity is the goal of individuation. To the binary mind, wholeness can seem irrational. To the whole mind the binary process can seem disconnected. There are times, however, when the two marry and the circle is squared, so to speak.

Business applications

A brief sketch of the relevance of quantum theory to the development of post Jungian analytical psychology has been presented. Quantum theory per se has a number of practical business world applications which fall outside the precise boundaries prescribed by Jungian analysts in clinical practice and which support the concept of the analyst/coach. According to Atmanspacher, a number of these were developed by Flohr (2000) and include models producing valid empirical results for improved decision-making models, questionnaire and survey responses and analysis, learning behaviour, agency and intention, machine learning language and so on.

Perhaps the simplest application to the corporate world is that of making money. According to Yukalov and Sornette (2016), a mathematical formula, 'the sum of a utility factor', has now been developed for the calculation of the quantum probability of an event. This is described as 'a rational evaluation of the considered prospect, and of an attraction factor, characterizing irrational, subconscious attitudes of the decision-maker. Despite the involved irrationality, the probability of prospects can be evaluated' (p. 12). From a Jungian perspective, such powerful (and now computerised approaches) bridge the worlds, but only in so far as supremacy is not claimed by rationality. The living mystery remains.

References

Ananthaswamy, A 2016, 'Quantum weirdness may hide an orderly reality after all', *New Scientist*, viewed 19 December 2019, www.newscientist.com/article/2078251-quantum-weirdness-may-hide-an-orderly-reality-after-all/.

Atmanspacher, H 2004, 'Quantum theory and consciousness: An overview with selected examples', *Discrete Dynamics in Nature and Society*, vol. 1, pp. 51–73.

Atmanspacher, H 2019, 'Quantum approaches to consciousness', *The Stanford Encyclopedia of Philosophy*, Stanford University, viewed 19 December 2019, https://plato.stanford.edu/archives/fall2019/entries/qt-consciousness/.

Atmanspacher, H & Primas, H 2009, *Recasting reality: Wolfgang Pauli's philosophical ideas and contemporary science*, Springer, Berlin.

Bohm, DJ, Hiley, BJ & Kaloyerou, PN 1987, 'An ontological basis for the quantum theory', *Physics Reports*, vol. 144, pp. 349–375, DOI:10.1016/0370-1573(87)90024-X.

Cambray, J 2009, *Synchronicity: nature and psyche in an interconnected universe*, Texas A & M University Press, College Station.

Castleman, T 2004, *Threads, knots, tapestries: how a tribal connection is revealed through dreams and synchronicities*, Daimon Verlag, Einsiedeln.

Everett, H 1957, 'Relative State Formulation of Quantum Mechanics', *Reviews of Modern Physics*, vol. 29, no. 3, pp. 454–462.

Feynman, RP, Leighton, RB & Sands, ML 1965, *The Feynman lectures on physics: quantum mechanics*, vol. 3, Addison-Wesley, Reading.

Flohr, H 2000, 'NMDA receptor-mediated computational processes and phenomenal consciousness', in T Metzinger (ed.), *Neural Correlates of Consciousness. Empirical and Conceptual Questions*, Cambridge: MIT Press, pp. 245–258.

Hameroff, SR & Penrose, R 1996, 'Conscious events as orchestrated spacetime selections', *Journal of Consciousness Studies*, vol. 3, no. 1, pp. 36–53.

Heisenberg, W 1930, *The physical principles of the quantum theory*, The University of Chicago Press, Chicago.

Hiley, B 1995, 'Nonlocality in microsystems', in J King & KH Pribram (eds), *Scale in conscious experience: is the brain too important to be left to experts to study?* Lawrence Erlbaum Associates Inc, New Jersey 315–336.

Jedlicka, P 2017, 'Revisiting the quantum brain hypothesis: toward quantum (neuro) biology?', *Frontiers in Molecular Neuroscience*, vol. 10, DOI:10.3389/fnmol.2017.00366.

Jung, CG 1952/1981, 'Synchronicity the acausal connecting principle', in *The structure and dynamics of the psyche*, CW8.

Jung, CG 1955/1989, 'Mysterium coniunctionis', in H Read, M Fordham, G Adler & W McGuire (eds), *The complete psychological works of C.G. Jung* (CW), CW 14, Princeton University Press, Princeton.

Langs, R 1976, *The bipersonal field*, Jason Aronson, New York.

Limar, I 2011, 'Carl G. Jung's synchronicity and quantum entanglement: Schrödinger's cat 'wanders' between chromosomes', *Neuro Quantology*, vol. 9, pp. 313–321, DOI:10.14704/nq.2011.9.2.376.

Mansfield, V & Spiegelman, JM 1996, 'On the physics and psychology of the transference as an interactive field', *Journal of Analytical Psychology*, vol. 41, pp. 179–202, DOI:10.1111/j.1465-5922.1996.00179.x.

Meier, CA (ed) 2001, *Atom and archetype: the Pauli/Jung letters, 1932–1958*, trans. D Roscoe, Princeton University Press, Princeton.

Narasimhan, A & Kafatos, M 2017, 'Exploring consciousness through the qualitative content of equations', *Cosmos and History: The Journal of Natural and Social Philosophy*, vol. 12, no. 2, pp. 184–191.

Rieffel, EG, et al. 2019, 'Quantum supremacy using a programmable superconducting processor', *Nature*, pp. 505–510, DOI:10.1038/s41586-019-1666-5.

Satinover, J 2001, *The quantum brain: the search for freedom and the next generation of man*, John Wiley & Sons, Inc, New York.

Spiegleman, JM 2003, 'Developments in the concept of synchronicity in the analytic relationship and in theory', in N Totton (ed), *Psychoanalysis and the paranormal: lands of darkness*, Karnac, London.

Williams, T 2016, 'John Duns Scotus', in *The Stanford Encyclopedia of Philosophy*, Stanford University, Stanford.

Young, T 1802, 'The Bakerian lecture. On the theory of light and colours', *Philosophical Transactions*, Royal Society of London, vol. 92, pp. 12–48, DOI:10.1098/rstl.1802.0004.

Yukalov, VI & Sornette, D 2016, 'Inconclusive quantum measurements and decisions under uncertainty', *Frontiers in Physics*, vol. 4, DOI:10.3389/fphy.2016.00012.

Part III

Corporate analytical psychology

Chapter 10

Background to Jungian coaching and consulting in business

John O'Brien

The Olympian ideal

Modern business coaching is based on sports coaching. As such it carries the fundamental aspirations and challenges of the Olympic Games of Ancient Greece. The aspirations are those of excellence and the Olympic ideals, which value the struggle more than the victory. The challenges are those posed by the practical reality of the human drive to win at all costs. Both were relevant issues for Ancient Greece. For development, the management of these opposite tensions requires a safe space, the suspension of warfare, an Olympic Truce, so to speak. The Jungian idea of individuation is the progression towards wholeness which occurs when a safe space is provided within which opposed forces can be held. For the Ancient Greeks, the safe space of the Olympic stadium was sacred (Murray 2014). This is apparent both in the culture and the mythology that first competitors to take part in the Games were the Greek gods and heroes. The Games took the form of human athletic competitions in 776 BCE and were held once every four years until 394 CE. Competitors in training were educated in the arts, philosophy and music, and subscribed to the Olympian ideals. According to Reid (2011), these five main ideals are subsumed under the idea of *Arête* (excellence and moral virtue). They include *Kalokagatheia* (nobility, beauty and goodness), *Andreia* (courage), *Eusebeia* (respect), *Sophrosine* (self-discipline) and *Dikiaosyne* (justice). According to Plato, *Kalokagatheia* implies harmony between body, morality and spirit. These ideals infused training and competition with the principles of fairness and sportsmanship. Summarising, Reid cites Plato's view that gymnastics are: 'chiefly for the sake of the soul' (2007, p. 161). To this end, competitors were supported by two coaches. *Paidotribes* (masseurs) taught wrestling holds and *Gymnastes* (sports scientists) taught training and nutrition.

An important feature of the Games was *ekecheria* or the laying down of arms. The tradition was sacred and it assured safe space for competitors and spectators alike. Peace was guaranteed for seven days before, during and after the Games (UN 2019). Notwithstanding the noble Olympian ideals, it is acknowledged that not all fully subscribed to them. For some, *Philonikea*, the love of victory, was more important than the struggle of the game. Furthermore, cheating, lying, unfair competition and commercial interest were not insignificant factors. Such aspects grew with the secularisation of the Games as it expanded from a Pan-Hellenic to a universal competition which continued as part of the Roman Empire until 393 CE. The opposite tensions of noble ideals and political and commercial interests seemed necessary for the Games to exist. The games required sponsors and sponsors required games. The management of this tension required the creation of sacred space and acknowledgement of the soul. What then of these ancient ideas is applied in Jungian coaching and consulting?

It is important for every Jungian coach and consultant (JCC) to see that the boundaries which create a safe space are secured so that soul work can take place, and the next is to assure that professional training and continuous support is undertaken.

The establishment of the modern Games

The spiritual dimension of the Games was not lost on Baron Pierre de Coubertin who revived the Games in Athens in 1894. Coubertin had been convinced by Thomas Arnold, the Headmaster of Rugby School in England, that Christian manliness could develop both the physical strength and moral fortitude for the advancement of the future leaders of an expanding empire. Organized sport naturally followed from such considerations. In Germany, a sports journalist, Carl Diem, inspired by Coubertin's vision not only introduced the Olympic torch into the modern Games but also picked up the spiritual torch from Coubertin and Arnold, and shortly after WWI, in 1920, he founded the world's first sports school at the Deutsche Hochschule für Leibesübungen (Chatziefstathiou & Henry 2012). In some sense, the structures for modern sports education were built as containers for the tensions between the drive for participation, harmony and peace and the drive for victory, imperial expansion and conflict, in other words, peace and war.

Sports psychology

Around the same time in the early 1920s, sports psychology was being introduced by Coleman Griffith in the US. Griffith keenly felt the opposite forces of the commercial drive for success and the psychology of developing individual players and teams. His sponsors were chiefly motivated by the business imperative to find low-cost ways of improving athlete performance, measured by results in the game, and thus introduced psychological coaching along with other methods such as hiring practitioners to put an evil eye on the competition during Games. Given the passionate support of public sport today, specialists in this art are no longer deemed necessary! Needless to say, in the inter-war years, despite Griffith's publication of *The psychology of coaching* in 1926, sports psychology enjoyed limited success.

Sports psychology started to develop again in the 1960s and the International Society of Sports Psychology in Italy was founded in 1965. In 1985 the Association for the Advancement in Sports Psychology was founded in the US, and the following year the American Psychological Association formed a Division for exercise and sports psychology. One of the drivers for the expansion of the industry was and remains the demand for psychologists to improve military performance under pressure. This is piquantly evidenced by the extensive application of positive psychology to fitness and resilience training for the US military (Seligman & Matthews 2011). Modern sports psychology is now largely focused on cognitive and psychological abilities in so far as they affect physical performance. For example, Grushko et al. (2018) include items such as attention and memory, time perception, anticipation and decision making, and sensorimotor coordination. They note that technology such as eye tracking, biofeedback and neuro-feedback is still being developed in support of psychological approaches and mental training is now routinely part of sports psychology. The trend is towards applied cognitive behavioural and biological methods.

With its emphasis on performance, sports psychology found a natural home in the business world. The cognitive approach pioneered by Tim Gallwey in 1979, with his publication, *The inner game of tennis*, was a landmark in the introduction of subjective methods of sports psychology and his work inspired a wave of executive coaches, such as Graham Alexander (2010) and Sir John Whitmore (1992) to apply practical psychology to business in the form of the GROW model.

The corporate coaching industry

The ideas of Barry Curnow, David Clutterbuck, Stephen Palmer and Dave Megginson were particularly influential in the 1990s as the coaching industry crystallised and the term 'coaching' became a 'catch all' for different methods of working with individuals and groups. A good overview of psychological developments in coaching is given by Palmer and Whybrow (2008) and useful perspectives on different approaches are given by Cox et al. (2010). A practical history of developments in that period is provided by Wildflower (2013).

To some extent, coaching followed the trends in psychotherapy with cognitive and behavioural approaches superseding early psychodynamic and later humanist and integrative schools. Popular business coaching literature suggests that that the explicit concern for soul fell by the wayside of these evidence based developments which promised quick returns. Coaching has now grown to a sizeable global industry and is increasingly influenced by positive psychology as advocated by Kauffman (2006) and it is expected that this trend will continue. Although the industry is unregulated, a number of research and accrediting organizations have established themselves in recent years. These include the Institute of Coaching (an affiliate of Mclean/Harvard Medical School) and the International Coaching Federation founded in 1995.

It can be argued that the loss of explicit focus on soul in the coaching industry merely reflects the wider Zeitgeist and that at this stage of its development, the industry has scaled in response to market demand for commodity. Through the lens of analytical psychology, it is perhaps the very absence of soul in the world of corporate coaching, which has constellated in the unconscious an unstoppable force for its return. A new pioneering phase has begun.

Consulting

Management consulting began with a clear focus on performance. Arthur D. Little was a Chemistry graduate from MIT, with a strong interest in providing professional technical services to industry. His firm, founded in 1886 grew to become a leading management consulting firm notably providing the white paper for the European Commission for the deregulation of telecommunications in 1968 and contributing to the privatisation of British Rail during 1994 to 1997. The movement from research and development to strategy was mirrored in the history of the industry. In 1893, Frederick Taylor had started his business in systematised shop management and manufacturing costs and in 1914 Booz Allen Hamilton, working with clients from both industry and government, was founded. The industry experienced considerable growth in the 1930s in response to US domestic conditions and again the 1960s as a result of internationalisation.

Deming's transformational ideas appeared in 1986 and 1994. Deming is largely credited with the success of the Japanese car industry. He exerted considerable influence on organizational consulting, especially on the transformation of management and leadership. His approach was based on four interdependent factors, which comprised his system of 'profound knowledge'. First, he advocated a holistic view of systems defined by the overall aim, towards which players support each other. Second, he stressed the importance of Shewhart's theory of variation (1986). Simply put, this is a statistical approach to quality improvement and waste reduction which distinguishes between stable and predictable patterns of variation in a system and surprise variations arising from unknown or unanticipated factors which fundamentally affect the system. Third, he emphasised the theory of knowledge. He argued that conveyance of knowledge predicts outcomes, takes into account historical failures and carries the risk of not being correct. From this perspective he counselled against basing future practice solely on current and historical practice, without reference to rational theory, and was therefore highly sceptical of case study teaching. The fourth element of profound knowledge was psychology. He strongly argued for intrinsic motivation in contrast to external motivation by pay and grades.

The realisation of the human value of people by management consulting was underlined by Peter Drucker in the 1970s. Concerning the responsibilities of leadership, in 1973, he wrote:

> In modern society there is no other leadership group but managers. If the managers of our major institutions, and especially of business, do not take responsibility for the common good, no one else can or will.
>
> (1993, p. 325)

Deming's work together with that of Argyris and Schon (1978) formed the basis for Peter Senge's *Fifth discipline* (1990).

Senge's Fifth discipline

Senge emphasised the need to look beyond individual actions and events to understand the problems of underlying systems which give rise to such actions. He looked as far and deeply as the spirit and his work shines like a jewel fashioned from the 'prima materia' of the consulting work and research of the previous ninety years. The five disciplines are as follows:

Personal mastery

Personal mastery is the discipline of continually clarifying and deepening our personal vision, of focusing our energies, of developing patience and seeing reality objectively. As such, it is an essential cornerstone of the learning organization – the learning organization's spiritual foundation (p. 7).

Organizations which can adapt are capable of learning. They are in touch with opposite realms of vision and material reality and this is embodied in their leadership. In Jungian terms they respond to a deep spiritual calling, made apparent in the symbol of a vision. This ignites a sense a purpose, and 'For such a person, a vision is a calling rather than simply a good idea' (p. 133).

> It goes beyond spiritual unfolding or opening, although it requires spiritual growth. It means approaching one's life as a creative work, living life from a creative as opposed to reactive viewpoint.
>
> (p. 141)

Senge notes the commitment of people with personal mastery, which in Jungian terms originates from the Self. They are creative, connected and concerned about the success of the organization. The development of personal mastery requires the relinquishment of mastery of others, and an inward focus which is not egocentric, but which analytical psychology would say serves the process of individuation.

Mental models

Senge uses metaphors that are wholly compatible with analytical psychology when describing mental models. In this process, we 'learn to unearth our internal pictures of the world, to bring them to the surface and hold them rigorously to scrutiny'. Such is the facilitating role of the analyst coach, to enable the client to consider 'deeply ingrained assumptions, generalizations, or even pictures or images that influence how we understand the world and how we take action. Very often, we are not consciously aware of our mental models or the effects they have on our behavior' (Senge 2006, p. 8). This view is wholly compatible both with Spitz's research into infant development and O'Brien's description of its effect adult functioning in Chapter 5 of this volume. This approach could be described as reality based psychology which recognises the practical value of 'the power of truth, seeing reality more and more as it is, cleansing the lens of perception, awakening from self-imposed distortions of reality' (Senge 2006, p. 125).

Shared vision

Senge argued that when individual vision is translated into a shared vision, then genuine commitment is given. In our experience of major corporates around the world, efforts to create shared vision are frequently based on values, goals and mission statements. After an initial burst of enthusiasm, they frequently fail. In our view, this is because they are created rationally rather than from the depths of the personal and collective unconscious. Corporate analytical psychology has both the missing tools and discipline that which Senge noted (p. 9) was required for the creation of a shared vision. In accordance with the premises of analytical psychology, Senge argued that shared visions must begin with the individual and develop in the group. This involves both harmony and conflict. In this respect, we might imagine or discern a natural musical developmental structure in group processes.

Team learning

His ideas can be summarised as 'the learning organization', in which leaders have the tasks of guidance, resource allocation, cultural management and vision, and the stewardship of core values which bring integrity. In Jungian terms, personal, interpersonal and surrounding space is created for reflection, connection and communion, which invites the infusion of spirit into teams. Dialogue is essential to team learning. It requires the suspension of firmly held assumptions and views and a genuine intention to think together with each other. This happens most profoundly in Jungian groups dealing with material from the unconscious.

Systems thinking

According to Senge, systems thinking brings together the other disciplines into a coherent body. It yields a holistic view which appreciates all the parts and their relationships to each other, giving orientation and motivation to its members. Without a holistic view, silo mentalities are likely to prevail and tribalism are likely to take hold (O'Brien & Weder di Mauro 2003).

Corporate consulting today

As of 2019, according to Consulting.com, the top five consulting firms by revenue are Accenture Consulting (at $17,310 billion), Capgemini Consulting, Tata Consultancy Services, Cognizant Technology Solutions and Deloitte Consulting. The top five by prestige are:

McKinsey & Company, The Boston Consulting Group, Inc Bain & Company, Deloitte Consulting LLP and PricewaterhouseCoopers. According to Consultancy.UK, the 'Big Four'; PwC, Deloitte, EY and KMPG still account for 40% of the global market. The industry is presently characterised by increasing competition from freelance consultants. The Big Four are the world's largest consulting firms, and account for nearly 40% of the global market. McKinsey & Company and The Boston Consulting Group figure prominently as do AT Kearney, Booze Allen Hamilton.

Jungian coaching and consulting work with organizations

Given the considerable resources of expertise and finance invested in the coaching and consulting industries over the last forty years, it is a little surprising to note that there is very little mention of analytical psychology in the literature, and only limited references to practice based on Jung's work, which Senge did not make explicit. There are some exceptions, for example, the 1992 publication by Murray Stein and John Hollwitz *Psyche at work*. Contemporary ideas on Jung's archetypes have been popularly developed but appear to be quite remote from Jung's original work and in some cases not connected with it at all.

Type psychology

Perhaps the most widely recognised application of Jung's work to organizations is the Myers-Briggs Type Indicator (MBTI). The MBTI is a widely used psychological instrument used for the development of people in organizations. According to the Myers-Briggs Company (2019), it is used by more than 88% of Fortune 500 companies in 115 countries. The MBTI Type Indicator manual instrument was developed by Isabel Briggs Myers and first published in 1962. The instrument indicates 16 type preferences arrived at through a combination of 'dichotomies'. These comprise the attitudes of introversion and extraversion and the functions of thinking and feeling, sensing and intuition, and in addition, judging and perceiving.

The MBTI instrument was inspired by Jung's publications on psychological types (CW 6), but has significant differences to Jung's original work. MBTI critiques from empirical psychology are summarised by Pittenger (1993). These include McCrae and Costa's (1989) evaluation of MBTI from the perspectives of Jung's theory of psychological types and the Five factor model of personality. The Five factor model, based on trait theory, includes Jung's extraversion as one of the factors. Similar instruments to MBTI include the Gray-Wheelwrights Jungian Type Survey (Mattoon & Davis 1995) and the Singer-Loomis Inventory of Personality (Karesh, Pieper & Holland 1994). The instruments are constructed differently and a full comparison is given by John Beebe who gives his own model (2006).

Type psychology was originally conceived with the individual in mind, but found application in a number of group and team building instruments, including those focusing on team competencies, for example, by Margerison (2001).

According to Steve Myers (2019), Jung did not approve the MBTI research and development undertaken in the US and raised several criticisms of it during the 1930s and 1950s. Notwithstanding this point, which seems to be well substantiated by Myers, the instrument was offered to trainee analysts at the C. G. Jung Institute as an option. On the basis of our consulting experience, if used according to the specific training and ethical guidelines provided, in the hands of a competent practitioner, and especially of a trained analyst, the MBTI and similar instruments can add a great deal of value. Keys to effectiveness seem to be the analytic competence of the analyst coach, and the education of users competent to differentiate the applications of the instrument for the required purposes in accordance with ethical guidelines.

Type psychology is most aligned with analytical psychology when used with Jung's central concept of individuation in mind and when it therefore takes into account the transcendent function. As such it is sometimes used to assist spiritual training. However useful, it represents a relatively small but not insignificant part of Jung's work.

Jungian work with groups

Jungian work with organizations was well underway in the United Kingdom as early as the 1980s. Notable pioneering work was undertaken by the psychiatrist and psychoanalyst Dr Tom Pitt-Aikens who consulted in the

United Kingdom at The Cassel Hospital, Stamford House, Finnart House Community Home with Education and the Feltham Borstal. His Jungian training had been gained at the Institute of Psychoanalysis in London.

His approach was pioneering in that his approach based on analytical psychology included systems thinking, family therapy and social psychology. It was applied not only to troubled adolescents in institutions but also to their families, social workers and the wider social systems. One of the features of his work was the establishment of a safe space which allowed for a disciplined focus on the thematic core of offending behaviour. The theme revealed and acted out by the adolescent shows commonalities between the individual and surrounding systems. During the process of structured consultations themes would become clearer and hidden family or transgenerational traumas would appear in surprising ways. The central theme was usually related to the idea of 'loss of the good authority', a concept articulated by Bruggen and Pitt-Aikens in 1975 and developed by Pitt-Aikens in 1989. Systems then adjusted and positive outcomes were achieved. A case example is the young man who repeatedly stole cars. A rescuing approach by social workers resulted in lenient treatment by a kindly magistrate who dealt with him on several occasions. It was not until the magistrate's car was stolen by the young man that a fuller meaning of the loss of the good authority represented by the delinquent behaviour was recognised and appropriate group consultation with all concerned addressed the underlying family theme satisfactorily.

As is often the case with pioneering clinical work, modification for commercial application followed, and key elements of this approach were used to great effect in consulting work with significant corporate leaders and executive teams from the early 1990s to date. Examples of both clinical and consulting work are given in the following chapters.

In the context of group psychotherapy, Ettin (1994) argues that Jungian theory finds a natural application in groups. It addresses the tension of opposites which occur such as the integration of the individual into the group between individual needs and group needs and authoritarian and democratic principles (Ettin, Cohen & Fidler 1997). His work builds upon that of the early group analysts, including Bion and Foulkes, and includes a shift of focus from the individual to the group as a whole.

The ground-breaking approach to Jungian work with groups, which is a foundation for working with groups in organizations, is provided by the work of Teresa Castleman (2003). Castleman describes the approach:

> Dream groups were inspired by my research in Lakota dream practices. I was struck by how communal their dreams were seen to be, benefiting the individual as well as the whole tribe. Some dreams were considered property of the whole community and would result in changes in ceremonial practice, a person's name, or which

direction the hunt might search for buffalo. I was eager to try the experiment of just how post-modern adults would react to listening to other's dreams as important, even vital material for all who hear. Decades of synchronicities, remarkable bonding, courageous acts of liberation and integrity were daily occurrences of over thirty-five years. Some in the Jungian world found it 'dangerous' to mix the psyches this way; others claimed that all of this was already written and tried in the first generation of Jungian analysts. I did not find any support for this notion, in particular my term: *the tribal unconscious* which is to differentiate from both the personal unconscious as well as the collective unconscious. The tribal unconscious lies between the personal and the collective – inviting 'objective dreams' that reveal actual, factual information about persons and situations that the dreamer could not have known, as well as connect each other through synchronicities. 'Tribal Dreams' as many who know my work call them, are a regular feature of dream work in a group setting.

(Teresa Castleman, personal communication, 25 November 2019)

Definitions

Since the 1990s, ample consideration by numerous experts has been given to definitions of coaching, counselling and mentoring. Acknowledging that debate, my purpose here is solely to define Jungian coaching.

The word *coach* derives from the name of the Hungarian village Kocs where the first horse drawn coaches were built in the 15th century (Merriam-Webster dictionary 2019). It also has resonances with the French word *coche*. Both imply carriage, transition from one place to another. The word has come to mean instruction, training or hints given by a tutor to help a student or athlete through examinations or performances. The International Coaching Federation gives a definition of partnering with clients in a thought-provoking and creative process that 'inspires them to maximise their personal and professional potential' (ICF 2019). Kauffman (2006) argues from a positive psychology viewpoint that coaching helps clients to 'shift attention away from pathology and pain and direct it toward a clear-eyed concentration on strength, vision, and dreams (...) from what causes and drives pain to what energises and pulls people forward' (p. 220). Both definitions describe what coaching does and how it is done and include a facilitative element.

Consulting has its origin the Latin *consulere* 'to take counsel' (Chambers concise dictionary 2004). The modern usage in management consulting has developed from advice giving and its connotations to include expert methodological help. An example is Edgar Schein's consulting method of appreciative enquiry.

Given the multidimensional nature of the Jungian work, in practical work with clients, all features are organically constellated and therefore we are using the terms interchangeably.

References

Alexander, G 2010/2006, 'Behavioural coaching—the GROW model', in J Passmore (ed), *Excellence in coaching: the industry guide*, Kogan, London, pp. 83–93.

Argyris, C & Schon, DA 1978, *Organizational learning: a theory of action perspective*, Reading, Mass, Addison-Wesley Publishing Company, Boston.

Beebe, J 2006, 'Type psychology', in RK Papadopoulos (ed), *The handbook of Jungian psychology: theory, practice and applications*, Routledge, Hove, pp. 130–153.

Bruggen, P & Pitt-Aikens, T 1975, 'Authority as a key factor in adolescent disturbance', *British Journal of Medical Psychology*, vol. 48, pp. 153–159.

Castleman, T 2003, *Threads knots tapestries*, Syren Book Company, St Paul.

Chatziefstathiou, D & Henry, IP 2012, *Carl Diem: Olympism in the shadow of fascism and the post-war rehabilitation (1912–1961)*, Palgrave Macmillan, London.

Consulting Industry Consultancy. UK Viewed 29 April 2020 https://www.consultancy.uk.

Cox, E, Bachkirova, T & Clutterbuck, D 2010, *The complete handbook of coaching*, Sage, Los Angeles.

Drucker, P 1993, *Management: tasks, responsibilities, practices*, Harper Collins Business, New York.

Ettin, MF 1994, 'Symbolic representation and the components of a group-as-a-whole model', *International Journal of Group Psychotherapy*, vol. 44, no. 2, pp. 209–231.

Ettin, MF, Cohen, BD & Fidler, JW 1997, 'Group-as-a-whole theory viewed in its 20th-century context', *Group Dynamics: Theory, Research, and Practice*, vol. 1, no. 4, pp. 329–340.

Gallwey, WT 1979, *The inner game of tennis*, Bantam Books, Toronto.

Griffith, CR 1926, *The psychology of coaching: a study of coaching methods from the point of psychology*, Scribner, New York.

Grushko, AI, Isaevb, A, Kaminskyc, I & Polikanovae, I 2018, 'Modern trends of sport psychology in Russian psychological society', *Papeles del Psicologo*, vol. 40, no. 1, Moscow State University, Moscow. pp. 64–73.

International Coaching Federation (ICF) 2019, *About ICF*, viewed 19 December 2019, https://coachfederation.org/about.

Karesh, DM, Pieper, WA & Holland, CL 1994, 'Comparing the MBTI, the Jungian type survey, and the Singer-Loomis Inventory of Personality', *Journal of Psychological Type*, vol. 30, pp. 30–38.

Kauffman, C 2006, 'Positive Psychology: 'The Science at the Heart of Coaching', in DR Stober & AM Grant (eds), *Evidence based coaching handbook: Putting best practices to work for your clients*, John Wiley & Sons Inc, Hoboken, pp. 219–253.

Margerison, C 2001, 'Team competencies', *Team Performance Management*, vol. 7, no. 7/8, pp. 117–122.

Mattoon, MA & Davis, M 1995, 'The Gray-Wheelwrights Jungian Type Survey: development and history', *The Journal of Analytical Psychology*, vol. 40, no. 2, pp. 205–234.

McCrae, RR & Costa, PT 1989, 'Reinterpreting the Myers-Briggs type indicator from the perspective of the five-factor model of personality', *Journal of Personality*, vol. 57, no. 1, pp. 17–40.

Murray, SC 2014, 'The role of religion in Greek sport', in Christesen P & Kyle DG (eds), *A companion to Sport and Spectacle in Greek and Roman Antiquity*, Wiley-Blackwell, Hoboken, pp. 309–319.

Myers, IB 1962, *The Myers-Briggstype indicator: manual*, Consulting Psychologists Press, Palo Alto.

Myers, S 2019, *Myers-Briggs typology vs Jungian individuation: overcoming one-sidedness in self and society*, Routledge, Abingdon. forthcoming.

O'Brien, J & Weder di Mauro, B 2003, 'Stimulating productivity in complex global organisations', *European Business Journal*, vol. 15, no. 3, pp. 112–121.

Palmer, S & Whybrow, A (eds) 2008, *Handbook of coaching psychology: A guide for practitioners*, Routledge, Hove.

Pittenger, DJ 1993, 'Measuring the MBTI … and coming up short', *Journal of Career Planning and Placement*, vol. 54, pp. 48–53.

Reid, HL 2007, 'Sport and moral education in Plato's Republic', *Journal of the Philosophy of Sport*, vol. 34, no. 2, pp. 160–175.

Reid, HL. 2011, *Athletics and Philosophy in the Ancient World: Contests of Virtue. Ethics and sport*, Routledge, New York, pp. 281–297.

Seligman, MEP & Matthews, MD (eds) 2011, 'Comprehensive soldier fitness', *American Psychologist*, vol. 66, pp. 1–87.

Senge, PM 1990, *The Fifth Discipline: the art and practice of the learning organization*, New Doubleday/Currency, New York.

Shewhart, W 1986, *A.Statistical method from the viewpoint of quality control*, Dover Publications, New York.

Stein, M & Hollwitz, J 1992, *Psyche at work: workplace applications of Jungian analytical psychology*, Chiron, Wilmette.

The United Nations and the Olympic Truce https://www.un.org/en/events/olympic truce/. viewed on 20.09.19.

Whitmore, J 1992, *Coaching for performance: A practical guide to growing your own skills*, Nicholas Brearly Publishing, Boston.

Wildflower, L 2013, *The hidden history of coaching*, Open University Press. McGraw-Hill Maidenhead UK & New York.

Chapter 11

Corporate analytical psychology topics

Nada O'Brien

Key topics are given in the form of conceptual categories of the energy transformation process which are considered in the practical work of corporate Jungian coaching and consulting. In this chapter we begin by describing the individuation process. This is the main premise upon which corporate analytical psychology is based, and from which it has derived its methodology and practical application. We then look into the energy view perspective in corporate settings, followed by the structural view. This includes the different layers of the unconscious and the archetypal actors of the psyche. These latter include anima, animus, persona, shadow and the ego–Self relationship. We explore the *field* phenomena in corporations and bring all these topics to life through a short case study. Finally, we offer a perspective on *corporate complexes* outlining the development of the concept with reference to Ferreira's chapter from this volume 'Introducing corporate cultural complex' and showing diagnostics and applications with reference to O'Brien's chapter from this volume 'Corporate complex: diagnostics and application'.

The individuation process

Fear and freedom, truth and power, performance and development, automatisms and good authority are frequently observed pairs of meaningful opposites found in organizational life. Opposites are fundamental to our existence; for example, the archaic instinctual demands and cerebral proclivities of modern human beings are often antagonistic. In corporations we frequently try to resolve the tensions between opposing forces which are impeding progress by introducing new procedures, changing business processes or systemic leadership training. From the perspective of corporate analytical psychology, these can be considered as substitute process formations which absorb energy (resources) and rarely bring renewed energy, but nonetheless carry encoded themes of the potential energy residing in the unconscious. Decoding aids identification and clarification of issues which have been kept in the dark, and as such are unconscious sources of energy disbalance. More importantly, when understood symbolically, the formations also contain clues as to how the potential energy can be integrated into consciousness. In other words, avoidance mechanisms also carry a coded guide to a solution.

Vignette

In a global financial services organization, systemic leadership training was introduced to address the problem of silo mentality and low performance. The topic evoked a 'frantic' charge. A palpable sense of urgency took the proportions of an existential crisis. The organization assigned this task in its totality to a recently appointed executive who came from a psychologically remote culture. The differences attracted the group able to project its creativity on her. The new training focused on cognition and attitudes towards the technical matters of business processes, which were being reorganized. Symbolically, it prompted thoughts about what was denied (the *movement*) in the organization, which was of such vital importance that caused such intense and libidinal charge of 'existential' importance. What potential was held frozen in the unconscious, and why did it appear demonic to the conscious ruling attitude?

That the collective had delegated this task onto 'a foreign creative feminine' invited our hypothesis of projection of the 'anima guide'. The evocation of this unconscious function of the group was manifest in the appointment. The assignment symbolised a creative and redemptive power, 'foreign' to the ruling conscious patterns of organizational life and opposing the conscious ruling attitude. It indicated a potential link to the frozen unconscious energy to be redeemed. The subsequent implementation challenges, setbacks and progressions followed the individuation map. An understanding of this guided the intervention strategies which facilitated the flow of the deeply hidden cultural issues which emerged safely and could be transformed. New values for the organization started to emerge in practice, change was set in motion, and significant advancement was made according to the capacity of the stakeholders during the given organizational cycle.

Whether the system in focus is the individual, group or organization, the principle of opposites seems to apply. It operates according to the equivalence principle. Substitute process formations carry symbolically encoded keys to the energy held in the unconscious, and these keys can unlock its potential and allow natural development to take place. As a rule, we observe the movement from parental complexes towards archetypal fields. For example, in the early stages of enquiry, a negative mother complex (absence of nurture, no creativity) might constellate, and this will be compensated for by the appearance of a foreign Anima guide. Symbols will show ego capacity and indicate ways of participating in the individuation journey arising from the tension of opposites for individuals, groups and the organization.

Energy view: the process of transformation of energy in organizations

The process of energy transformation in organizations can be generally observed in the variety of different forms which life development takes in its repeated attempts to reach satisfactory realisation. We find it in the patterns of career development of individuals and in the life history of organizations, where the underlying developmental requirements are thematically one and the same. But the attempts of realisation are expressed in different forms. Examples include business process improvement and reforms of HR strategies. The underlying organizing patterns can be detected in the dynamics between opposite poles. Observed in this way, we can see remarkably symmetrical intrinsic, interwoven and reflected patterns of events, human relationships, business processes and market dynamics. The dynamic of the process of transformation is best described through the analogy of the change process as it takes a form of *three times* in fairy-tales (O'Brien 2019).

'Three times' in fairy-tales

Organizational development is a process of energy transformation. A real change can occur if there is enough value created which can affect the (unconscious) automatic repetition of old redundant patterns of being. The way is paved for new movements by escaping neurotic circles of repetition. The main condition for change is the creation of a safe space for this newly available energy (however small) to flow. As stated, securing this condition is the first and most challenging task for Jungian coaches and consultants and it requires continuous awareness of one's inner dynamics, secured by the capacity to hold and respect boundary conditions. A results oriented, quick problem-solving mindset (see 'directed thinking' in Escamilla's chapter on 'Neuroscience and Jung' from this volume) poses a challenge to the creation of safe space. From the point of a directed thinking mindset, it can appear that 'nothing is happening' in the initial process of Jungian coaching. The counter-transference anxiety of the Jungian coach or consultant (JCC) is frequently articulated as a pressing urge to 'prove' the development to the client by making a premature interpretation, thereby disrupting the holding process. On some occasions, we have found that the need for the safe space is so intense that at the very beginning of the first session there might be an out-burst of tears, even before any problem has been introduced. This is usually a surprise to the client, because it comes out of nowhere, without any obvious reason. Immediately afterwards, a sense of relief is felt and genuinely human conversation begins to flow. The intensity and unexpectedness of the outburst prompts curiosity and opens space for complex and rich transformational work, within which the irrational is acknowledged. 'Our mania for rational explanations obviously has its roots in our fear of metaphysics, for the two were always hostile brothers' (CW 10, para. 387). After all, 'our cerebral consciousness is like an actor who has forgotten that he is (only) playing a role' (CW 10, para. 332).

An important facet of both leadership and consulting success is the acknowledgement of the powerful flows of libidinal energies which run our thoughts and behaviour. We must be able to allow intense inner personal experiences without acting upon them, or making a split by completely detaching from them. This comes as a result of a long and complex maturation process and it requires a gradual buildup of energy in order to go through the experience. It gives an objective position from which one can observe what is running (through). It involves constant navigation of the roads between the old and the new, until the inertia of the old and the fear of the new no longer possess strong enough energy to pull back from the newly acquired position.

The regressions and trials which accompany steps forward are not only inevitable but also necessary for mastering the wide spectrum of intense inner experience which creates defensive resistance to change. They are our most critical source of learning and they challenge to its limit our capacity to hold safe space. However, once when the 'critical mass' of the transition is acquired, the *metanoia* has taken place and the new position has been established for long enough, new vital energy provided for the developmental cycle becomes the possession of the client and it supports new patterns. Change is real and the new reality is here to stay. Until it changes.

Working with symbols brings the essence of analytical psychology in its full richness and complexity. If the change which is required by a client is real, i.e. not of superficial nature but signifying deeper development which brings new added value, then the flow of the new energy stirs the cords of trauma through the chambers of the unconscious. It is interesting that, like the piper at the gates of dawn, *the new* always comes by touching, one way or another, the gate of trauma. What is this intricate connection between trauma and the release of vital energy which brings new developments to the (inner and outer) world? Well-known cross-cultural and timeless images of the hidden treasure guarded by a monster reflect this particular phenomenon which marks a nodal point of the developmental process. Success in the hero's quest is portrayed in the slaying of the monster and the bringing of the treasure home, into the newly acquired kingdom. In our practice such an image was spontaneously painted by the leadership team of a highly successful law firm facing fundamental change.

It is this multilayered quality of trauma which gives birth to defences and resistances to the energy transformation process. Defence mechanisms aim to protect the Ego, the central entity of consciousness from the potent forces of the unconscious. Defence mechanisms of a client are also sources of information about the nature of the trauma. Defences exist with a reason and are to be respected. Analytical psychology helps us to recognise the unique ways in which the client's transformation is naturally guided. We will be informed by the psyche's symbols, articulated in the client's own business language (or artistic expression) of safe and productive ways, unique to the client, of working with defences. The symbols support the forces of the unconscious, which aid transformation and strengthen the ego complex through turbulence. Symbols indicate the required form and timeliness of JCC interventions.

Structural view: structure of psyche in corporate context

While there is an increasing trend of using the concept of archetypes in relation to organizational life, where there is a lack of scientific and clinical grounding in Jung's analytical psychology, approaches can be misleading and dangerous. Nonetheless, Jung's work on archetypes is fundamental to his work and can lead to the greatest depths of knowledge and development. Work with archetypes requires many years of rigorous analytic training, supervised clinical experience and personal development.

The most common tendency is to define a specific number of 'organizational archetypes' and interpret them literally as definitive aspects of organizational life, even in some cases as people. Jung himself emphasised that theoretically there could be any number of archetypes (CW 9i, para. 99) and that we can never grasp their meaning given their multidimensionality and rootedness in the deepest layers of the unconscious. We can rather only catch glimpses of meaning reflected in their multifaceted manifestations. Therefore, the structural view of psyche on the organizational level is offered as an orientation of thinking in lieu of literal and fixed definitions.

The archetypal makeup of psyche suggests adaptation between inner and outer worlds. The archetypal patterns of animus, anima, persona and shadow are considered in this context. Ultimately, it is the relationship with the Self which encompasses the whole. The archetypal energies are constellated in a compensatory way to the conscious limited ground, motivating the development towards wholeness. For example, we may notice depression in an organization. We might ponder about the withdrawal of energy in terms of (failed?) adaptation to the demands of individuation. We might consider the ways in which depression is compensatory to the conscious prevailing mode of being. What is in disbalance? Which psychic values need to be acknowledged, allowed into the conscious realm and lived, so that the flow of more balanced energy, enriched with new ways of being, can be re-established? What is the state of the relationship between animus, anima, persona, shadow and ego? How does the Self manifest through different constellations and where does the new potential lie? How does it manifest in the different aspects of organizational life?

Anima and animus

Detecting and discerning anima constellations in corporate life, we explore the organizational *ambience*: the prevailing moods; the sources of inspiration, animation, fascination and obsession; the emergence of ideas finding their forms; and the psychological space for imagination (Pardo 2011). We enquire further. What is the relationship towards the unknown? What are the irrational hints of the new organizational modes, values and thinking? What are the relational styles in the organization? How does the organization care about the employees? How does the organization *express* itself? Which forms do the inevitable episodes charged by affect take in the organization? What is the emotional stamina of the organization to hold challenging situations and crisis? How does listening happen? What are the styles and patterns of the renewal of vitality?

In the archetypal field of the animus in an organization we can investigate the underlying source of authority which determines conscious opinions, thinking patterns, attitudes, convictions, operational procedures and the ruling logic. It might be vested in a person, a group, procedures or history. But it will be there in the archetypal field. We try to understand the underlying ways of discernment, deliberation and reflection. We consider the types of 'organizational heroes' in order to come in contact with the constellated aspects of the animus. We ponder the 'general and absolute truths' as well as tricky patterns of the organization, and we note organizational expressions of humour!

Furthermore, we seek insight into the animus and anima relationship (*syzergy*). What is the situation with the energy behind the ruling, espoused principles of the organization. Does it feel powerful, alive and strong? Does it spring from the depths of their souls and resound through the group, animating it? Who really owns it? Does the decision-making process on the basis of disembodied general principles without allowing exceptions or on a case by case basis? Does the organization provide space, time and conditions for reflection, considering what is going on? Is there a capacity for staying in the unknown and dealing with uncertainty? How does the organization handle the affect charged complex episodes? What are the organizational ways of supporting the new developments and renewal (*child motif*)?

Persona

In persona we look for the patterns of adaptation towards the outer world and relationship to true identity. Edgar Schein's artefacts and basic assumptions (1984) is a useful starting point for looking into the organization's mask to the world and for considering its relationship to the real values and emerging identity. In this way we can reflect upon the congruency of the organization's formal presentation to the world (for example, in investor presentations, customer relations, market positioning and stated values) with everyday practice. We are mindful of the fact that these archetypal constellations work in relation to the dominant ruling attitude of the organization. Furthermore, we observe the ways of the adaptation to the internal world and how these multidimensional adaptation ways and patterns work and relate. By way of an example, the scientists of a pharmaceutical company were genuinely inspired to create new medicines to combat disease. An inspiring vision was written on this basis. A disenchanted sales force had written its own vision statement in the back office washroom. 'Flog more pills!'

Shadow

There is now a wide variety of approaches to corporations solely focused on organizational shadow. As stated earlier, very few are actually based on Jung's work. We are mindful of the fact that the shadow archetype produces fascination. Caution and humility in approaching it are necessary. Work with clients in analytical settings and with corporations has sharpened our understanding of the shadow archetype as potent unredeemed forces residing in the unconscious. It is both the source of renewal and vitality. Holding the key for new development it is at the same time entwined with trauma and threatens the ego in demonic forms. Untrained work with shadow can precipitate personal psychosis and organizational disintegration.

It is not within the JCC's gift to redeem the shadow. This happens through the process of the unconscious becoming conscious, led through its own subterranean paths according to the laws of the underworld. Tokens of redemption might be found in acts of integration of those aspects of life or energy quanta which were cast down from the conscious realm. Shadow resides in the dark corridors and basements of the corporate soul, which are unseen. Here close to core identity, trauma is guarded. This is where child labour is used in sweatshops, where animals are blinded to produce cosmetics. We approach the actual sources of fear and fascination which suck the vital energy of the organization into unseen vortexes of depression. We do not make the connection between carnage on our roads and the alluring image of the fast car. Speed is glamourous. We can delegate its shadow aspects to our ambulance staff and police, at least until we have to pick up our own child from the road. Given the multilayered origins of the shadow, its power and impact are amplified with the accumulation of transgenerational energy, carrying the cultural and collective potential of destruction and renewal. For every glorious victory there is a defeat. We know this from sport and we feel it in warfare. The enemy in the night outside is the shadow that we cast in the daytime.

We are mindful that every client on every level (individual, group, organizational) brings a certain capacity of working with the shadow. The ways of engaging with it are intrinsic to the client. We are also mindful that only so much development is asked for in any particular cycle of growth. More darkness than the soul can bear at any single point in time should not be revealed.

Major facets of unconscious energy are initially contaminated with the shadow. Analytic sensitivity and discrimination are therefore essential when dealing with the transformation phases. Ego defences inform about which style of analytic 'jam session' should take place with the shadow. A high level of musicality is demanded in this *danse macabre*, as is the case with the interactions with the 'Underworld'. To approach the shadow in cavalier fashion, too ambitiously and too quickly can result in release of powerful forces from the unconscious for which the ego structure might not be stable enough to interact and can cause grave consequences. Following the intrinsic ways of the process of the communication between the conscious and the unconscious provides a safe guide for this kind of work. It can vary from silent witnessing, containing the tensions and staying in uncertainty and suffering, to active interventions, but the essence is always compassion.

Shadow work leads to the enlargement of consciousness and to inner and outer connection.

Ego–Self relationship

'He *must* obey his own law!' (CW 17, para. 300).

Corporate analytical psychology is concerned with understanding the unique laws inherent to each organization. Their own unique patterns when fully lived, bring the ultimate realisation of inherent potential. Put another way, each organization is a unique constellation of individual, group and collective psyche which, in realising its potential, bring new values to the world. Success is full participation in the wider ecosystem.

> True personality is always a vocation (…) But vocation acts like a law of God from which there is no escape. (…) He *must* obey his own law. (…) The only meaningful life is a life that strives for the individual realization–absolute and unconditional–of its own particular law. (…) To the extent that a man is untrue to the law of his being (…) he has failed to realize his own life's meaning.
>
> (CW 17, para. 300)

The field

We are mindful that our experience of unconscious happens through symbols. Symbols occurring in and around work with clients knit a story. The dyadic relationship with the client is more than the sum of two integers. A third dimension, a common intersubjective field is created. This forms a stage upon which archetypal images perform their eternal dramatic plots. The field is of great interest to corporate analytical psychology. Relevant theoretical perspectives include Jung's alchemical nature of transference (CW 16), analytical object and interpretation (Schwartz-Salant 1988, 1992) psyche, soma and physics (Mansfield & Spiegelman 1989), categorisations of relationships between mutual process and the interactive field (Mansfield & Spiegelman 1996), the attachment theory perspective (Knox 2009) and, more recently, the interplay of personal and cultural complexes (Calland 2019).

The field's characters and plots are made of motifs, whose underlying source is of mythical nature, with interactions of archetypes at the core. Corporate analytical psychology observes the field as an archetypal mirror of the constellated work with the organization. We look for the meaningful relation of the narratives shared by our clients in the organization, common occurrences in the field of psyche and soma. We take into consideration the manifest information of the organization which directly or indirectly comes our way, never by chance. In the following case description, it was the constellated field which provided most information and guidance for our work.

Application of the topics: case study

In order to ground these concepts in more concrete situations in organizational life, we will describe an assignment with one multinational corporation. The case, highly complex in nature, was informed by a rich pool of images, complex episodes, synchronistic events, narratives on different levels and business developments, so given the scope of this chapter the assignment will be presented only through chosen red threads.

We were approached by the HR department of an international subsidiary and given the presenting problem of 'too much talking in the executive board meetings'. The meetings would last too long. Important decisions were not made. The same people would talk. The same people would not talk.

The HR team had invested a lot of expertise and effort in communicating the company's values to the employees, designing competencies, company behaviour models and making them familiar to the staff. Yet at all levels in the organization, the meeting dynamics and communication issues did not change. Further enquiries revealed that the common actors in 'overtalk' situations in the executive team were the business silo heads, and this was reflected in meetings between their subordinates at different levels of the organization.

Our engagement comprised of individual coaching with the national CEO and the executive team members, observation of their team meetings and few engagements with the top 100. During the first round of individual coaching sessions, more than a half of the clients reported frustration with their fellow team members. Similarly, there was a strong theme of poor communication. Subordinates lacked timeliness in reporting and or did not communicate at all. The communication issue was pervasive at all levels and detracted considerable value from business. In one case an executive read in the newspaper that a company employee in his division had committed suicide. The employee's team leader had known about the matter but had not followed the simple procedure, or used common sense to inform the executive. Media interest was distressing for the family of the deceased, his friends and colleagues and posed an ungrounded threat of reputational damage to the executive and to the company. The problem could have been avoided by a simple act of communication.

Our executive board meeting observations informed us that the group energy was being directed on the object, elaborating on the outer objective situations and establishing a logical order from different perspectives. This dominating principle (apparent extravert thinking function) prompted us to ponder about the unconscious motivations, beliefs and personal, subjective arena in the unconscious. A curious theme which surfaced in the individual sessions was a sort of surprise that one should even talk about personal ideals or ponder about 'self-understood' issues such as relating to a topic in the organization. As if they were 'yes of course' aspects of the organizational life, one does not talk about them and yet it seems that there was no aware-ness that they were actually not lived. In terms of the conscious orientation patterns of the group, our thoughts and early hypothesis were around the tension between the opposites of extravert thinking and introvert feeling (the latter being the inferior function). Despite the impression of 'coldness' on the manifest level, we were mindful of the strong *feeling* libidinal charge which potentially exists in the unconscious but being introverted, does not flow towards the object. We wondered about the potential ways of this unconscious charge unfolding in the course of our work.

The CEO, who was a Western European, in his early 40s, open-minded, constructive, intellectually ingenious, was determined to create 'a speak up' culture, enhancing both vertical and horizontal communication throughout the organization. He was disturbed to learn the result in an anonymous survey of the top 100 that despite all the efforts and the accepted 'speak up' culture on the manifest level, the issue of not communicating dramatically expressed in one of the employee's survey statements: 'If we speak up, our heads will be cut off!'

During individual coaching with executive members and the CEO a number of topics were raised. These typically included business issues and situations, complex episodes, dreams and events from private lives. Narratives carried a number of themes and images. These included, for example, the absent (or prematurely deceased) father, the forcibly dislocated and accultur-ated girl, female prostitutes, spouses in empty silence, a cold and uptight mother figure, children with disorders (autism spectrum), and frantic pace and corporate offices. Curiously enough, when our clients were asked if they initi-ated informal meetings with their colleagues (i.e. picked up a phone and talked or met over coffee to discuss relevant issues) the question met with huge surprise. It was as if there was some sort of an unconscious predisposition (fundamental bias) that this is not what one would normally do! The images which surfaced when we pondered about this together with our clients revealed a deeply rooted cultural complex. In accordance with unspoken patriarchal codes some things were self-understood and expected. One did not explicitly communicate regarding those things, and it was expected that they should be approached by the other party (of different rank) and not vice versa. Furthermore, the (international) firm had a historical legacy of dramatic national relations which dated way back in time, which in addition surfaced the protestant-catholic dialectics.

We noted a sense of 'unapproachability'. Our counter transference took the form of bodily chill (with a sense of horror to some extent), a sense of definite, irreversible loss, longing and sadness. It had a quality of dignity around itself which one 'has to' silently respect and not question. It was as if there was a taboo of sadness and loss one simply does not touch. Furthermore, when clients were speaking about the other party not communicating about business relevant issues, there was a sense of deep disappointment, hopelessness and betrayal. It was the kind of betrayal that a father would have in the old days with regards to his son, for not following in his footsteps. It was also the other way around, that of a son not being able to rely on his father, as our phantasy would have it. And yet, one does not talk about it.

The transference brought the images of unifications of things otherwise not belonging to the immediate world of the individual. Science and art, strange and common, matters of spirituality and business were routinely brought to the table. In addition, there was a sense of welcoming, cherishing and nourishing something personal, original and creative which they would 'pour' into that safe and playful space. Our fantasy named it as *Inspiratrice*. These were projected onto our roles so the sessions were awaited with curiosity and the expectations of something new and 'unusual'. Through our peer reflections and supervision, we became mindful of these projections and took precautions against the indulgence of our self-view of being special and quirky (always as a compliment to a Jungian!). In this respect, there was a potential hazard of identification with trickster energy in the form of the King's Fool and Advisor, or as an inspiring anima with a power to 'carry away'. These archetypal energies were eventually realised to a greater extent in the group itself. Meanwhile, they informed us about the developments in the *field* and provided us with new lenses through which we observed the process of substitute formation and the underlying dynamics working towards a new balance.

Structurally, we pondered the relationship between animus and anima constellations, appearing in the forms of initial coldness, non-relatedness and prostitution, attitude towards the feminine, and sadness and absence. We considered persona in her dignified, untouchable style in the meeting place of the inner and outer world. The organizational attitude towards customer issues in general (including marketing style) was 'We will present our products and services in proper and dignified ways but will not "impose" them on the customers'. We reflected upon the shadow carrying something 'horrific' which could not be spoken, but paradoxically manifested itself through silence or *silently*. Yet, both the advisory and inspiring energies aiding the transformation process sprang from the shadow, which stood in opposition to the conscious attitude of the company.

The motif of 'the head being cut off' provided us with the additional insight into the dynamics of the collective unconscious, in so far as the head not being connected to the rest of the body indicating a potential schism. The apparent schism was between intellect and emotions, 'cultured' and 'archaic' man, control and spontaneity, duty and fun. It was not surprising to learn that the most frequently reported reasons for absence from work were stress related bodily disorders (mainly migraines). We enquired about the organizational 'modi vivendi' and the provisions of safe space and opportunities for any form of informal socialising, for just being together in a human, spontaneous way. There were many highly structured events such as offsites, but they over-crowded and overwhelmed with unprioritised business issues. They absorbed available time and energy. Apart from a few timid individual initiatives, there were no provisions for freer human interaction. Furthermore, we learned that the CEO would frequently be 'missing' from the meetings where his presence was expected and that he himself would not initiate communication oppor-tunities to solve issues with his colleagues. The impression was given that most meetings were regarded as an 'unnecessary waste of time' and that there was an underlying anxiety of any potential emotional involvement. Thinking in Jungian terms, this ruling was turning potentially anima-ting energy into *animosity* and freezing the relational capacity. The sense of communion would deteriorate and the espoused values, competencies and behaviours would live on the paper and in the cloud of political correctness. Logos principle (reason, discrimination, judgement) became over-dominating in regard to the relating principle (Eros) so in potential relating situations (i.e. meetings), the outcome was too many words lacking energy to move the process forward.

Considering the reasons why strong logos principles were dominant, we realised that there had been a historical attempt to unify what had grown into a diverse multinational corporation by the imposition of the culture which had served the parent company. In time it had created hardened schisms that calcified the energy flow. On the manifest level there was a communication issue, and at a deeper level the conditions for *communion* were absent. The nodal point in this process we learned only after we had completed our engagement.

Over the course of three months we noticed a change in the field. Images brought up in the client sessions were of spouses communicating with non-verbal gestures, for example, a red rose, bursting into tears, deep sadness, a sense of pressure release. Images of vital female characters wearing colour-ful clothes appeared as did valuable books, the making of art out of natural materials and curious maidens from a faraway country. Images of mature male figures as witty advisors to captains on sea journeys, were accompanied by landscapes of the shores, oceans with powerful winds and, interestingly enough, a great deal of small talk about food, dance and singing!

We supported the narratives guided by the client's respective styles of communication. (Some preferred business consulting language, others more personal or more explicitly symbolic ways.) In all cases, content and process analysis took place and the business application and added value to the organization was kept in mind. The boundaries of our consulting team peer reflections and supervision provided a container for reflection and potential transformation.

The HR client created different provisions for spontaneous, informal human interactions. The first 'meeting over coffee' initiatives were made by the clients themselves and we were sometimes asked to mediate the sessions with the CEO. (We used this invitation to support the client to develop communication with the CEO themselves.) Given the more specific symbols which were surfaced in the sessions, a spectrum of opportunities for different interactions was created. These included intense direct contact weekly sports events, weekend clubbing, singing, dancing and jazz evenings. It was important that these provisions were chosen and designed by the clients themselves and it was curious to us that there was strong presence of music in these activities.

With regards to the *child motif*, which at the beginning of our involvement had an autistic feature (due to traumas, as informed by the narratives), it was mentioned that music could be a potential way of 'involvement with the world', something like a bridge. It is worthwhile noting that autism is defined by social interaction and communication impairments, repetitive patterns of thought and behaviour and the reduced sharing of emotions and affects (DSM 5). Autism seen through the lenses of analytical psychology appears as being in a special world with its own rules and values as a reaction to transgenerational trauma (Kalsched 1996). Symbolically, connecting such a world to music, which is one of the deepest mediums of inner and outer *communio* (O'Brien 2019), was a token of potential progress of a great significance. Furthermore, the story of a late teenager who wanted to apply for a visa to stay in the country of the international subsidiary in order to explore the country's world of music and theatre was also indicative of development towardsunification of opposites.

In order to acknowledge the changes, and to celebrate the flow of new life energy we supported the HR client to invite the executive board members to design the first of many regular monthly informal dinners (one of the new initiatives they had decided upon) using carefully chosen symbols implicitly resonating with their field. These events became socialising rituals 'indigenous' to the organization. The invitation was communicated in a playful, light-hearted way, creatively challenging the executive leaders to a game. They readily and enthusiastically accepted, self-organized (without our facilitation) and invested a lot of creative thought and effort into the task. This first dinner was a success and we heard a lot of spirited anecdotes reported from this first special event. The level of enthusiasm, creative effort and care invested in preparing this event by the clients themselves demonstrated the energy charge released and made available to be channelled into the more interactive, spontaneous and relational modes of being necessary for superior business performance. This event and other spontaneous 'spin off' initiatives in the following months eventually resulted in a new structuring of formal meetings with different dynamics. They were characterised by humour, more fluent and spontaneous communication and a more satisfactory decision making process. New and disconfirming data was encouraged. Constructive challenge grew to the point where organizational strategy process was redesigned and significant improvements were made to the different divisions to provide a connected market facing service. Both our client and we felt that the journey had taken a different course from that which we might have expected twelve months previously and that the energy available for change was now being channelled in a new and productive ways.

We completed our engagement with full awareness that the proper analogy of the ending would be that the hero in a fairy-tale has reunited with his beloved but that 'the evil forces' somewhat transformed, are not banished from the newly acquired kingdom. We remain mindful that these forces, 'which obstruct meaningful vitality' (Evans 1964, p. 47), are awaiting somewhere in the organizational shadow to constellate new oppositional poles sometime in the future to prompt a new cycle of self-discovery.

The images produced in the course of our engagement show a movement from parental complexes to the more archetypal images of animus and anima (Kast 2006, p. 125). These mediate the relationship between ego and the unconscious, and their appearance indicates a step forward in the process of the ego's separation from the parental imagoes, mirroring an approach towards the Self and fulfilment of core potential. Executive board members became more 'independent', taking the initiative for change more into their own hands rather than waiting for the instructions from the absent 'father' (CEO and/or external authority). The CEO, in his 'absent ways', which now revealed a dislike of negative patriarchy, supported the new activities and restructured the meetings to increased efficiency; openness towards emerging values and guidance (Kast 2006, p. 127).

A few months after the completion of our engagement, during the course of our work with another client in a different part of the world, without any mention of the multinational corporation in question from our side, we learned that the pivotal figure in the organization's history was the late father of the family currently running it. He had been a close collaborator of a national leader who had supported the Axis powers and had committed large scale atrocities in WWII. Since that time, the company had kept growing, changing its identity and outfits, and in time only a very few well informed individuals knew that fact. It was a family taboo, a secret kept away from the world, engulfed with profound shame and guilt. It was the secret which nobody spoke about. We were astonished that, uninvited, this information found a way to us. Learning this new information we were reminded that 'the unconscious is the future in the form or disguise of the past' (Adler, p. 407). It seems that the story had found its own way to be communicated, through the scattered images of the many narratives which our clients had felt safe to be express, not knowing their meaning in the familial and collective unconscious, but which they had been courageous enough to own and transform. All *in a veil of silence* shielded from the direct, explicit rationalisation, but vividly *musical*, tuning in to something new.

What had made this 'organizational father' act in such a way and make such choices? Apart from the comment that he was a sort of an absolutist type of a leader, we were not given any information about his early history and had not researched it. We were wondering what kind of extreme conditions in the early environment of this individual and what transgenerational traumas contributed to his profile. From a type psychology perspective Jung's comments seem apposite. 'Some have their reason in thinking, others in feeling. Both are servants of Logos, and in secret become worshipers of the serpent' (Jung 2009, p. 280).

It is a remarkable fact that a great number of issues which arrest the flow of the life energy in corporations have at their deepest core shame and guilt and an absence of any means for expression. Furthermore, once when some of the core plots do come to the surface, they are, as a rule, connected to some form of collective trauma. We often find ourselves working 'with' or 'in the presence of' people from the past, victims and perpetrators of atrocities who are long time deceased but whose stories somehow come to light. We often feel as if we are still living in WWII due to the vast majority of cases dealing profoundly with the events which took place then and were not processed. We wonder if we are collectively living in a time of taboo where not asking questions (or not having the safe space for it) takes the form of abyssal detachment from trauma through consumerism, living in virtual reality which limits the production of our own images (What they might show?!) and an extreme 'speeding up' of the pace of life as a frantic 'high', an escape from a life debilitating sadness of humanity?

Shame, guilt and trauma are a mysterious threesome which seem to reside in the deepest chambers of the human psyche. Shame and guilt engulf victims and perpetrators and rescuers alike. These issues were illuminated in the contribution to research in this field on Nazis and their followers made from a Jungian perspective (Marks 2011). Marks adds to the spectrum the motifs of humiliation which were consistently found in the individual, group and national levels. These topics raise eternal questions of human nature which is capable of *unspeakable* atrocities. As an analyst, Jungian coach and consultant and as a human being, one finds it hard to look into this abyss. Perhaps, one might look at it *silently*. An answer might be found in the narratives written by the archetypal hand itself. And there is the fairy-tale of The Green Maiden.

'The reason for evil in the world is that people are not able to tell their stories' (Jung 1976, in Lafontaine 2019).

References

Calland, R 2019, 'Race, power and intimacy in the intersubjective field: the inter-section of racialised cultural complexes and personal complexes', *Journal of Analytical Psychology*, vol. 64, no. 3, viewed 26 November 2019, DOI:10.1111/1468-5922.12503.

Evans, RI 1964, *Conversations with Carl Jung and reactions from Ernest Jones*, Van Nostrand Reinhold Insight Books, Princeton.

Jung, CG 1932/1981, 'The development of personality', in *The development of personality*, CW 17.

––––––– 1934/1970, 'The meaning of psychology for modern man', in *Civilization in transition*, CW 10.

––––––– 1936/1970, 'Wotan', in *Civilization in transition*, CW 10.

––––––– 1936/1990, 'The concept of the collective unconscious', in *Archetypes of the collective unconscious*, CW 9i.

––––––– 1946/1985, 'Psychology of the transference', in *The practice of psychotherapy*, CW 16.

––––––– 2000, *The collected works of C. G. Jung* (CW), eds. H Read, M Fordham, G Adler & W McGuire, trans. RFC Hull, Princeton University Press, Princeton.

Jung, CG 2009, *The red book: Liber Novus*, ed. S Shamdasani, W. W. Norton & Company, New York.

Kalsched, D 1996, *The inner world of trauma: archetypal defenses of the personal spirit*, Routledge, Brunner-Routledge, New York.

Kast, V 2006, 'Anima/Animus', in R Papadopoulos (ed), *The handbook of Jungian psychology*, Routledge, Hove, pp. 125,127.

Knox, J 2009, 'The analytic relationship: integrating Jungian, attachment theory and developmental perspectives', *British Journal of Psychotherapy*, vol. 25, no. 1, DOI:10.1111/j.1752-0118.2008.01098.x.

Lafontaine, L 2019, *Carl Jung on evil – quotations*, blog, viewed 19 December 2019, https://carljungdepthpsychologysite.blog/2019/05/03/carl-jung-on-evil-quotations/#.Xf-mPJNKjIU.

Mansfield, V & Spiegelman, JM 1989, 'Quantum mechanics and Jungian psychology', *Journal of Analytical Psychology*, vol. 34, no. 1, DOI:10.1111/j.1465-5922.1989.00003.x.

Mansfield, V & Spiegelman, JM 1996, 'On the physics and psychology of the transference as an interactive field', *Journal of Analytical Psychology*, vol. 41, no. 2, DOI:10.1111/j.1465-5922.1996.00179.x.

Marks, S 2011, 'Hidden stories, toxic stories, healing stories: the power of narrative in peace and reconciliation', *Narrative Works*, vol. 1, no. 1, viewed 13 November 2019, https://journals.lib.unb.ca/index.php/NW/article/view/18476.

O'Brien, N 2019, 'Who is listening: a psychoanalytic view on listening phenomena', *New Sound International Journal of Music*, vol. 52, viewed 26 November 2019, www.newsound.org.rs/pdf/en/ns52/08_OBrien.pdf.

Pardo, E 2011, 'Homage to James Hillman', Myth and theatre festival dedicated to James Hillman, viewed 26 November 2019, www.pantheatre.com/pdf/1-james-hillman-homage-gb.pdf.

Schein, EH 1984, 'Coming to a new awareness of organizational culture', *Sloan Management Review*, vol. 25, no. 2, viewed 26 November 2019, https://sloanreview.mit.edu/article/coming-to-a-new-awareness-of-organizational-culture/.

Schwartz-Salant, N 1988, 'Archetypal foundation of projective identification', *Journal of Analytical Psychology*, vol. 33, no. 1, pp. 39–64.

Schwartz-Salant, N 1992, 'On the interactive field as the analytic object', *Chiron Conference*, printed for participants, Einsiedeln.

Chapter 12

Introducing corporate cultural complex

Carlos Ferreira

When applied to leadership development in business schools and to the corporate world, analytical psychology stimulates self-awareness and authenticity. It supports individual consciousness and enables groups to better collaborate with society and the environment, creating a better and more integrated path for human and organizational development. This combination delivers equitable, sustainable and prosperous organizations.

The story of the growth of corporate culture began at the end of the 19th century. The Industrial Revolution and Victorian imperialism ushered in the first corporations. Entrepreneurs founded their own companies and implemented management systems which were strongly rooted in personal and family values. During the second half of the 20th century, after the two Great Wars, with the boom of the American empire, intellectual leadership of the business schools naturally transferred to the United States. The public company management model erupted, bringing about the end of the great family companies and the introduction and development of first principles of corporate governance Sampson (1996). With 21st-century globalisation, a new corporate reality has now been established in the lives of over 1 billion workers. Corporate, rather than family values are now predominant in Western society.

Organizational culture as a group phenomenon arises from the creative drive of individuals. But it can also be the greatest restraint to the full expression of individuality (Machado & Péricles 2010). One of the aims of *analytical development* (Ferreira 2010) is to support and protect the personality of individuals engaged in the mass culture of the corporate world. Business schools which have focused on leadership frequently challenge the status quo:

> Our current leaders (especially in business, but also in government and other spheres of public life) have lost legitimacy. (…) If there is a model, does it need to be revisited, re-examined, and revised in the light of the widespread failures in leadership?
>
> (Nohria & Khurana 2010, p. 3)

Some of the key questions, therefore, are: 'How can we develop a leadership discipline from personal achievement (getting ahead and gaining power) to a serious professional calling with ethical and social responsibilities?' and 'How can we support the human existential journey through work with practical and symbolic meaning?'

The impact of corporations on the daily life of 21st-century citizens is profound. Psychologically, corporations are arenas for: the projections of identities; searches for meaning; constellations and projections of personal, familial and cultural complexes; the development of new defence mechanisms, and the production of the corporate experience of psyche.

> Individuals are altered as well as a result of the interplay of ego consciousness, personal unconscious, social systems, and the collective consciousness and unconscious.
>
> (Stolz 2006, pp. 3–4)

> Replacing social roles of the past, which were carried out by traditional religions, family, schools and government, it is mainly within corporations that the 21st-century cosmopolitan citizen lives in society.
>
> (Bologna 2006)

Within corporations, the dynamics of individual psyches interact with collective psyches, changing each other and collaborating towards the expansion of contemporary collective consciousness, building culture. In business articles in newspapers and magazines, good news is often personalised by the attachment of the names, pictures, background, styles, decisions and results of individuals. But when the news is bad, the 'proto-protagonist' is the administrative council, the board of directors, the headquarters, human resources, the market, the crisis or even the competition. 'Bad news' reports often have very clear subjects. But they are depersonalised.

Many corporations are managed through financial and market business performance targets driven by shareholder accountability. They may also constantly strive for efficacy and efficiency. But those which lack the balance of human objectives such as customer and staff satisfaction may also become depersonalised to the point where they exhibit antisocial Shadow characteristics. Examples include manpower exploitation in countries with large numbers of people below the poverty line; superficial, short-term relationships with suppliers, employees and clients; poisoning, death and genetic mutations in employees, clients and inhabitants of areas surrounding the factories; billion-dollar frauds; lawsuits and so on. Super rewards to successful executives chasing aggressive market capture at all costs, reinforce images of successful careers.

The question should then be asked; 'What does it mean to be successful in the corporate environment?' Corporations have promoted social advances and new levels of comfort and health never experienced before by the human race. Yet the angst felt by a substantial proportion of the corporate population due to professional and personal dissociation is nowadays more present and more relevant in social health than hysteria was in the late 19th century (Cartwright & Cooper 1995). It would be interesting to know what Adler, Freud and Jung, among others, might have to say about the burnout epidemic. At the same time, analytical development observes and explores not only the individual but also the collective dynamics of the psyche in this new system of social organization which, despite coming into force only a few decades ago, already plays a central part in the lives of billions of people around the world.

Corporate complexes might be the source of the sensation of not feeling alive inside corporations. What does it mean to 'dress up' the ego, the centre of consciousness with a fixed professional Persona? What are the implications of living the fixed persona? Dale Stolz (2006) argues that one cannot live a role; one can only live one's life. The corporation is fertile, well-tended ground for 'giving wings' to the fixed persona and for reinforcing aspects of the Shadow that may be either useful or detrimental to the business. The Persona acting in the corporation can be partially regarded a mask of the ego that feeds itself from the benefits of the corporate 'mother'. Such an ego escapes responsibility when it finds a protective and projected shadow of anonymity in a delegated corporate 'other' role, such as legal, audit, regulatory, marketing person, boss or subordinate and so on. It can avoid taking responsibility. To these roles it can attribute all evil, blame and negative content. The dilemma is that Persona is necessary for survival but must not be identified with. The role is not the person. Healthy adaptation requires flexibility of Persona, and conscious awareness of it.

Corporations encourage both competition and teamwork. In their negative aspects, the maxim 'every man for himself' can mean self-centredness, narcissism and tyranny, and 'one for all and all for one' can imply loss of personal identity. The positive aspects are responsibility towards oneself and one's colleagues. Increased self-awareness (of both aspects) brings new ways of seeing, and of respecting and valuing the other. This provides a potential way that will enable the renaissance of the individual human being in corporations. In a meaningful corporate environment, we might imagine a process that goes beyond individuals and extends to teams. Classical analytical psychology and leadership development approaches are not independently sufficient to deal with these corporate issues and it is time we address the questions that need to be jointly tackled. As a result, new perspectives might emerge so that the world of productivity, one of bottom-line pragmatism, is able to prosper with awareness of its Shadow, while enabling individuals to feel alive. It is encouraging to note that the theme of the leader in crisis and the paths to self-knowledge is presented in specialised literature on the subject of leadership development (Boyatzis & McKee 2002).

The self-realisation and personal self-fulfilment concept most commonly held is that of the ego gratification. But as the ego is confronted with the Self, deeper development is achieved. Realisation initially stems from the ego, since

> only the conscious ego is capable of realizing psychic contents, but with continuous and stable egocentric identity, with more human kindness, (...) instead of realizing itself, the ego helps the Self trail the path to realization, in what could be called an existential self-realization.
>
> (von Franz 1990, pp. 11, 18)

In organizations in which the personal egocentric realisations of the leader dictate objectives (and cascade through the company), the meaning of each individual's work tends to become empty of meaning. The culture can become one of subservience and shallow values. Such is the straight path to disengagement and to 'the terrible feeling of not being alive within the corporation' (Kets de Vries 2006, p. 6). In contrast, where the leader and senior executives are searching for existential self-realisation, the realisation of the whole body of employees may also be thus reflected. The meaning of each individual's work may be an expression of that self-realisation, more profound and truly felt, and may give space for a feeling of accomplishment in broader life. This naturally promotes collaboration and a real sense of the collective. Exploration of the unconscious and connection to the Self in the search for meaning, are effective ways of achieving sustainable organizational performance. They yield sustainable organizational performance based on personal and professional development with soul.

The corporate cultural complex

In analytic sessions, part of the analyst's task is to identify and work with the client's personal complexes with the aim of facilitating the release of psychic energy for creativity, soulful productivity and healthy social interaction. Modern theories now also recognise 'cultural complexes' and 'corporate cultural complexes'.

In this intense age of global economics, we are frenetically connected through fast communication media, landline and cell phones, internet, cloud computing, online services, online news agencies, Twitter, Instagram and Facebook. The role of companies in the formation and identification of groups and cultures is now profound. Moreover, corporations are the main actors in the world of economic and market disputes between warring companies and economic blocks. They define new forms of human conflicts. Each has its own culture. By observing corporations as strong devisers of culture and consequently in the centre of class and market conflicts, cultural complexes allow us new perspectives concerning the psychological nature of individuals and companies.

The core of images and values that originate from a corporate view of the world, related to power, technical rationality and profit makes corporate complexes different from personal or cultural complexes. Nowadays corporations are transnational, global entities that act somewhat independently of traditional cultures (Stolz 2006). Corporate complexes are also cultural complexes developed by traumas and conflicts inherent to this specific group. For this reason, we use the term 'corporate cultural complexes'.

Stolz (2006) notes that corporate complexes may trigger collective angst and destructive situations in the organization. He cites many examples, such as the 'cult of CEOs', a projection of the king complex, providing a list of cases in which the main executive of a corporation was tried and arrested for corruption and abuse of power, among other crimes. Alternatively, names such as Lee Iacocca (Chrysler), Jack Welch (GE), Bill Gates (Microsoft) and Lou Gestner (IBM) are renowned and influential executives who directly support the corporate complexes of the 'ideal' company, with its group defence systems of dependency and idealisation. The alluring power of the mythical image of the hero generates the endless search for the charismatic, brilliant leader offering salvation, or redemption from 'non-productive' and 'trivial' jobs inside the company (Stolz 2006, pp. 240–241). Corporate complexes in action, channel a powerful affective core and a set of unconscious images which impact individual and collective subjectivity, 'exerting meaningful influence on careers, investments, products, services, availability of jobs and the very lives of millions of workers' (Stolz 2006, pp. 240–241).

Among the case studies presented by Stolz, four corporate complexes have been highlighted: ideal corporation, social defence, dependency complexes and the complex of the person-in-role (Stolz 2006, p. 254). Defined as corporate complexes, since they are comprised of both individual features and those of the cultural group to which they belong, they typically have unconscious content, and operate in the overlap between the individual's unconscious and the collective unconscious. They are manifest in rational daily life, which is frequently results oriented, and defined by tasks, which are requirements of the corporative world.

The constellation of the first, the ideal corporation complex, can be observed when desires and personal complexes of a certain individual merge, in a fantasy, with the culture and objectives of the corporation in which they work. This is a potentially narcissistic corporative complex which aligns personal desires to the corporation's ambitions and virtues in an apparently perfect harmony. This leads to the illusion of being in a safe and perfect work environment, probably generating behaviours which are at odds with reality.

The second is the social defence complex. One of the main elements in the process of creating the image of the organization in the mind of an individual is the way it usually gathers elements of the social system and the corporation structure to be extensions of his/her own personal defence system.

Corporative procedures, practices, cultural patterns, 'modi operandi' and structures defend the individual from perceived psychological threats and protect the group from potential external threats. An example of a defensive corporate complex is the vacation period. Often, in many corporations, middle and senior managers view business trips as a substitute for vacations. How is this defensive? Being away from work for a 'long' period may bring about the fear of leaving the corporative territory in danger. Many managers feel guilty for being away, for abandoning their dedicated workmates. At first sight, these individuals seem to be too good to be true: they are committed to the group; they are never tired and are always willing to self-sacrifice. But they might also fear being scapegoated in their temporary exile from the group. They tend to be obsessively driven, highly self-critical and ultimately prone to burnout.

The third complex, the corporate complex based on dependency, is probably the most widespread in corporations nowadays. Individuals have many needs that corporations can easily cater to, potentially leading to dependency, such as the need for authority figures in place of the parents, the need for safety and salvation, for which people pay a high price, including their own freedom, or the need to feel special, to feel chosen.

Lastly, the person-in-role complex, when constellated, can be observed, for instance, in people who are usually 'pleasant, bright, and caring individuals', transformed into automatons who act in ways in which they would never act by their own will. Being responsible for a certain post inside a certain corporation, which has its own culture, affects the way individuals present themselves, playing roles for specific audiences, with the objective of carrying out their tasks, reaching their objectives and accomplishing things. The use of this mask to adapt to the world, a mask that is required, healthy and necessary to all relationships in our daily life, typically goes unnoticed. A mature individual should have different personas which fit appropriately to social situations and the business world. The problem is not having a Persona, but the pathological identification with it, in which one's inner life is neglected, and which can lead to inflation and alienation from reality (Stolz 2006, p. 286).

While Stolz's definition of the corporate complex is of interest, it is not necessarily a third psychic structure, different from individual and cultural ones. It is in fact a cultural complex inherent to corporative culture, in other words, 'a corporate cultural complex'. Such distinction is important as it characterises differences in the nature of traumas and conflicts that have led to a certain corporate cultural complex. New ways of understanding and possible transformation can be developed from this premise.

Corporate organizational culture has values which are good enough, since they were able to build the society we now live in. As it declares its identity, it also 'excludes and represses aspects which are deemed troublesome and distressing', that become part of the 'organizational Shadow' (Ziemer 1986,

p. 119). The cost of failing to reintegrate the denied contents to the conscious is present in the daily life of companies in the form of ruined reputations, missing funds, loans that go unpaid and many of those responsible being rewarded with promotion. The traumas originated by this process enable the formation of affective cores, feeling-toned, constellating the corporate cultural complexes.

Discussion and conclusion

The hypothesis of complexes in a collective context, being constellated from conflicts and traumas characteristic of a certain culture rather than from a single individual, is, in our opinion, a turning point in consciousness development. Just as early psychoanalysis presented a new opportunity for self-awareness through dialogue and the exploration of personal complexes, the dynamics between consciousness and unconsciousness, and the quest for the real self, cultural complexes open a new door for exploring collective awareness.

The most remarkable and admirable traits of a culture also generate a specific Shadow shared by the individuals within that culture. In some cases the collective Shadow might be constellated as cultural complexes in particular individuals. The pathology of complexes takes place when a certain amount of psychic energy is no longer available to the ego and constitutes the feeling toned, core of a complex. The phenomenon is reproduced when individuals from the same corporation share the same traumatic effect created by conflicts inherent to that particular group. The amount of psychic energy that would be available for building and developing a group or organization begins to be diverted into the constitution of the affective cores of corporate cultural complexes, in the affected individuals in that group.

Corporate cultural complexes may give rise to new research possibilities within the developing field of corporate analytical psychology. These presently include: recruitment; assessment and development; organizational culture; and development and business improvement. In this latter discipline cultural barriers to progress are few but the most difficult to remove. Research might also include items such as the diagnosis and management of trauma based complexes and of complex contamination. The established scientific methods of investigation and measurement of the impact the personal complexes of leaders could be targeted towards specific roles. It could also be developed for corporate cultural complexes, which are discernible, for example, in artefacts, rituals, business practices, process definitions, brands and marketing actions and so on.

The study of corporate cultural complexes will make a unique contribution to business schools. For aspiring and established leaders, it can enhance self-knowledge and self-development and build a foundation for: sustainable consciousness; development, mindfulness; meaningfulness and transformational leadership. This can be the bedrock of a new work culture more fitting the needs and the profiles of 21st-century people. Society demands authentic leaders, who can combine self-confidence with humility and who are recognised as integers and trustworthy characters. Corporations need leaders able to recognise their own reasons, feelings, desires and strengths and weaknesses, and who can perceive not only how their unconscious feelings and emotions affect behaviour but also what triggers them. These are leaders who can be responsible for their acts, consonant with their principal/agent obligations and with their personal values. They can deal with reality (Kets de Vries 2006).

By exploring the unconscious, unfolding some of its contents, promoting a deeper connection to the Self, analytical development establishes a new perspective on leadership, one supported by current neuroscience (see 'Neuroscience and Jung' in this volume). By going beyond physical, emotional and mental explorations and by opening a spiritual connection, an authentic meaning of work can be reached providing genuine existential self-realisation. In other words, leadership development can have soul. Three decades ago, von Franz argued that the time had come to pay more attention to the individual's internal path towards the Self, because only someone who was supported by the Self can truly be ethical (von Franz 1990, p. 25). It is now high time to cross the river.

References

Bologna, JEB 2006, *As grandes mudanças do século XX*, viewed 20 February 2019, www.podbr.com/2006/06/06/as-grandes-mudancas-do-seculo-20.

Boyatzis, R & McKee, A 2002, 'Inspiring others through resonant leadership', *Business Strategy Review*, vol. 17, no. 2, London Business School, pp. 15–19.

Cartwright, S & Cooper, LL 1995, 'Organisational marriage: 'hard' versus 'soft' issues?', *MCB Personnel Review*, vol. 24, no. 6, pp. 26–35.

Ferreira, CA 2010, *Corporate complexes: the cultural complexes at workplace*, MS dissertation. Pontifical Catholic University of São Paulo, São Paulo.

Kets de Vries, MFR 2006, *The leader on the couch: a clinical approach to changing people and organizations*, John Wiley & Sons Ltd, Hoboken.

Machado, JR & Péricles, P 2010, 'O mal-estar na organização – a relação entre cultura organizacional e seus potenciais efeitos restritivos sobre a capacidde humana de criar soluções e realizar mudanças', *ESPM Magazine*, viewed 25 February 2019, http://bibliotecasp.espm.br/index.php/espm/article/view/992.

Nohria, N & Khurana, R 2010, *Handbook of leadership theory and practice*, Harvard Business School Publishing, Boston.

Sampson, A 1996, *Company man – the rise and fall of corporate life*, Random House, New York.

Stolz, DE 2006, *I am not I: the many faces of psyche in the workplace*, PhD thesis, Pacifica Graduate Institute, Carpinteria.

von Franz, ML 1990, *Psicoterapia*, Paulus, São Paulo.

Ziemer, R 1986, *Mitos organizacionais - O poder invisível na vida das empresas*, Editora Atlas, São Paulo.

Chapter 13

Corporate analytical psychology methods

Nada O'Brien

Diagnostic methods

Diagnostic methods comprise the analysis of process and content. Process analysis takes into consideration all phenomena which occur in and around the relationship between the Jungian coach and consultant (JCC) and the client. Transference, countertransference and intersubjective field give an initial diagnostic orientation which is refined throughout the process. Content analysis is multilayered. It brings closer to consciousness the many types of content communicated in a session. As well as manifest, verbal content (narratives) it includes proto-narratives (Nattiez 2013), the wide spectrum of communication media in the coenesthetic sense. Synchronistic phenomena are precious (although highly coded) diagnostic indicators. In other words, we take into consideration all occurrences which take place within and around the session and use them as diagnostic information.

We are mindful of the narratives (presented problems) which clients choose to share within the session and we consider them both on the manifest and symbolic levels. Given the fact that a large percentage of narratives are presented in business-related discourses (for example, a client might talk about efficiency and return on investment), special consideration is given to learning the languages of this multilayered pool of meaning. Solid experience and understanding of corporate life is necessary to appreciate the set plots presented in the narratives which, when considered symbolically, reveal the underlying dynamics of the client situation. We must speak fluent business language and understand the structures and dynamics and nature of business and its environment. The motifs we encounter in the corporate context take typical and specific forms and carry highly relevant libidinal charges which can easily be overlooked if a coach is not experienced and knowledgeable about corporate life. Therefore, if a client is talking about 'efficiency' or 'business', it carries multilayered implications of *corporate complexes* (see the chapter 'Corporate complex: diagnostics and application' from this volume). It is important to emphasise that this is an important specificity of corporate analytical psychology, because it does not only require familiarity with the particular profession of the client (such as accountancy) but also of its inter-relationship with the other business disciplines and its contribution to the enterprise as a whole. It demands both personal experience of corporate life (as a senior corporate employee or consultant) and knowledge of how the complex corporate business world works. Presented narratives in business language can then constellate themes and reveal woven maps of complexes, on individual, corporate and cultural levels. In turn, the complexes can reveal potential archetypal sources. There is a trend of crudely 'translating' different corporate structures and dynamics into Jungian language (for example, the HR department as the 'Mother complex' or the CEO as 'king') and to generalise these and other literal translations into fixed frame-works. This practice is contrary to the spirit of Jung's work and can be quite damaging. Our focus is on the facts presented by the unconscious and their unique manner of unfolding, their semantics and their contexts.

Proto-narratives bring forth points of the client's energy charge, especially in relation to the narratives, and they provide diagnostic orientation. The entire choreography of non-verbal expression (the coenesthetic dimension of communication) gradually outlines style of expression of the client's uncon-scious. This helps the JCC to learn about and attune with the client, devel-oping deeper layers of mutual communication and rapport.

As in general Jungian analysis, dreamsareprecious sources for diagnostics (with special attention to the initial dream). The Word Association Experi-ment and different techniques using symbols and the body are also com-monly used. As mentioned earlier, most of the clients initially bring a business-related issue as a presenting problem, and this is also considered an important source of diagnostic orientation.

Clients are, however, informed about the value of communication with the unconscious and asked to pay attention to their dreams, and to inner and outer events which interest or move them. Many clients choose to relate dreams or snippets during sessions, usually either at the beginning of the process or at some significant point thereafter, although there is no particular requirement put from the JCC side. Another important aspect of the diagnostic process is the consideration of the body. Different forms of somatisation are frequently reported in a majority of cases, as 'by the way' parts of the narratives, and they are often quite obvious in the non-verbal communication.

What might follow creates a rich painting with interwoven themes rele-vant to business, personal and psychological life. Although somatisation in this context indicates particular states related to the body, and meaningful to the client situation and the individuation process, it does not necessarily sig-nify pathology. However, there is extensive research on corporate related ill-nesses, an area for Jungian research. In addition to the medical approach, we would consider somatic dis-ease also as a manifestation of psychic reality which aims to draw the attention of consciousness.

Intervention methods: Jungian coaching and consulting

Taking a broad view on the questions of psychological intervention, corporate analytical psychology is first and foremost rooted in analytical process with the core aim to facilitate the individuation process. By following the client's symbolic lead, corporate analytical psychology offers the best and safest way of facilitating the individuation process. The JCC is equipped to appreciate a presented business issue symbolically. According to the particular diagnostic indicators, the JCC might be guided to work within the corporate discourse, using the presented narratives with business-related problems, without acting or speaking in any explicit analytical manner whatsoever. However, most clients move from the exclusive use of corporate discourse to broader life issues. The corporate world offers a fertile stage for consultants to work in a Jungian way. Techniques include holding, witnessing with empathy and developing the capacity for symbolisation. There must be competent familiarity of work in the intersubjective field and good enough attunement. Sometimes, complex episodes will occur and will need to be processed. Symbols will be engaged with in more or less explicit ways.

As in classical analytical work, the terms such as 'holding' or providing a 'container' signify the virtue of being in the tension of opposites and facilitating the flow of energy without acting it out by premature problem solving or decision making. Patience brings a ripening of the fruit of the opus, a symbol which unites and transcends the opposites. The result of this transcendent function is a flow of new life, a unique and by no means rational or predictable solution to an irreconcilable tension of opposites. This unique solution makes an inscription in the collective depository of deep human knowledge, enlarging consciousness with a glimmering ray which makes the darkness visible.

Temenos and time and space boundaries

As in classical analytical work it is essential to secure a safe space for the process to unfold in a transformational way. In this regard, the territory of the safe space and the marking of its boundaries reflects another specificity of corporate analytical psychology. In principle, coaching and consulting practice takes place in the organization itself, in private consulting offices or in typical corporate-friendly spaces (such as private rooms in business clubs or the Institute of Directors). This respects the codes of business with which clients are familiar. The choice of the meeting space for the initial 'chemistry check' meeting (also having the option of the JCC office) is highly informative. Choices of meeting times add a further analytical perspective about the process development and form a special dimension of the relationship.

The very nature of corporate life is somewhat extreme in terms of the volatility, pace and demand for reactivity. Therefore, rescheduling and interruptions of the sessions by urgent, unexpected business events put pressure on clients to behave reactively, which differs to the settings of the guarded space in the analyst's office. However, our experience has taught us to consider these events as material brought into the analytic frame, and therefore meaningful in that regard.

Corporate analytical psychology sees the safe space first and foremost as a symbolic space between the JCC and a client reflecting the meaningfulness of their connection, the potential of their relationship, the mutual readiness for the transformational work and the JCC's capacity for holding. The material meeting space should ideally secure the boundaries for privacy and scheduling should ideally secure regularity and continuity. It is, however, a common error for aspirant or trainee JCCs to mistake the outward tokens of temenos for holding capacity. Rigid insistence on the trappings merely communicates that the coach does not feel secure. With experience, a mature coach internalises the boundaries and can with increasing therapeutic manoeuvrability go into the client's busy office space, facilitating temenos. Temenos is only to be literally interpreted at the novice stage, although this does not preclude the 'ideal' conditions noted earlier.

As the process progresses, the tendency in the large majority of cases is to move out of the client's office towards the JCC's office or, in some cases, to scenography which reflects current inner psychological landscape (for example, the open sea view, natural environment or artistic environment). In time, the quality of attunement creates a relational rhythm, which, like music, will find its own form. The importance of regularity and continuity prompts clients to reduce reactiveness to the outer pressures of life and to participate with awareness in securing and internalising temenos.

Boundaries between Jungian coaching and consulting and analysis

The fact that a client engages a consultant signals that the dynamics of the organization might be ready for transformation. This is limited to the extent that the JCC–client relationship and its participants can process development at that moment. This depends upon the capacity of the ego structure to receive the flow of the new energy coming from the unconscious. The developmental demand of the client is deeply connected to the transformational issue of the organization.

As we learn from the principles of quantum nonlocality and coherence, an intervention in however small part of a whole affects the entire system (Laszlo 2007, pp. 42–49). Given the corporate framework, Jungian coaching and consulting is a process which responds to the demands of the client's individuation process for that given period. In comparison to classical Jungian analysis, it does not always have the usual long-term perspective, although it has to be long enough to provide a safe container for the ongoing transformation process, and this will vary from client to client. This is one of the key ethical features of Jungian work in corporate framework. It is 'easy' to impress a client by using different techniques which might stimulate archetypal imagery, cause fascination and create an impression of 'a quick fix' and coaching success. The danger accompanying this is profound, because archetypal images carry potent forces from the unconscious without securing the necessary containment for them to be processed and integrated to a certain degree. It can cause regression, neurotic symptoms and acting out of complex episodes which are harmful to the client and to others. If the ego structure is not sufficiently stable, it can cause a psychotic episode and trigger pathological states. As with any other client matter, the process and content analysis should guide the further steps, such as the proper timing and manner of relationship closure and/or continuation of work in the form of conventional analysis or some other form.

Some issues which a client might bring (certain psychological disorders or traumatic experiences) might not be well enough contained within the Jungian coaching and consulting framework. The water is sometimes too deep and a return to the shore is indicated. Therefore, the JCC should be fully aware of his or her own limitations and be familiar with appropriate support and referral networks. This is also relevant to the JCC's personal fitness to practice, and underlines the necessity of supervision and continuous professional development which are 'condiciones sine quibus non' for this kind of work.

References

Laszlo, E 2007, *Science and the Akashic Field*, Inner Traditions, Rochester.
Nattiez, JJ 2013, 'The narrativization of music. Music: narrative or proto-narrative?', *Versita*, University of Montreal, DOI: 10.2478/hssr-2013-0004.

Chapter 14

Corporate complex
Diagnostics and application

John O'Brien

Corporate survival depends upon adaptation to changing external conditions. Necessary internal changes might be spontaneous and require strategic adjustment and operational realignment. The social system is always critical to speed cost and success and the most significant barrier to successful adaptation is usually found in corporate culture.

For systemic clarity, in this chapter, we consider *corporate complexes* as the unconscious patterns of the organization as a whole. Individual complexes are explained in Chapters 4 and 5. Notwithstanding the 'group as a whole' perspective, it should be noted that the corporate complex also appears to some extent within the individual and vice versa. Furthermore, a corporation sits within a wider culture and will necessarily carry aspects of the broader cultural complex and vice versa.

Organizational culture framework

Edgar Schein

Corporate complexes can be understood within an organizational and leadership development perspective with reference to Edgar Schein's useful approach and method for the analysis of organizational culture. While a full account of his work is not possible in this chapter, significant aspects relevant to corporate complex are highlighted. To some extent, the rationale for a Jungian approach to organizational development and leadership emerges from an appreciation of the limitations of Schein's seminal work in this field.

Schein stated that one of the most interesting aspects of culture is that 'it points us to phenomena that are below the surface, that are powerful in their impact but invisible and to a considerable degree unconscious' (2004, p. 14). He defines culture in term of basic assumptions which are learned through problem solving in response to basic survival issues. The psychoanalyst Wilfred Bion (1961) used the term in his work describing the psychodynamic processes in his groups which he had studied with Tavistock colleagues during the 1940s.

Schein used a learning theory framework to explain how survival methods become second nature in groups success formulae and are taught to new members as the 'correct ways' of seeing, thinking and feeling about things. Schein's methods include an in-depth approach based on anthropological enquiry. He categorised visible and invisible aspects of culture. Observable features include espoused values; formal philosophy; the unwritten rules of the game; climate, special embedded skills and competencies; thinking habits; mental models and shared language; shared cognitive frames used to induct new members; shared meanings; and root metaphors (symbols). His method of enquiry also takes into account invisible phenomena such as values and beliefs and he describes the formation of culture as a 'striving toward patterning and integration' (Schein 2004, p. 17). The ways that an organization typically defines truth are noted by Schein as: traditional dogma, truth revealed with authority, rational/legal, truth resulting from adversarial debate, pragmatic and scientific truth.

Beyond Schein

His approach appears to resonate with analytical psychology in a number of ways. For example, the description of invisible underlying patterns which strive toward integration seems to reflect the teleological aspects of Jung's theory of individuation, which describes the journey towards wholeness. There is also recognition of 'the unconscious'. In his terms, there is more to culture than superficial rationality. However, from the perspective of analytical psychology, his work is limited in three main respects. First, analytical psychology acknowledges striving toward patterning and integration from a deeper perspective. Universal patterns in groups and organizations are formed in the interplay between infinite numbers of archetypes. These are found at the heart of complexes which are by definition, unconscious. Complexes give rise to values and beliefs, which are mostly accessible to consciousness. The patterns are represented in fairy tales, myths and legends that contain skeletal organizing structures and patterns.

Second, the 'striving towards' is a fundamental process of individuation. As such analysis is based on the positive direction of the psyche and its realisation as part of the whole. It is not a closed system but an open one, which allows for the individual and collective experience of the numinous, an essential element without which corporations experience soullessness. A key limitation of psychoanalysis in this respect is that from both the Jungian and some post Freudian standpoints, Freud was in the grip of the Moses complex which replaced the mystery of the God image with Freud as the father of psychoanalysis (O'Brien 2019). Regardless of the psychoanalytic influence on Schein's work, the City of London Corporation has carried the motto *Domine dirige nos,* or 'God lead us' since 1633, and 'In God we trust' remains the official motto of the US. Schein's idea of root metaphors as integrating symbols would seem to be consistent with Jung's approach, but on closer inspection it does not significantly include the dimension of the numinous in Jung's definition (see the chapter 'What is Jungian coaching and consulting?' from this volume).

Third, analytical psychology recognises *psychological truth*, a category omitted in Schein's list. In our current post truth era, some relationship to psychological truth seems to be a much needed foundation for the establishment of good authority in corporations.

Diagnostics and application

Given that the system in focus in this chapter is the corporation as a whole, armed with an overview of Schein's work and with a professional understanding of Jung's work, we will now address the following questions:

1. How can the corporate complex be identified?
2. How can the potential energy locked therein be quantified (what is the potential value added)?
3. How can this energy be made available for spontaneous and planned adaptation?
4. What is the refutable theory which can predict future corporate outcome?
5. Where has it been tested and what were the results?

1. Identification of complexes

A clinical method of diagnosing complexes in individuals, the Word Association Experiment (WAE), was designed and developed by Jung and has been confirmed by continuous research to date, as described in the previous chapters of the book. The experiment is based on the identification of complex indicators elicited by the empirical measurement of physiological, verbal and behavioural responses to stimulus questions of subjects. Subsequent interviews enquire into associations, projections and meaning and take into account the interviewer's influence as a participant observer. Complexes are thereby identified.

We cannot (nor would wish to) connect the organization as a whole to measurement instruments such as functional magnetic resonance imaging and galvanic skin response metres. It is helpful that one of the analytic competencies developed by training in the WAE is the identification of complex indicators without the use of the test. During the course of our consulting work with major corporations over some thirty years, we have categorised indicators of corporate complexes. These indicators are quite specific in that they point directly to blockages of energy, to cultural barriers which impede business performance, all set in a framework of the individuation process.

Methods of identifying complexes can be playful. For example, 'once upon a time' the executive team of a pharmaceutical company, as part of a teambuilding exercise was invited to improvise a fairy tale. After some initial hesitation and nervous laughter, the members around the boardroom table with great imagination and enthusiasm took sequential turns to add to the story, which spontaneously and according to fairy tale tradition ended after the third round. The motifs of the created narrative informed about the underlying existential anxiety and power game around the potential merger which was not discussed explicitly. These themes weaved a map of the *nodal points of meaning* for the individuals involved, the group and organization as a whole. They indicated, in their symbolic and coded ways, what actually matters for the people, what the underlying dynamic is and, taking into consideration of the whole narrative, the direction of the energy flow towards a more optimal balance of the opposites. What was not possible to discuss for the group on the manifest level, became so creatively attractive to play with on this created symbolic stage, revealing the intrinsic ways forward. From this and other suchlike narratives can be deduced the complexes and archetypes in play at the point on the individuation journey where the organization finds itself. Individual reflection and careful debrief (resounding or bringing back the images to the client) can also provide similarly useful information for participants and examples of these are given by von Franz (1996) and Stein (2000). When the images and chosen analytical creative challenges were represented to the group, it facilitated the translation of these into corporate cultural complexes, acknowledgement of the depth of the situation and challenges they were dealing with, present practical challenges, future risks and immediate and directional decisions supporting potential.

I have noted two methods of surfacing the unconscious dynamics of the organization, the observation of complex indicators and spontaneous folk tales. There are many more which include most forms of artistic (symbolic) expression and which can be incorporated into the normal calendar of team building or offsite events. A combination of approaches can yield substantial insight into corporations wanting to become aware of their current positions and to understand where corrections and adjustments to conscious standpoints are required and to release energy for new developments.

Complexes take various forms. Although they might shape shift or reverse, they are formed around an identifiable pervasive and persistent theme which invites consideration of the archetypal organizing patterns.

The value of dealing with the complex can be calculated by the direct and indirect, immediate and downstream,the impact of suboptimal decision making plus the opportunity cost of consumed energy which could be productively employed elsewhere. Sometimes awareness of the complex can make the difference between survival or dissolution of the form.

2.   New adaptation

Identification of complexes yields root causes of issues relevant to the whole organization at a level deeper than core beliefs and values. Once aware of complexes, organizations can make significant forward progress.

3.   Theory of corporate complexes

The most clearly stated definition is given by Singer and Kimbles (2004). Expanding the idea of group complexes, they state that cultural complexes 'can be defined as an emotionally charged aggregate of ideas and images that cluster around an archetypal core' (p. 28). A comprehensive Jungian approach to cultural complexes, supported by case studies, is given by Singer and Kaplinsky (2010). Corporate complexes can be defined accordingly within the added condition of the boundary of a corporate entity.

The possibility of a refutable scientific statement of complex theory, and therefore of corporate complex theory according to Jones (2013), was considered limited as Jungian approaches, premised on the psyche, 'cannot be adequately served by the methods of natural science' (p. 408). However, according to Roesler and Uffelen (2018) recent extensive research into complex theory more than adequately establishes the diagnostic capability of the WAE as on a par with standard diagnostic measures with the additional advantage of also identifying issues such as low self-esteem and shame and guilt. Samuels also explains that Jungian theory has been based on Jung's methods which were proven in practice, and that the conceptual convenience of theory although implicit was not explicitly stated by him. Thus, the recent proof of effectiveness of complex theory is a solid addition to the science, and the developments in quantum physics hold promise of scientific articulations of the psyche.

4.   Testing and results

WAE research methods for analysing the corporate group as a whole to identify the corporate cultural complex. This work has been undertaken by us in so far as corporate themes have been discernible at the individual and group level. Amongst leaders who have undertaken the WAE results have been achieved and simpler methods of applying the approach have since been developed (O'Brien 2019).

So far, we have typically worked to two clusters of outcome measures for consultancy work with corporations. The first is a return on capital employed. In this case the contextual method for our work was provided by a major consultancy group using the Balanced business scorecard (Kaplan & Norton 1996), which granulated top level financial objectives into sub objectives including quality, people, financials and operations. Each category was further granulated through several layers to the individual. A significant corporate cultural complex took the form of top down management based on a military style chain of command and machine bureaucracy structure which stifled adaptation to technological innovation and customer responsiveness. This was evident not only in business processes, reports and direct observations, but also in typical tokens of the culture such as shoe cleaning equipment on each floor, silver service in the executive suite and strict hierarchical allocation of car models and parking spaces. In-depth interviews and group observations revealed the pervasive theme of controlling (non-gender specific) masculine authority, which on reflection could be described as a collective negative father complex. Support and interventions built on this hypothesis and method contributed to the achievement of all client set goals and created readiness for transformation. The theory of our approach was only partially articulated and described in publication (O'Brien 1995) but created a great deal of interest which contributed to the early growth of the coaching industry.

In a different corporation, the executive team had already discerned that a key success factor was staff engagement. On discussing this with the client firm, a US international banking organization, we discovered that a silo mentally, both between different national subunits of the organization and between the units themselves. Staff members were exceptionally bright and highly skilled in their disciplines, typically graduates from the top US and European business schools. Specialist focus, however, sometimes came at the cost of loss of focus on team and corporate goals. For example, research and development produced superb information that traders found difficult to read and act upon in a timely manner. Much effort was wasted in bickering between the two global divisions. On reflection, we might consider the phenomenon as a manifestation of single minded expertise value developed as an early survival response of the organization. In response to such situations, the complex could be used to the client's advantage. As they were experts in evaluating business success factors, and understood the survival value of their expertise, they were able to gain awareness of emotionally charged non-value added decision making which detracted from collective performance and spontaneously adjust their internal systems accordingly. The complex might be termed a 'compete, kill or die' or 'collective insecure overachievement complex'. Substantial improvement was facilitated by education and consulting on complexes at the individual and group level.

References

Bion, WR 1961, *Experiences in groups*, Tavistock, London.
Jones, RA 2013, 'Jung's "Psychology with the psyche" and the behavioral sciences', *Behavioral Sciences*, vol. 3, no. 3, pp. 408–417.
Kaplan, RS & Norton, DP 1996, *The balanced scorecard: translating strategy into action*, Harvard Business School Press, Boston.

O'Brien, J 1995. 'Mentoring as Change Agency – a psychodynamic approach.' *The Journal of the British Asociation for Counselling*, vol. 6 no. 1, pp. 51–54.

O'Brien, J 2019, 'The Moses complex', submitted to *Culture and Psyche*, San Francisco.

Roesler, C & Uffelen, T 2018, 'Complexes and the unconscious. From the association experiment to recent fMRI studies', in C Roesler (ed), *Research in analytical psychology*, Routledge, London.

Schein, EH 2004, *Organizational culture and leadership*, Jossey-Bass, San Francisco.

Singer, T & Kaplinsky, C 2010, 'Cultural complexes in analysis', in M Stein (ed), *Jungian psychoanalysis: working in the spirit of C.G. Jung*, Open Court Publishing Company, Chicago, pp. 22–37.

Singer, T & Kimbles, SL 2004, 'The emerging theory of cultural complexes', in J Cambray & L Carter (eds), *Analytical psychology contemporary perspectives in Jungian analysis*, Routledge, London, p. 28.

Stein, M 2000, *Psyche's stories. Modern Jungian interpretations of fairy tales*, ed. L Corbett, vol. 1, Chiron, Wilmette.

von Franz, ML 1996, *The interpretation of fairy tales*, Shambhala, Boston.

Part IV

Application of corporate analytical psychology

Jungian coaching and consulting

Chapter 15

What is Jungian coaching and consulting?

Nada O'Brien

Jungian coaching and consulting is a professional practice which facilitates the individuation process in organizational contexts. It operates in the scientific framework of corporate analytical psychology. The profile of Jungian coaches and consultants (JCC) comprises theoretical mastery of analytical psychology and business related sciences as well as professional experience in Jungian analytical work and organizations. The competencies of Jungian coaches and consultants include those of analysts, coaches, consultants and business professionals. Additionally required is sensitivity to the real issues of corporate life and its potential for transformation, in Jung's terms, individuation. This enables mastery of the bridging function, which can only be developed through clinical practice and by operating in the corporate world over a long period of time.

The practical framework takes the form of business coaching and consulting and is specified by a contract. This means that a Jungian coach or consultant with the appropriate experience and qualifications can be engaged for providing services to support corporate issues, such as culture change, leadership development and specific projects. A JCC is able to access business competencies and language in order to better understand the needs of the individuation process of the client. In the process of engagement with the presenting issue, insight will be gained into the underlying dynamics of the individual, team and organization, as well as of those of the environment (relevant aspects of the markets, national culture and Zeitgeist). The transformation potential and map can thus be comprehensively understood.

While the Jungian analytical lenses and discourse are familiar to the JCC, the practical framework is business coaching and consulting. Therefore, the 'translation' skills play a very important role. For example, the presenting issue could be erratic, bipolar leadership of executive team decision making. The diagnostic process might have revealed that the underlying issue might be a mood disorder. Instead of talking about 'anima possession' with the client, the JCC engages with the topic using language that the client can understand and appreciate. This is also a diagnostic token of the attunement with the client and reflects the translation skills of the JCC profile. This skill is not just a result of training and experience but is unique to the client relationship.

Jungian coaching and consulting assignments

Facilitating the individuation process as a core framework of this work follows Jung's guidance: 'Learn your theories as well as you can, but put them aside when you touch the miracle of the living soul. Not theories but your own creative individuality alone must decide' (Jung 1942, p. 361). This implies the ability of being in *not knowing* and exploring the symbolic, encoded communication with the unconscious. At the same time, the consulting engagement comes with a clear goal, ultimately related to measurable improvements. In general, coaching and consulting engagements are directed towards leadership, management and culture and measurably linked to the purposes of the organization, be they profit, social benefit or a mixture. For example, a coaching assignment may be to help a manager to develop certain leadership skills, which will eventually be measured by the success of team meetings and exceeding set business targets. A consulting task might be to enable personal and professional development in a CEO and executive team, or to help the CEO to navigate the organization through times of uncertainty. There are also many cases when the CEO or HR director hires a JCC to engage with a third party beneficiary (an individual, team or teams working on a mission critical task, such as information technology transformation). At the outset, there is a set engagement with an agreed time scale and fee. Goals are made explicit and frequently reminded. The JCC is bound to honour commitments made to the organization and to the clients involved. At the same time, the core commitment of a JCC is to facilitate the individuation process, which is basis upon which corporate analytical psychology has been developed. A further matter is the potential for there to be discrepancy between the set goals defined by the organization and the explicit goals and implicit individuation needs of the immediate beneficiary.

In reality there is often a natural and healthy tension between the interests of the organization and those of the individual and the JCC works fairly and squarely in the areas of overlap (see Chapter 25) In competitive environments, the common goal can usually be best achieved by acknowledging both differences and unities, and the management of internal and external opposites is a key leadership competency which creates dynamic alignment.

There is always an expectation and responsibility to deliver added value. The JCC must understand how to bridge the specific corporate ways of measuring success, while setting safe space to work with psyche. (Professionalism and track record can build confidence in the 'invisible' symbolic tokens of change which deliver hard core measurable results.) But is sometimes the case that JCC's essential role of facilitating the individuation process is asked for but not valued. A bridge might not be offered to allow a JCC to honour commitments to all parties without a loss of the professional ethics and personal integrity which are essential to the work. It is here, in this apparent split, dissonance and schism where we find the definition and purpose of Jungian coaching and consulting. It is also here where we reach for *meaningfulness* as the cornerstone of Jungian coaching and consulting work.

The split

At the core of every issue we have been engaged to work with there is usually some form of split. For example, there might be a dichotomy between intellect and emotions, modern and primitive, spiritual and material, conscious and unconscious, knowledge and faith, masculine and feminine, money and soul, and so on. The money and soul dichotomy is an important issue to get to grips with.

Thinking psychologically, money is a symbolic form of psychic energy. It represents energy value, the capacity to invest and undertake projects and the power of exchange. James Hillman (1982) observed the money and soul split through the lens of Western culture, focusing specifically on the Christian paradigm. The Biblical phrase 'Render unto Caesar the things that are Caesar's' might connote occasions when material wealth is exclusive to the salvation of the soul. Perhaps the most striking example is the betrayal of Jesus by Judas, for which he is paid thirty pieces of silver. But considering money as 'an archetypal dominant' Hillman states:

> Money is like the id itself, the primordially repressed, the collective unconscious appearing in specific denominations, that is, precise quanta or configurations of value, i.e., images. Let us define money as that which possibilizes the imagination. Moneys are the riches of Pluto in which Hades' psychic images lie concealed. To find imagination in yourself or a patient, turn to money behaviors and fantasies. You both will soon be in the underworld (the entrance to which requires a money for Charon).
>
> (Hillman 1982, p. 5)

He sheds light on the mythological background of the term *moneta* (the etymological source of the word 'money'). Moneta was the Roman goddess in whose temple money was coined and whose Greek equivalent was Mnemosine (memory, imagination) the mother of Muses.

> Money is thus a deposit of mythical fantasies. It is a treasury that mothers and remembers images. (...) It belongs in the constellation of the Muses, necessary to imaginational culture, and hence it does become devilish when imagination is not valued (as in Christianity). The ugliness, the power corruption, the purely quantitative nature of money today are not its fault, but that of its having been severed and then fallen from the Gods from which it came.
>
> (Hillman 1982, p. 7)

From the perspective of the collective unconscious, money has archetypal qualities and thus has a powerful effect on consciousness. This is especially so if the attitude towards it is one-sided; by regarding it as God or the Devil. In other words, it carries 'divine' qualities. Hence Hillman's metaphor, 'fallen from the Gods', which in Jungian language translates into 'numinous'.

The numinous effect 'causes a peculiar alteration of consciousness' (CW 11, para. 6). It is emotionally intense and indicates an experience of the Self. It is the valueof an archetypal event (CW 18, para. 596). Shortly before his death, Jung reflected on the situation in the world in terms of the loss of numinosity:

> No wonder the Western world feels uneasy, for it does not know how much it plays into the hands of the uproarious underworld and what it has lost through the destruction of its numinosities.
>
> (CW 18, para. 581)

Jung sees the loss of numinosity as a core reason for the general absence of spirituality and morality and considers our times disoriented and in a constant state of schizophrenia (CW 18, para. 581). That which is oppressed comes back from the unconscious with an overwhelming power which carries fascination, lowers the level of collective consciousness and becomes the ruling trend of the time. Therefore, phenomena such as incredible greed, reckless exploitation of natural resources and inhuman cruelty can be seen as a reaction to stripping the world of its key asset, the numinous aspects of soul. Pushed deeply into the unconscious, it returns in a destructive way.

> Since energy never vanishes, the emotional energy that manifests itself in all numinous phenomena does not cease to exist when it disappears from consciousness. As I have said, it reappears in unconscious manifestations, in symbolic happenings that compensate the disturbances of the conscious psyche. Our psyche is profoundly disturbed by the loss of moral and spiritual values that have hitherto kept our life in order. Our consciousness is no longer capable of integrating the natural afflux of concomitant, instinctive events that sustains our conscious psychic activity. This process can no longer take place in the same way as before, because our consciousness has deprived itself of the organs by which the auxiliary contributions of the instincts and the unconscious could be assimilated. These organs were the numinous symbols, held holy by common consent.
>
> (CW 18, para. 583)

Jung concludes that in modern times our unconscious tries to heal the split by producing symbols. From this perspective, the journey of producing and experiencing images requires money. It is the means of paying for the psychological work and of experiencing the outer world in an imaginative way.

Jungian coaching and consulting work is always in liminal space, bridging the two worlds, facilitating the exchange of different currencies, be it a fish, gold, development or a consulting fee. It requires the careful negotiation of new pathways, meeting obstacles which can only be overcome at the 'third' attempt. It is exactly here, in the worlds divided by schisms and in front of apparently impossible engagement tasks, where we reach for meaningfulness, the core method of our work.

Meaningfulness

Given that the JCC's standpoint is that of analytical psychology, the underlying dynamics of the individuation process are always kept in mind. Careful observation of what is presented and felt as a dilemma can reveal the central developmental 'plot' situated in the unconscious. Consequently, applying the Jungian lenses in this way gives a different perspective on seemingly impossible task engagements.

Every client is meaningful to our own individuation processes, and the next step for a JCC is to reflect upon the particular engagement coming their way in relation to their own inner journey. Is it meaningful and in which way? How do the presented themes, motifs and the symbolic nature of the engagement resonate with the JCC's own journey? We consider this initial process as a preliminary chemistry check of the field. We wait for occurrences from the unconscious (for example, dreams or synchronistic events) to guide us before the engagement is accepted. We see how the soul reacts. It is only after this initial experience and reflection that further steps are taken towards a decision (such as the mutual chemistry check with the client and the formulating of an engagement agreement). Once the underlying 'plot' can be reasonably discerned and hypothesised, a response to the request for a proposal can be made in the client's business discourse and if accepted, an agreement made. This agreement should secure a good enough operational framework for the explicit and implicit client needs to meet.

Who are the clients?

We are repeatedly impressed and humbled by the cultural, ancestral and collective dynamics which play their parts in our work. They extend far beyond the client's personal biographical issues. Likewise, an initial client's request for consulting extends beyond the presenting package into teams and organizational processes, structure and dynamics and so on. Once when the transformational work takes off, without exception, the patterns of old, cultural, religious and racial patterns of conflict come to the surface. These are sometimes several hundred years old, wearing an outfit of the current Zeitgeist and with a present survival drama attached. They come in symbolic form, without the participant's awareness that these old patterns are being unwittingly enacted. They are experienced as unbridgeable divisions.

It can be astonishing to be presented with a business problem which, on a manifest level, is not that difficult to solve, and for which there is a rich pool of management expertise and traditional coaching and consulting available. The relatively simple problem can bring the organization to a standstill. In such cases, the disturbing dynamics underneath might well have been 'covered up' by everyday civilised and proper behaviour. This explains how a simple business problem can sometimes stir disproportionally intense irrational reactions, which trigger basic survival instincts. Antagonised will only agree 'over their dead bodies'. This organizational field of latent existential threat strongly affects the ability for reality checking and decision making processes. It generates profound cognitive biases. From an energy perspective, it is as though a person is being exposed to the overwhelming forces of a hurricane or an earthquake. The ego, as the central complex of consciousness is impacted by potent forces from the deeper layers of the unconscious in such a way that individuals, groups or whole organizations are infected by and act upon them.

Given that corporations embody the modus vivendi of the collective, their shadows will carry the vital counterparts, which surface disruptively. These notions are useful for consultants to keep in mind, not only for diagnostics, but also because of the experience they will encounter in the client's field. The transference and countertransference process is likely to be deep and intense, given that the contents of the unconscious will carry not only the individual trauma of the client, but also that of the collective Zeitgeist, and this is particularly so in multinational organizations.

Defence mechanisms and resistances to change

The need for protection from the overwhelming impact of the unconscious gives rise to defences in the form of a fear/power axis in the organizational structure with its accompanying excessive need for control. It also emphasises the need for providing a safe container and holding mechanism. It is important to bear in mind that the automatisms driving repetitive automatic behaviour and resistance to change are in most cases products of the defences against trauma, and the unconscious per se. These automatisms could be seen as strict rituals which keep the conscious busy, diverting focus away from potential cracks where the underlying trauma could creep in. This can be well illustrated with the excessive levels of 'busyness' frequently found in corporate culture. This is also a feature of the increasing pace of life associated with the current Zeitgeist. Yet it is not the object of the 'obsession' or extreme focus wherein the source of the problem lies, but what it is that is being avoided so by this extreme behaviour (CW 7, para. 133–138).

The client's presented issues are the beginning of a thread woven into a multidimensional mosaic of forgotten, hidden, unknown, unborn and unlived ancestral lives. To the extent that they did not have space and time to be incorporated they continue their 'time travels' through the generations. When they surface, they need to be recognised and given enough time and space within the conscious life of the organization for the energy to take its appropriate form. They will signpost new roads to success.

Alternatively, if automatic patterns take over our conscious positions and faculties, they create automatisms which imprison and calcify the natural movement which is sensitive and open to change and bring new creative solutions. No wonder, then, that one of the meanings of '*corporare*' is 'to kill'. It can be necessary to allow the natural and dignified death of the rigid corpus which no longer reflects the essence of the organization and prevents the generation of new solutions. The work of Jungian consultants in organizations can support participants in the proper ways of burying the dead and celebrating life. These often can take the form of process observation, reflection and feedback of formal business meetings and offsites. Meetings become more efficient and effective and offsites become simultaneously wilder and more reflective, as the expression of the raw instinctual side of human nature takes place through artistic and adventurous expression. Business meetings spontaneously incorporate a symbolic dimension which helps members to see below the surface of things, to manage opposites and to deal with uncertainty.

Symbols function as *rites of passage*. They are the vital link between archaic and cultural man, and link something vitally important but unknown and present knowledge. Working with symbols and supporting the development of the symbolising capacity is the core method of Jungian coaching and consulting work.

Who are the consultants?

It is curious to experience how groups and individuals in organizations refer to Jungian coaches and consultants. An entire spectrum of projection onto the JCC takes place, in much the same way as it does in analytical work. In this way clues are given about the present underlying state of affairs in the organization. For example, projections onto the JCC can say something about the level of trust, the state of good authority, the main defences and the readiness for change in the organization.

Fairy tales

An excellent model for illustrating the complex network of the various roles of JCC is the Jungian approach to fairy tales. Jung and his associates considered fairy tales as the best illustrations of the anatomy of psyche (von Frantz 1996, p. 11). Archetypes manifest to consciousness as images or symbols. They interact to form universal plots which are found in their purest symbolic forms in fairy tales. The types of symbols, the manner of their appearance and their interactions (the plots) are governed by natural laws.

Jung emphasised that the idea of energy is not based on a mechanistic view of the very substance moving in space but on the relationships between different appearances of it. Archetypes are the formulae, the universal patterns by which libidinal dynamics are organized. Fairytales provide the maps of these formulae and relationships, portraying the interactive dynamics of the archetypes of the collective unconscious.

Both in diagnostic and intervention phases, it can be helpful to identify the respective roles constellated in the organization and the consultants. These might include: the dominant governing principle of the organization (i.e. the King); the state of vital energy of this principle (the Queen); the main obstacles for transformation (e.g. the Evil Witch or Monster); the direction of the transformational process and its unique ways of movement, strengths and challenges; the very goal of the transformation (the Hero and his journey); and the aiding forces of the transformational process (e.g. wizards and helping animals).

Corporate analytical psychology teaches discernment of how these major roles are constellated through the stakeholders of the organization. They do not necessarily align with individuals as one might expect, for example the King or Queen energy might not be expressed through the CEO or HR director, as commonly claimed by so pseudo Jungian approaches. Training in Jungian analysis safeguards the superficial, potentially dangerous, literal projections of fairy tale characters onto the concrete individuals, so that, for example, a leader is seen as a King or an HR professional as a Witch, or alike. The images are forms constellated from complex, multidimensional patterns of energy. Specific types of energy 'run' through different stakeholders at different times. Their interactions (plots) are constellated in different situations of corporate life at different times. The respective underlying dynamics (fairy tale plots) serve as a precise and reliable framework for JCC work. An analogy can be drawn between the JCC's role and the forces aiding the transformation.

Projections are not gender specific and they come with their Shadow sides. The JCC needs to become aware of the projections cast upon them by clients and not to identify with them. At the beginning of the relationship, and in certain circumstances, there might be a significant amount of negative projection, especially where there is mistrust in the organization. One can witness the gradual transformation of this negative projection during the change process. It is also possible that the client's projection onto JCC does not take a form of aids to the transformation process, in which case there should be an analysis of what role is projected, how it stands in relation to the transformational process itself and if it might also be a comment on the JCC's underlying dynamics. It is not unusual that the projection changes, so that along the course of the transformation process, there are different roles projected onto JCC. The clients' projections are not without a 'hook', which implies that the JCC's underlying dynamics will be truthfully reflected in the projection, but only to a certain degree.

Inflation is a common challenge of the JCC. The saviour complex is often constellated, which, together with all other variety of inflated roles, only feeds the neurotic circle, and does not actually help the client at all. It robs the client of internal change agency and most cases ends with the metaphorical crucifixion of the consultant. Individual and group supervision are necessary safeguards. Continuous work on self-awareness, and healthy grounding in humility defend against inflation and are a requirement of the JCC's professional, personal and ethical integrity.

Summary

In the context of corporate analytical psychology, 'meaningfulness' signifies the transformation work which reduces impulsiveness, reactivity and automatic behaviour. It yields new ways of being, bringing new awareness, releasing vital energy and creativity. It brings a deeper understanding of human relations. Projection is recognised for what is. The capacity to tolerate disturbing situations is enhanced and the sense of maturity and responsibility to work through difficulties grows. It creates space for authenticity. As a rule, it also brings humour, spiritedness, motivation and inspiration into the field. Humour helps deal with the overwhelming intensity of difficult issues by creating different perspectives from which solutions can be generated. This is a movement from one sidedness.

Meaningfulness in operational business contexts delivers an improved reading of present reality and future probability both in the internal world of the organization and in the external world (political, economic, social, technological, legal and environmental). It brings the organization closer to its genuine identity. The business processes, problem solving mechanisms, new solutions and products change accordingly and reflect the uniqueness of the organization, bringing something new to the market and facilitating improved returns on investment. Meaningfulness makes it safer to process difficult and controversial issues.

It is meaningful for people to tell their stories, impregnated with symbols. In a particular global company, executives meet in a circle, with no table in the middle. Reportedly, after a while it feels like discussion around the camp fire and natural changes occur which radiate through the organization. 'The reason for evil in the world is that people are not able to tell their stories' (Jung 1977 in Lafontaine 2019).

References

Hillman, J 1982, 'A contribution to soul and money', in R.A Lockhart, et al. (eds), *Soul and money*, Spring Publications, Dallas, pp. 31–43.

Jung, CG 1932/1981, 'The development of personality', in *The development of personality*, CW 17.

————1938/1989, 'Psychology and religion', in *Psychology and religion: East and West*, CW 11.

————1942, *Contributions to analytical psychology*, London.

————1961/1989, 'Healing the split', in *The symbolic life*, CW 18.

————1977, 'The synthetic or constructive method', in *Two essays on analytical psychology*, CW 7.

————2000, *The collected works of C. G. Jung* (CW), eds. H Read, M Fordham, G Adler and W McGuire, trans. RFC Hull, Princeton University Press, Princeton.

Lafontaine, L 2019, *Carl Jung on evil – quotations*, blog, viewed 19 December 2019, https://carljungdepthpsychologysite.blog/2019/05/03/carl-jung-on-evil-quotations/#.Xf-mPJNKjIU.

von Frantz, ML 1996, *The interpretation of fairy-tales*, Shambala, Boston.

Chapter 16

Entering the system

Organizational consulting and the psychology of the transference

Laurence Barrett

As we engage with any organization, whether it is at an individual, team or enterprise level, we are entering a living system of complex interrelationships that is both conscious and unconscious; 'a social arena within which we enact the undertow of our emotional inheritance' (Armstrong 2005, p. 92). Within this system, individuals and groups, each with their own goals and assumptions, compete and cooperate for resources, status and power and will be influenced at an unconscious level, by underlying complexes of feelings and associations arising from past experiences.

For any consultant seeking to work in a psychodynamic way, this creates a challenge. Our role is to help the forces shaping that 'social arena' to emerge into consciousness and be realigned in ways that support its development. Making sense of these forces requires a degree of distance and objectivity, but as we enter the system, we become part of it. We exert influence upon it which may be intentional or simply because we are present. The underlying forces within the arena also exert influence upon us and may provoke responses based on our own emotional inheritance. We both change the system and are changed by it.

Our capacity to work effectively therefore requires us to understand the conditions by which we enter those systems and the effect that we have on them, simply through that act of entry. We need to consider how we are being used by the individuals we encounter, as an object within the system (Winnicott 1971) and what roles the system expects us to take up. In particular, we need to understand what may be unconsciously projected onto us and why. These projections often arise from the imagined effect of the consultant on the existing network of relationships within the system, and on the possible changes to the social identities of its constituents. For this reason, every consulting assignment has the potential to create an existential struggle for those involved, where the very basis of identity may be challenged. From this tension may arise a new transcendent position of opportunity, and the possibility of individuation, but that journey may be a long and arduous one, and success is by no means guaranteed.

As we receive these projections, we may then be influenced by our own 'valency' (Bion 1961) to follow established patterns of behaviour or take up particular roles which may feel familiar to us and yet be inappropriate for a particular assignment. For example, a system that is unable to take responsibility may project a need for a patriarchal figure to direct it, and a consultant with a valency for directive behaviour may find themselves irresistibly drawn into this role.

The psychology of the transference

Understanding this exchange of projections and in particular having an appreciation of the psychology of the transference and its implications therefore becomes a critical first step in any consulting assignment.

The term 'transference' was first used by Freud, who described how in certain situations a 'whole series of psychological experiences are revived, not as belonging to the past, but as applying (…) in the present moment' (Freud 1905/1953, p. 116). We may 'transfer' the attributes or emotions from past experiences and relationships and project them onto the person of another, making a false connection. We may interpret their behaviour on the basis of a shadow from the past rather than the reality of the present. This may then arouse within others a response, or countertransference, where their behaviour is based on their own emotional inheritance and their expectations from this are projected back onto us, to continue the cycle.

Although transference has typically been used to refer to the dynamics of relationships between therapist and patient, it is increasingly understood as having a much broader application, and as providing insight to the functioning of organizational systems (Armstrong 2005; Kets de Vries 2011; Maccoby 2004). Here leaders, either as part of the system or as mythical figures from the past, may become objects for transference, as followers seek to orient themselves in the system through familiar relational patterns. Leaders may also project aspects of their own unconscious onto their teams, creating and maintaining the system as a mirror of their own psychology: They might 'concoct organizations as a means of defence against psychotic anxieties, thereby generating a fundamental cause of problems within those organizations' (Jaques 1995, p. 343).

The projections of the transference can also originate beyond the personal experience of individuals and be founded in the 'cultural unconscious' (Henderson 1990) of the system itself. This is the layer of the unconscious where we find the deeply held experiences or beliefs of a group being re-enacted as a living history. They may also be archetypal, arising from the deeper collective unconscious and the shared experiences of humanity itself. Here the consultant might be seen as a saviour, perhaps imbued with mystical qualities who will shepherd the system towards a future promised land or as an embodiment of threat itself, a terrifying invader who will disrupt the balance of a carefully negotiated status quo and whose intention is to plunge the system into a period of chaos and darkness: or as a scapegoat who can be sacrificed to atone for the mistakes of the past and for whom failure is then inevitable.

This archetypal dimension extends the transference beyond a simple repetition of past relationships and suggests a more teleological function where 'the understanding of the transference is to be sought not in its historical antecedents but in its purpose' (CW 8, para. 146). The transference may then be seen as an unconscious attempt by the client to create a 'template' in the form of the consultant for the attributes to which the client aspires but which they cannot yet accept in themselves (Perry 2008). Clients may begin to activate their own developmental processes, by bringing their unconscious into a more tangible, conscious form. As Jung suggests, an individual 'clings by means of the transference to the person who seems to promise him a renewal of attitude' (CW 8, para. 146). The figure of a consultant who is then idealised as a powerful and directive figure may then serve to constellate the paternal archetype in the client themselves; 'The healing agent is transpersonal but is first experienced in personal terms' (Salman 2008, p. 65). It is this archetypal dimension that places the transference at the centre of Jungian work:

> The transference phenomenon is without doubt one of the most important syndromes in the process of individuation; its wealth of meanings goes far beyond mere personal likes and dislikes. By virtue of its collective contents and symbols it transcends the individual personality.
>
> (CW 16, para. 539)

A mutual entanglement

Crucially for consulting work, Jung also saw the transference as a mutual entanglement, 'a dialectical process where both parties bring conscious and unconscious elements of their personalities and where both are transformed (potentially on an equal basis) by their interaction' (Samuels 2006, p. 181). This reciprocal relationship was represented by Jung in a model that he referred to as the 'counter crossing transference relationships (...) the "marriage quaternio"' (CW 16, para. 422). If we re-imagine his model for a consulting or coaching context, we may view the transference as essentially consisting of four simultaneous exchanges between two people.

The first exchange (Line A) can be interpreted as the conscious or 'real' relationship between consultant and client (Groesbeck 1975; Perry 2008; Samuels 2006). Here the consultant will be briefed on an assignment, and the ostensible primary task agreed, a briefing which may disguise the underlying forces at work in the system or reveal them through subtle nuances.

Line B represents the relationship between the conscious and unconscious elements of the consultant and clients' own inner worlds, and those elements of their individual unconscious that may be emerging or hidden, but which

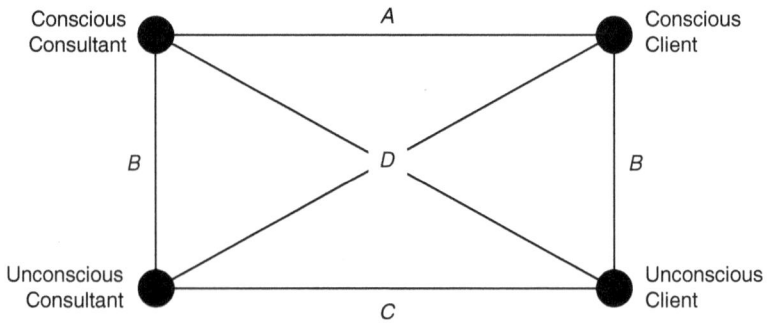

Figure 16.1 A Model of the Transference

will drive the transference response to the other. They represent the degree which we have a developed self-awareness and insight into the unconscious complexes that shape our behaviour.

Line C represents the unconscious projections between the two, of which neither are fully aware and where feeling toned archetypal symbols may be exchanged, often through the vector of physical attributes such as age, gender or race.

Research (Dieckmann 1976) has also suggested that archetypal images and associations may be constellated simultaneously in both parties and perhaps even anticipated by one or other of them, becoming a conscious part of their shared narrative. Stephens et al. (2010) suggested that as an understanding or rapport begins to be felt between two individuals, the brain responses may begin to mirror each other and overlap; effective communication in effect becoming a single (and empirical) act performed in alignment by two separate brains. Similar findings have been made by other more recent research (Nummenmaa et al. 2012). This phenomenon has been termed 'neural coupling'. We may also receive these projections in the form of a projective identification, where we identify with the projected feelings of another, and then mirror their emotional state as our own; we feel what they are feeling. This mirroring may then trigger a countertransference on our part, changing the way we then combine with the system. If we are able to notice these projective identifications, through our own reflective capability, they may provide us with valuable insight into the unconscious processes of our clients, in what is termed 'syntonic' (Fordham 1957) or 'reflective' (Samuels 2006) countertransference.

Lines D are the respective transference projections between the consultant and the client. One line represents the consultant's conscious awareness of the client's unconscious, perhaps through behavioural nuances or revealing symbols. The other line represents the client's possible awareness of the consultant's unconscious, creating a mutual human connection and perhaps also a source of vulnerability. These exchanges are where we may create the insight and trust needed to surface unconscious material in the service of the assignment. With 'D' we can begin to form the mental models and hypotheses which allow an appreciation of the mind of the other, and its effect on our own state in what may be referred to as 'mentalisation'; 'an imaginative mental activity that enables us to perceive and interpret human behaviour in terms of intentional mental states' (Fonagy et al. 2007, p. 288).

Through a developed awareness of the possible interplay of these exchanges we can reflect consciously on the dynamics of our relationships. We can consider what belongs to us, what belongs to our clients and what arises as a result of the alchemy of that combination; what is the new system that is created by us both. 'Thus, the analyst is simultaneously a guide, a participatory role model and a catalyst for the patient's "inner healer"' (Sedgwick 1994, p. 23). We can mediate the development of the system and support individuation within the system, as a catalyst and container, while ourselves being transformed by the process.

However, in his original diagram, Jung made it clear that the transference projections of the quaternio are not simply part of a closed system restricted to two individuals. This is particularly important when we consider the potential complexity of organizational consulting. The projections may reflect a highly dynamic exchange of symbols and feelings that may extend far beyond the relationship of the two individuals concerned. They may include the influence of team dynamics within the organization, or its evolving cultural unconscious. They may also be affected by the leadership of the organization, who might be present either physically, in symbol or myth, or perhaps even as ghosts of the past. The environment will also play a factor, as, unlike the relative calm and stability of a therapy room, this may be a variable beyond the control of the consultant. The psychogeography of the system will influence behaviour, perhaps creating conditions where complexes may be triggered more readily, and the transference and other projections may be intensified.

We can then imagine the quaternio as less a single 'crystalline' form, and more as a complex and dynamic aggregate of interrelationships. Here the consultant may be receiving multiple projections at any one moment, placing a considerable burden upon them. Fordham suggested that 'the whole analytic process is a mass of illusions, delusions, displacements, projections and introjections' (Fordham 1996, p. 172) and this may be multiplied many times over in a large organization.

Understanding the importance of boundaries

To survive these unconscious processes, and ensure we can operate effectively, consultants must then develop a sensitivity to and awareness of the boundary conditions that define that system, above and below the surface of consciousness, and the possible impact we may have on that system as we cross those boundaries. With physical artefacts or other visible symbols of our inner worlds (Schein 2004), boundaries mark the intrapsychic and inter-psychic spaces of the system. We can see them in the way our clients dress, the way they greet us and the words they use to define themselves and their organization.

Boundaries define the organizational system within its larger context and establish the identity of the system as an enterprise, and by extension of those within it: They define the nature of its tasks and the structures that mark the limits of authority and leadership (Armstrong 2005, p. 103). In the context of Jung's quaternio, they may be conscious or unconscious, and reflect both intrapsychic and interpsychic dimensions. Boundaries exist as much in the mind as in the physical world, reflecting the fantasy of relation-ships as much as their concrete reality. Boundaries provide the reference points by which individuals, including consultants, orient themselves within the system and make meaning of the system, as they reveal the relationships and social structure from which the system is created (Lawrence 1999).

From a psychoanalytic perspective, boundaries define the often uncon-scious and unexamined assumptions of individual and group identity and may reveal that real motivation for organizational change has more to do with the maintenance of this identity and the territory associated with it than with rational organizational function; many change programmes are simply 'the organizational equivalent of a dog urinating on a lamppost' (Stokes 1994, p. 127).

Boundaries also provide that sense of continuity and containment, without which the world may be experienced as chaotic and overwhelming (Stapley 2006). In Jungian terminology, it is through the perception of boundary that the 'vas hermeticum' (CW 16, para. 402) is created, the imagined sealed vessel that is required to contain the intrapsychic turbulence of individu-ation, particularly in the presence of transference projections.

Understanding boundaries may then help us to appreciate how any per-ceived challenges to that identity may be received, and how that may mani-fest in the system, and in particular in the transference onto a consultant whose presence itself may provide that challenge. Through understanding boundaries, we may begin to unpick what belongs to whom in any exchange and avoid the addictive, and potentially narcissistic preoccupation (Peters 1991) of an increasing spiral of transferential interpretations.We may better appreciate the symbolism of our entry into the system and subsequent presence within it, and be better able to work with their effect.

Without this understanding, the consultant may overemphasise boundar-ies, misinterpreting them or misapplying their own, and so miss the mutual humanity of the encounter. In not appreciating their role in the context of relationships within the system, they may risk an inflation of their own capability or a lack of trust and openness on the part of their clients. They may also underemphasise boundaries, and as a result enter what is termed a 'participation mystique', where they may not be able to distinguish themselves from the system and instead become bound to it by 'a direct relationship which amounts to a partial identity' (CW 8, para. 781). Here the consultant may be exposed to projections, including projective identifications, which they experience as their own feelings and impulses rather than as originating elsewhere in the system. They may then become 'drawn into the vortex' (CW 8, 15f) of transference and countertransference, and risk unconscious contagion from the neurotic symptoms of the client or the system as a whole. The state of mind of the system is replicated in the client and then replicated in the consultant. In this sense boundaries serve not only to maintain an objective task focus for a consultant, but they may also serve to protect them from psychological and perhaps resulting physical symptoms.

Boundaries are above all dynamic and subject to a constant process of renegotiation and evolution, driven by the dynamics within the system and its interactions with other systems. Individuals will be building new relationships with new allies and new rivals, and they may be developing themselves, providing new perspectives. As we enter the system, the boundaries will be disrupted further, and new exchanges of projections will be activated, requiring a constant vigilance on the part of a consultant (Lawrence 1999).

An ethical dimension

The failure to manage boundaries may then have significant ethical implications. A consultant may enter the system with a degree of power and influence that is magnified by their novelty, or the symbolism of the entry itself, as an act of transgression that punctures the containing vessel of the system. Despite the mutuality of the transference, the relationship is often asymmetrical (Fordham 1978) and the credible but unwary consultant may then influence their client in ways that are unhelpful or potentially damaging. They might enter a dangerous 'folies a deux' (Kets de Vries 2006, p. 140) and, in an exchange of transference and countertransference, encourage their client's projections with wild interpretations or act out their own impulses.

Imagine, for example, a consultant who is seeking to support an executive team through a complex and chaotic turnaround. They may be idealised by that client, who sees the consultant as a paternal figure, supplying the wisdom and authority that may be lacking in the system. This may activate the consultant's own valency and they may 'act out' the role of an archetypal father. Trapped in a 'narcissistic soup' (Kets de Vries 2010, p. 24) of interpretation and direction, the consultant may then increasingly adopt a controlling working style, becoming in effect the team leader, and so prevent the development of agency and leadership within the system.

Some conclusions

Psychodynamic consulting within organizations is a challenging undertaking where the consultant is required to navigate a series of complex and overlapping systems. Their boundaries are fluid and often permeable, and perhaps even intrusive as each system jostles for space. In contrast to dyadic therapy, the object of the work may be unclear, and the work environment may be complex and unpredictable. The consultant may be working with teams whose membership changes and whose dynamics are significantly shaped by absent figures, leaders or stakeholders, who are always present but only in fantasy and often in exaggerated or archetypal forms. In these teams, the 'emotional undertow' of the unconscious may belong to one or more individuals or originate beyond the boundaries of the team itself. Boundaries may also not be defined by clearly defined roles or structures, but by subtle nuances and symbols, which may be presented in a form unfamiliar to the consultant yet charged with feeling for our clients and part of a clearly understood (if not consciously acknowledged) *lingua franca* within the organization. As we enter and move across the system, we may then receive transference projections from multiple actors in multiple encounters and yet must be able to make sense of the origin of these projections and the implications for their work.

Nathan Schwarz-Salant, in his description of therapy as 'a strange endeavour of two people mutually constellating the unconscious' (Schwartz-Salant 1984, p. 29). Organizational consulting is equally strange, but the number of people constellating the unconscious in any one system may be many more than two. With this in mind, we must enter the system with a degree of caution and maintain the 'evenly suspended attention' recommended by Freud (1981), being sensitive to the symbols of the system and their possible meanings. Above all, we must understand the boundaries of system, including those of our own role, so we can appreciate what may belong to us, what may belong to our clients and what may be created by our combination. Only then can we make ethical choices in the service of the consulting task and protect ourselves from the 'vortex' of transference and countertransference.

References

Armstrong, D 2005, *Organization in the mind*, Karnac, London.
Bion, WR 1961, *Experiences in groups*, Routledge, London.
Dieckmann, H 1976, 'Transference and countertransference: results of a Berlin research group', *Journal of Analytic Psychology*, vol. 21, pp. 25–36.
Fonagy, P, Gergely, G & Target, M 2007, 'The parent-infant dyad and the construction of the subjective self', *Journal of Child Psychology and Psychiatry*, vol. 48, pp. 288–328.
Fordham, M 1957, 'Reflections on image and symbol', *The Journal of Analytical Psychology*, vol. 11, pp. 85–92.

Fordham, M 1996, 'Analytical Psychology and Countertransference', in S Shamdasani, (ed), *Analyst-Patient Interaction: Collected Papers on Technique*, Routledge, London, pp. 159–175.

Fordham, M 1978, *Jungian psychotherapy*, John Wiley, New York.

Freud, S 1981, 'Recommendations to physicians practicing psycho-analysis', *The standard edition of the complete psychological works of Sigmund Freud*, vol. 12, The Hogarth Press and the Institute of Psycho-Analysis, London, p. 111.

Freud, S 1905/1953, 'Fragment of an analysis of a case of hysteria', in J Strachey (ed), *The standard edition of the complete psychological works of Sigmund Freund*, vol. VII, Hogarth Press and Institute of Psychoanalysis, London, p. 111.

Groesbeck, CJ 1975, 'The archetypal image of the wounded healer', *Journal of Analytical Psychology*, vol. 20, pp. 122–145.

Henderson, J 1990, 'The Cutlural Uncosncious', in J Henderson, *Shadow and Self: Selected Papers in Analytical Psychology*, Chiron Publications, Wilmette.

Jaques, E 1995, 'Why the psychoanalytical approach to understanding organizational is dysfunctional', *Human Relations*, vol. 48, pp. 343–349.

Kets de Vries, MFR 2006, *The leader on the couch*, Wiley, London.

Kets de Vries, MFR & Engellau, E 2010, 'A clinical approach to the dynamics of leadership and executive transformation', in N Nohria & R Khurana (eds), *Handbook of leadership theory and practice: a Harvard Business School Centennial colloquium*, Harvard Business Press, Boston, pp. 183–222.

Kets de Vries, MFR 2011, *Reflections on groups and organizations*, Jossey-Bass, San Francisco.

Lawrence, WG 1999, *Exploring individual and organizational boundaries. A Tavistock open systems approach*, Karnac, London.

Maccoby, M 2004, 'Why people follow the leader: the power of transference', *Harvard Business Review*, viewed on 15 December 2019, https://hbr.org/2004/09/why-people-follow-the-leader-the-power-of-transference.

Nummenmaa, L, Glerean, E, Viinikainen, M, Jääskeläinen, IP, Haria, R & Sams, M 2012, 'Emotions promote social interaction by synchronizing brain activity across individuals', *PNAS (Proceedings of the National Academy of Sciences of the United States of America)*, June 2012, vol. 109, no. 24, pp. 9599–9604.

Perry, C 2008, 'Transference and countertransference', in P Young-Eisendrath & T Dawson, (eds), *The Cambridge companion to Jung*, Cambridge University Press, Cambridge, pp. 147–169.

Peters, R 1991, 'Transference as a fetish', *Free Associations*, vol. 35, pp. 56–67.

Salman, S 2008, 'The creative psyche: Jung's major contributions', in PYoung-Eisendrath & T Dawson (eds), *The Cambridge companion to Jung*, Cambridge University Press, Cambridge, pp. 57–75.

Samuels, A 2006, 'Transference/countertransference', in R Papadopoulos (ed), *The handbook of Jungian psychology*, Routledge, Hove, pp. 177–195.

Schein, EH 2004, *Organizational culture and leadership*, Jossey-Bass, San Francisco.

Schwartz-Salant, N 1984, *Archetypal factors underlying sexual acting out in the transference/countertransference process*, Chiron, Wilmette.

Sedgwick, D 1994, *The wounded healer: countertransference from a Jungian perspective*, Routledge, Hove.

Stapley, LF 2006, *Individuals, groups and organizations beneath the surface*, Karnac, London.

Stephens, GJ, Silbert, LJ & Hasson, U 2010, 'Speaker-listener neural coupling under-lies successful communication', *PNAS (Proceedings of the National Academy of Sciences of the United States of America)*, August 2010, vol. 107, no. 32, pp. 14425–14430.

Stokes, J 1994, 'Institutional chaos and personal stress', in A Obholzer & RV Zagier (eds), *The unconscious at work: individual and organizational stress in the human services*, Routledge, Hove, pp. 121–128.

Winnicott, DW 1971, *Playing and reality*, Tavistock Publications, London.

Chapter 17

Jungian group work
Individuation in and of the group

Laurence Barrett

Human beings are group animals. Our success as a species has been founded upon our ability to gather together in increasingly complex organizations, created from webs of relationships, which exist as much in the mind as in concrete roles and hierarchies (Armstrong 2006).

Recent neurobiological research has even suggested that our very capacity for thought must be considered in the context of these relationships. Through the process of neural coupling, the patterns of brain activity in different individuals may align as those individuals experience understanding and empathy. Communication between human beings may even be seen as a single cognitive process where the physical patterns of brain activity within individuals may be shared and may allow us to intuitively predict the behaviour of others (Stephens et al. 2010). These predictions may then create the foundation of trust needed to experience our relationships as supportive and protective, creating the spaces where we can be safe to nourish ourselves and invest more time in the relationships binding us together. We may physically share an understanding of the world in which we inhabit and our place within it.

However, groups may also be a source of anxiety and stress as members may need to compete internally for resources, power and status. A number of 'cultural complexes' (Singer & Kimbles 2004) may form for a group, based on the history of the groups own emotional experiences and these may establish norms with which members are required to identify. These identifications may then begin to overwhelm the personalities of the group members, in what Jung described as 'an alienation of the subject from himself for the sake of the object, in which he is (...) disguised' (CW 6, para. 738). We may sacrifice our own personalities and potential to fit into the groups of which we are part. Members who fail to adapt to the group might then be persecuted or expelled and may become preoccupied with the vigilance and negotiation required to take up the roles that the group requires of them. This preoccupation may then lead to a spiral of defensive behaviour where the group as a whole loses sight of its purpose and creates rigid and impermeable barriers to any possible changes within (Feldman 2004). In an attempt to preserve the status quo of the group, the group may then repress the development of its members.

This paradox has preoccupied philosophy and psychology since Aristotle described man as a 'political animal'. It was perfectly summarised by Wilfred Bion (1961) in his reflection on group work:

> The individual is a group animal at war, not simply with the group, but with himself for being a group animal and with those aspects of the personality that constitute his 'groupishness'.
>
> (p. 168)

We have evolved to participate in groups and yet fear becoming consumed by them. We need groups and yet hate ourselves for doing so.

Jung and groups

Like many of his peers, in part influenced by the overwhelming impact of contemporary mass movements, Jung chose to focus on the establishment of a psychology of the individual and a way to better facilitate the process which he termed 'individuation'. Through individuation, we may bring ourselves more fully to consciousness and in doing so, release ourselves from the unconscious influence of our social context which has shaped our identities. Instead of simply allowing ourselves to be defined by the roles and expectations of society, we may begin to make more conscious choices and more fully realise our potential. Jung felt that groups created a pressure to reinforce unconscious patterns from early life, and suggested that the larger the group, the more insidious its influence:

> The bigger the group, the more the individuals composing it function as a collective entity, which is so powerful that it can reduce individual consciousness to the point of extinction. (...) The group and what belongs to it cover up the lack of genuine individuality, just as parents act as substitutes for everything lacking in their children. In this respect the group exerts a seductive influence, for nothing is easier than a perseveration of infantile ways or a return to them.
>
> (CW 10, para. 891)

For Jung, individuation was either a solitary process, occurring naturally and unconsciously (Jacobi 1983) or one which was supported and consciously experienced under the guidance of a well-trained therapist. Within the sealed vessel of the consulting room and the analytic relationship, analyst and patient would be able to work without the danger of contamination by the collective. This dyadic method of psychotherapy was formed in its earliest days and Jung was highly critical of any changes to the format, particularly those which attempted to provide individual psychotherapy within a group context:

> the modern tendency to treat the psyche by group analysis, as if it were a collective phenomenon. The psyche as an individual factor is thereby eliminated.
>
> (CW 14, para. 59f)

It is then perhaps not surprising that Jung's concerns have become a pervasive theme in the development of analytical psychology itself. Accordingly, the potential of Jungian group work during Jung's early work was been largely unexplored, either theoretically or in analytic training.

This has begun to change in recent years, however, with the development of a substantial body of literature on the cultural unconscious (Henderson 1990; Singer & Kimbles 2004) and a handful of well-considered publications on Jungian group work, in particular the work of Louis Zinkin, who has successfully combined the traditions of both analytical psychology and group analysis. Zinkin has suggested that far from being a danger to the individual, membership of a group may actually create the possibility of individual development and that many of the features of the analytic relationship, a group of two, may in fact provide less support to individuation than a well-designed group experience (1998c).

Individuation in the group

As useful starting place in understanding the possibility of individuation within groups, is the recognition that without groups we cannot experience ourselves as individuals and therefore cannot begin to develop a sense of self.

Winnicott (1958) suggested we can only have the experience of being alone if we have developed the capacity to be in the presence of another (either physically or as a phantasy object). The foundation of emotional maturity and resilience is the capacity to recognise the difference between self and other and to tolerate being alone in their presence. Without the existence of the group the individual has no context, within which they can ground or centre themselves, and are therefore unable to fully participate in society. We may then only begin to develop as individuals through the relational fields of the groups we belong to (Zinkin 1991 in Colman 1998, 2000).

Despite his apparent misgiving Jung seemed to share this sentiment, and stressed that the process of individuation was only possible in the setting of a group:

> There is no possibility of individuation on the top of Mount Everest, where you are sure nobody will bother you. Individuation always

means relationship (…) collectivity is the worst position if you dissolve in it; but if you can hold onto yourself while still keeping in touch with it, that is the ideal condition. (…) Individuation is impossible without relationship.

(Jung 1997, p. 1367)

He further emphasised this within his psychology of the transference (CW 16), where he described the combination of mutual projections between individuals in a dyadic group as the catalyst through which the self is able to emerge. In the spaces of individuation, we allow new ideas to provoke new associations and new possibilities. These ideas may be both intrapsychic, where images from the personal or collective unconscious are allowed to surface, and interpsychic, emerging from our interactions with others at both a conscious and unconscious level. In being exposed to a far greater range of this 'prima materia' than we may encounter in a dyadic relationship, we may fuel the transformative potential within the group. When groups are at their best, they somehow become more than the potential of any single member and bring together all the knowledge, experience and talents within the group which in turn revitalises the group and creates new perspectives. Prompted by others, individuals may then themselves access their potential more fully, combining with others in new and transformative ways. According to Zinkin (2000) 'the group personality often seems more spontaneous and shows a much greater range of resources than when restricted to the clinical relationship of doctor and patient' (p. 104).

In the group, the role of the consultant is then to help make meaning from the web of symbols, projections and interactions. We are not simply observing the individual, but the individual in context, where that context is in itself a dynamic and unpredictable system whose constituents are changing, potentially with every interaction. This demands a significant degree of sensitivity and a practice of attention from the consultant to the patterns of the group interactions and their possible meanings, including the feelings and associations of the consultant themselves as an 'instrument'. Interpretation by the consultant becomes secondary to the development of dialogue and the insight arising from that for the group members themselves (Zinkin 1998c; Armstrong 2006). The consultant may stimulate and provoke participants as a catalyst but must not fall into the trap of becoming a parental, wisdom figure. Indeed Foulkes, the founder of group analysis, suggested that for a developmental group, it is sometimes important that the leader does not understand the dynamic of the group, as that understanding may be taken as approval and provoke an infantile transference, blocking learning: 'Not understanding is important for the possibility of learning something new' (Foulkes 1990, p. 294). A well-developed reflective capability is therefore essential, and the consultant must be able to maintain 'an evenly suspended attention' on the individual members of the group, their interactions, the group as a whole and of course on themselves.

Individuation of the group

However, the role of the group in the individuation process may be more than simply the provision of contrast and stimulus and might have the potential to become the crucible necessary for individuation to happen at all. Jung used the alchemical metaphor of the sealed vessel or 'vas hermeticum' to describe the feeling of containment necessary for an individual to bear the discomfort of development work. Within the 'vas hermeticum' of the analytic relationship, the personality could be heated, distilled and reformed, and the group may provide a similar container.

In working with groups, consultants often feel a moment when the group appears to resonate in a generative and supportive way. Members may begin to produce shared symbols representing an emerging sense of group purpose, which aligns its members without constraining them; 'the group collective constructs some sort of image, a kind of we-production rather than an I-possession' (Zinkin 1998c, p. 152). At this point the group may become both container and contained, an experience of the group as a 'matrix' described by Foulkes as:

> The hypothetical web of communication and relationship in a given group. It is the common shared ground which ultimately determines the meaning and significance of all events and upon which all communications and interpretations, verbal and non-verbal rest.
>
> (Foulkes 1964, p. 292)

Here, members may both contribute to the group and take from the group, the experiences or ideas that are most meaningful for them, while still maintaining a sense of connection to other members and to the group as a whole. The group may still experience tension, but the matrix formed by the relations within the group, will allow those tensions to be held so that sense can be made of them, which in turn informs the individuation experiences of the members. In this way a state of interdependence is created where the group becomes an archetypal image of wholeness and integration, containing its members who themselves have the maturity to contribute to the containment of the group. In these groups we may begin to see 'an indescribable sense of wholeness which far transcends the created universe' (Zinkin 1998b, p. 190).

In his studies of the rites of passage within traditional and modern societies, Turner (1969)described this feeling of connectedness as 'communitas', a sacred bond extending beyond social roles and relationships. As the participants of these rites cross the threshold between their past and future identities, through what is termed 'liminal space', their existing social roles are broken down and they begin to interact as 'human totals'; 'integral beings who recognisably share the same humanity' (Turner 1982, p. 269). In relinquishing their former roles, individuals become free to take up new roles in new ways, developing not simply the individuals within the group, but the group itself and the society of which it is part. The parallels between these rites of passage have been explored elsewhere (Moore 1991; Barrett 2019) but Turner's emphasis on communitas still tends to be downplayed in Jungian thought.

An important role for a consultant may then be to support the development of group as a matrix, helping the group to individuate through the surfacing and integration of its own 'prima materia'; the unconscious of its members individually and as a collective. This matrix in turn becomes the container which is able to support the development of the members and a virtuous circle is created.

We may begin by bringing attention to the diverse perspectives within the group, and then helping participants amplify the symbols arising from the group as a 'we-possession'. In understanding the group as a developing entity in its own right, members may then participate a more conscious way, choosing to take up different roles and to relate to each other in different ways. In one memorable workshop, a group was experiencing some challenges to role boundaries which were not being directly expressed. Over the course of the day one of the large windows in the room began to bang as a warm wind began to blow outside, which became increasingly irritating and distracting to the group. My co-facilitator wondered aloud about the meaning of the distraction and the group began to reflect on the wind as a symbol of the underlying turbulence within the group. Gradually, irritation became laughter, and the tone of relationships began to change. The group was able to form its own container, and the banging window became a symbol of those moments when the group felt unsafe as boundaries were tested. The underlying discomfort had found symbolic expression which the group was then able to tolerate and work it in the service of individuation.

Another role may be as a 'trickster' figure, adding new ingredients to the 'vas' and provoking the group as a whole, as a catalyst for development. Poetry, imagery, music, video or simply an unconventional opinion or perspective may be used, not as a means of teaching, but as a provocation to new associations which may break established patterns of behaviour or surface new symbols for the group to amplify. This is important not simply to support individual development but to enable the individuation of the group itself through the integration of the other, including those voices from the margins that are rarely heard (Feldman 2004). In introducing this 'prima materia' we may provide the fuel needed to ignite the tension of opposites and raise the heat needed to transform the contents of the 'vas'.

The group's role as its own container does not, however, exclude the need for leadership, particularly in the early stages of its development, and a consultant may be required to provide an archetypal parent (Perlman 1995; Barrett 2019) or a boundary figure. We must become the 'vas hermeticum' or 'primary skin' (Feldman 2004) within which our clients can feel contained and be able to explore the group without fear of the group falling apart. Without the visible boundary markers of the analytic consulting room, we may need to create the symbols of the boundary with whatever comes to hand, and these must be robust enough to withstand the heat of the groups own individuation process and the invasive effect of the systems beyond. These markers may be physical, in the arrangement of chairs or perhaps the visual imagery of the space; they may be in the form of music or language; or they may simply be in the simple rituals of time and the rhythm of group meetings. However, the consultant must still take up the role in such a way that the group is able to develop its own connections and interpretations, and 'find its own way through the free expression of ideas, feelings and fantasy' (Zinkin 1998a, p. 185).

When groups are able to develop this matrix and discover their own potential, it is possible to understand Zinkin's contention that

> the oneness, the unity of the group, need not be, as Jung feared, a loss of individuality in the mindless mob-like group but on the contrary is found in the formation of a superior mind, greater, higher and richer than any of the individual minds.
>
> (Zinkin 1998a, p. 189)

Beyond the group

As a matrix or communitas is formed and both the individuals and group embark on their individuation process, we may then see the effects move to a wider stage. Turner suggests that 'it is through communitas that the transformatory power of the liminal space is extended through the development of participants, to the very society within which the space exists' (Turner 1969, p. 97). The individuation of the group and its members may create the foundations needed to enable those members to in turn influence other groups and then beyond to society as a whole.

Perhaps our goal as Jungian coaches and consultants is not simply to support our immediate clients but to contribute in some small way to the individuation of the world itself. This contention was made by Hillman and Ventura (1992), who, in a critique of psychotherapy as a methodology, expressed disappointment that 'we continue to locate all symptoms universally within the patient rather than also in the soul of the world' (p. 154). They go on to argue that 'maybe the system has to be brought into line with the symptoms so that the system no longer functions as a repression of soul, forcing the soul to rebel in order to be noticed' (Hillman & Ventura 1992, p. 154).

Perhaps instead of accepting that individuals must inevitably struggle against repressive groups, we may work to support the individuation of the groups themselves, creating groups, organizations and perhaps even societies with genuine therapeutic potential.

References

Armstrong, D 2006, *Organization in the mind*, Karnac, London.

Barrett, LJ 2019, 'Working with groups: communitas and the rites of passage', in J O'Brien & N O'Brien (eds), *Introduction to corporate analytical psychology*, Dosije Studio, Belgrade, pp. 91–118.

Bion, WR 1961, *Experiences in groups*, Routledge, London.

Colman, W 2000, 'Models of the self', in E Christopher & S McFarland (eds), *Jungian thought in the modern world*, Free Association Books, London, pp. 3–19.

Feldman, B 2004, 'Towards a theory of organisational culture', in T Singer & SL Kimbles (eds), *The cultural complex: contemporary perspectives on psyche and society*, Routledge, Hove, pp. 251–261.

Foulkes, SH 1964, *Therapeutic group analysis*, Allen & Unwin, London.

Foulkes, SH 1990, *Selected papers: psychoanalysis and group analysis*, Routledge, London.

Henderson, JL 1990, *Shadow and self*, Chiron, Wilmette.

Hillman, J & Ventura, M 1992, *We've had a hundred years of psychotherapy and the world's getting worse*, Harper Collins, New York.

——— 1959/1964, *Civilization in transition*, CW 10.

——— 1997, *Visions: notes of the seminar given in 1930–1934*, Princeton University Press, Princeton.

Jacobi, J 1983, *The Way of Individuation*, Meridian, New York.

Moore, RL 1991, 'Ritual, sacred space and healing', in N Schwarz-Salent & M Stein (eds), *Liminality and transitional phenomena*, Chiron, Wilmette, pp. 13–32.

Perlman, MS 1995, 'Toward a theory of self in a group', in M Stein & J Hollwitz (eds), *The psyche at work: workplace applications of Jungian analytical psychology*, Chiron, Wilmette, pp. 174–193.

Singer, T & Kimbles, SL 2004, *The cultural complex: contemporary perspectives on psyche and society*, Routledge, Hove.

Stephens, GJ, Silbert, LJ & Hasson, U 2010, 'Speaker-listener neural coupling under-lies successful communication', *PNAS (Proceedings of the National Academy of Sciences of the United States of America)*, August 2010, vol. 107, no. 32, pp. 14425–14430.

Turner, V 1969, *The ritual process*, Aldine De Gruyter, New York.

Turner, V 1982, *From ritual to theatre*, Performing Arts Journal Publications, New York.

Winnicott, DW 1958, 'The capacity to be alone', *International Journal of Psycho-Analysis*, vol. 39, pp. 416–420.

Zinkin, L. 1991, *Your self: Did you find it or make it?* Unpublished paper for discussion at the Analytic Group of the Society of Analytical Psychology, 2 November. Cited in, W Colman 2000, *Models of the Self,* in E Christopher & SH McFarland Soloman (eds.), *Jungian Thought in the Modern World*, Free Association Books, London.

Zinkin, L 1998a, 'A gnostic view of the therapy group', in H Zinkin, R Gordon & J Haynes (eds), *Dialogue in the analytic setting: selected papers of Louis Zinkin on Jung and on group analysis*, Jessica Kingsley Publishers, London, pp. 181–194.

Zinkin, L 1998b, 'Grail and group', in H Zinkin, R Gordon & J Haynes (eds), *Dialogue in the analytic setting: selected papers of Louis Zinkin on Jung and on group analysis*, Jessica Kingsley Publishers, London, pp. 159–173.

Zinkin, L 1998c, 'Is Jungian group analysis possible?', in H Zinkin, R Gordon & J Haynes (eds), *Dialogue in the analytic setting: selected papers of Louis Zinkin on Jung and on group analysis*, Jessica Kingsley Publishers, London, pp. 149–158.

Zinkin, L 2000, 'Exchange as a therapeutic factor in group analysis', in D Brown & L Zinkin (eds), *The psyche and the social world: developments in group-analytic theory*, Jessica Kingsley Publishers, London, pp. 99–117.

Chapter 18

Jungian coaching and consulting
Organizational transformation

John O'Brien

The hero

In the early 1990s an unusual quote appeared in the world of management consulting

> Only a few achieve the colossal task of holding together without being split asunder, the clarity of their vision, alongside an ability to take their place in a materialistic world. (…) To my mind these last are the supreme heroes in our soulless society.
>
> (Irene Claremont de Castillejo)

Cited by David Whyte in 1994, it has since found its way into many books on coaching and has been found meaningful in different ways to different audiences around the world.

A quarter of a century later, by chance it came to our notice that Irene, who had been married to an investment banker, had graduated as an analyst from the original C. G. Jung Institute in Kusnacht, Zurich in the 1950s, around sixty years previous to our own graduation there in 2016. The words seem as relevant today as they were when they were discussed by the great and the good in the Waterloo room of the Institute of Directors in London twenty-five years ago.

The original text reveals the expression of the hero archetype in corporate life. Claremont makes two fundamental points. The first is that individual heroism begins with awareness of shadow.

> It requires all the qualities of a hero to turn from the pleasant harmless 'persona' mask which one has so carefully cultivated, and which one really believed one was, to find the elements of cruelty within oneself of which one had no idea (…) One can recognize the hero in modern young and women of a particular indefinable spiritual quality. They are the visionaries who refuse to lose their vision and yet do manage to live in the materialistic

world in which they find themselves, holding the opposites together within them rather than going out as preachers or reformers.

(1974, p. 51)

The difficulty of the task is not underestimated. Claremont describes the fate of many for whom the visionary light fades, and the consequences for those who are burnt out by the vision or lack of channel for its expression. The loss of soul is often labelled as mental illness and its rediscovery can become the province of the Jungian coach and consultant (JCC).

So who are the supreme heroes to which Claremont refers?

Artists at least have a form in which they can hold their own conflicting opposites together. But there are some who have no artistic recognized form to serve this purpose. They are artists of the living.

(1974, p. 52)

What can this mean for today's corporate world?

The hero is an archetype, not a person. Leaders who are unconsciously identified with an archetype lack humanity and are being run by the archetype. The hero, representing life energy and individuation is a particularly seductive archetype. The leader who continually chooses the heroic option will sooner or later meet certain disaster. However, the leader who is able to choose when to allow space to the hero archetype, being fully aware of its shadow (anti/hero aspects) might be a soulful person on the individuation journey. In this case is heroism is a companion and not a master. As archetypes lure us into one-sidedness, we lose awareness of their dualistic nature.

One sidedness

The experience of 'being spilt asunder' is not fun. But it may sometimes seem so.

According to Jung, there is a fundamental split in human nature, a severance from the experience of wholeness. Archetypal at its core, it is apparent at different recursive levels in time and space. For example, at the individual neurophysiological level, there is a division between conscious and unconscious systems. This can be observed in the autonomic nervous system and in its subdivision into sympathetic and parasympathetic systems which activate fight/flight/freeze and relaxation responses respectively (Benson 1974). At the developmental level, in the mother–child system, the management of the split (separation) is necessary, and the timing and mode of this transition is one of the critical arts of parenting. Within the mental system, binary process, or splitting into opposites is a necessary part of thinking, but it is only part of mental processing. In Jung's type psychology it has its logical counterpart, an opposite, equally rational, feeling function. The process of becoming whole, or individuation, is one in which growth occurs through consciousness of the opposite tensions. One sidedness leads to disruptive energy from its opposite appearing symptomatically and it signals a loss of soul.

A particular one-sidedness of the modern organizational era is the binary thinking upon which many of the finest endeavours and achievements of humanity have been built, an exemplar field being information technology. It is reassuring to note that one-sidedness contains the seeds of the own incorporation of the opposite, as evidenced by the growth of quantum approaches to computing, to the awareness and incorporation of opposite psychological types and to the dynamism between completion and collaboration. Truly competitive teams collaborate superbly, and truly collaborative teams are highly competitive.

Rational thinking organizations

Particular organizations such as science, financial services, engineering, information technology manufacturing and so on demand emphasis on binary thinking. It is not surprising that despite the best efforts and processes of Human Resources to apply appropriate competency, the mental processes necessary for success become the subcultural criteria for advancement. As the individual develops, to the extent that safe space is in place, the integration of opposite functions might occur and it is this integration which is necessary for leadership through the different levels of an organization. Maturity brings the potential to lead and manage the whole organization with the diverse parts fully respected and supported. Harmony is not achieved through a one-sided imposition of functions, but through the containment of the inherent tension between opposites. This supports dynamic evolution.

Where the containment is not adequate, then splits are acted out. At the individual level this can take the form of the bipolarity, typically of mood issues such elation or depression at career and life cycle transition points. Reflected in performance, this can appear as over and underachievement, or sustained over achievement at an unsustainable personal cost resulting in symptoms characteristic of depression, burnout and chronic fatigue syndrome. At the organizational level, this can appear as cyclical waves of over and underperformance within broader waves of which the organization is unaware. In this case interference from the broader waves is experienced as game changing and can be highly disruptive. An example of bipolar activity at societal level is the economic cycle, which can be partly described in terms of long (Kondratiev) and short (Elliot) waves, but which in all cases is characterised by general moods of elation or depression. On the upswing, the experience of 'being spilt asunder' can be somewhat alluring and lead to incautious risk management. On the downswing it can lead to underinvestment and starvation of key activities incorrectly identified as unnecessary for survival. Amplitude (intensity) and frequency are affected by a number of factors including the individual and personal complexes at play.

Here are some key tensions of opposites which can be occasions for the split to be acted out:

Hierarchical structure versus market structure

With increased size and complexity, for efficient resource allocation organizations develop hierarchy. Cross functional working grows more complex and is impeded by the vertical hierarchical lines. The tension often gives rise to tribalism. The group to which one belongs blames the other group for inefficiencies and attempts to solve the problem through tribal dominance, imposing values and mindset on the other. Exertion of control can give rise to fear which exacerbates the issue and destroys concern for anything outside the tribe which sub- optimally contributes to return on investment.

Individual versus collective interest

As fear increases, individual interest predominates. A collective resistance to change sets in. At the same time, early in the corporate career journey, personal achievement orientation usually dominates. As advancement occurs either through specialisation or hierarchical promotion, this must give way to team achievement. Specialisation requires communication with other disciplines and promotion requires team leadership. At the most senior levels, the long term well-being of the corporation becomes the paramount concern and institutional leadership is needed. This naturally leads to a concern for the environmental context.

Tribal versus corporate interest

People at all levels in the organization are usually able to explain the real power structure which affect them in terms of tribal dynamics and in great details. The structures differ from those on the organizational chart and the behaviours and values differ from those on the corporate website. They might both add value and destroy value, but they are highly resistant to change.

Results versus process

There is a common conflict between results and process orientations. Results focus, regardless of the means, can lead to bullying, sub optimisation of resources, lack of root cause problem solving and stifling of innovation. Process focus without results can lead to lack of purpose and productivity. For the sake of brevity, an example is given which incorporates all of the above themes, which affect individuals, teams and organizations.

Case example: individual

A senior executive in his 50s, who was responsible for a global function in a large corporation, had made several culture and process improvements to his critical part of the organization. He had reached a ceiling barrier as a result of lack of cross functional working between silos. Several internal and external consulting attempts had been made to promote collaboration across divisional and regional boundaries to no avail. His personal life had become troubled and there was risk of his family fragmenting. He could not see a productive way forward and beginning to experience depression and a sense of meaninglessness, he became increasingly disengaged from the executive team.

His early life and career had been characterised by a strong and vital sense of mission as a medical professional. This vitality was being consumed in an inner conflict between being creative and productive and fitting into a team which he felt was driving only numbers. Considered more deeply, it became apparent that a family theme was constellated. His childhood had presented him with some dilemmas, and in fact these had been repeated in family crises through the generations. The survival dilemmas of ancestors trying to protect deeply held human and religious values in the face of the brutal realities of warfare and economic oppression had to some extent inspired his career motivation to become a doctor. He described himself as now working without feeling, without soul. One can imagine the effects on his personal life.

Oppression, fear and economic necessity can stimulate striving for justice, harmony and financial stability. But when the hidden price of success is the loss of soul, the same demons reappear albeit in different guises. Externally, they come as work colleagues, as uncooperative other divisions and the unreasonable boss. Internally, complex and archetypal images appear in dreams. Without one's innate sense of morality, a collective corporate complex can take over and the person finds themselves back on the personal ancestral battlefield or in the concentration camp. There is real risk of fragmentation, of no recovery.

At this stage of the individuation journey, heroism is needed. This is the heroism of facing one's own shadow, and no longer being a reformer or healer but connection with Self. Then the tension of opposites is held, and creative energy is once again at one's disposal and external problems can be resolved with the leader as a new model of change agency. Transformational leadership requires leaders committed to the natural process of transformation.

In this typical case, the leader enjoyed many years of reintegrated family life, contributed to the successful global development of his function and his firm, and went on to pursue his mission in both discovery and development with most agreeable private equity backing delivering to those world populations most in need.

Case example: organization

Organizational culture change is sometimes identified as critical to the success of an industry. This can be one of the 'below the surface' drivers for acquisitions and mergers. The added value of acquisitions and mergers is somewhat debatable, and the costs thereof are extremely high. The main beneficiaries are the senior managers (not the shareholders) of the acquiring company. If less disruptive and low cost alternatives of achieving cultural renewal are available, it is sensible to consider them.

A common strategy is for a firm to ask for the help of an investment bank to provide an analysis of its vulnerability to takeover, to target its own weak areas and then to address them as though they were fighting a hostile takeover attempt. If organizational culture is identified as one of these areas, then facilitated transformation provides a low cost/high impact solution which empowers and revitalises incumbent management and brings new vitality to the organizational hard systems via the human activity.

Consulting to organizations

A regional international bank had identified the requirement for culture change, but at the same time was strongly invested in the prowess of the Human Resources function, which had skilfully designed and rolled out several very sensible in-house leadership and management development programmes. The need was expressed as 'We are doing a great job, but we can learn from you'. In practice, this translated into the therapist's dilemma when confronted with a client who implicitly gives the message 'Help me, I am suffering, but do what I tell you because I know best'. It is similar in essence to requests for training as analyst/coaches; 'Please just accredit us, we know what we are doing, and we know more than you and do not really value analysis anyway'. On the surface, however, all the survey boxes were favourably ticked.

During the initial diagnostic phase, individual senior managers revealed a number of culture barriers arising from a difference of national characteristics with the parent organization which manifested in an inability of the mixed executive team to candidly discuss issues of concern. A pool of fear cascaded through the organization which led to distorted information. The individual reports were consistent with group observations where performance was measurably hampered by below the surface themes of blaming, scapegoating, distortion of information and in fact the complete obverse of the values and behaviours advocated by Human Resources.

The issues mirrored inter-regional issues and relations with HQ where a number of concerns arose from a confusion of corporate ownership and management. These issues reflected family and partisan conflicts with deep historical roots, the language of which appeared in interviews, observed meetings and the subculture.

Deeper insight (analysis alone) empowered the Human Resources Director and CEO to work with greater awareness of cultural barriers, and in particular with the shadow aspects of corporate life. They were able to deploy their internal capabilities appropriately and to achieve greater alignment with an HQ driven global development rollout.

Putting it together

A European national energy company had run into serious problems of safety, profitability and staff morale. The industry has a science/engineering/operational mindset. In its principal country, public concern had grown and in accordance with its stated policies and plans, the government had decided to close several operating units. However, the full consequences of closures would have been detrimental to the national interest and the public good.

The Board, CEO and Human Resources Director agreed that a turnaround required a substantial transformation effort. A programme was developed which included the 'up close and personal' development of the CEO and executive team, the specialist and support directors and their teams and the operational managers and key personnel. The diagnostic phase identified a universal theme of lack of trust following miscommunication and changes of policy between government and business leaders, which led to demoralisation of staff who had been promises had not been kept. The culture of the organization was quasi-military in that of necessity all members were trained to conform to instructions. The culture was one of public spiritedness and there was a real concern to get the work done well, together with a frustration that things were not working as they should.

Consultants worked one to one with leaders of the different parts of the organization providing space for them to be heard and to integrate and put in practice parallel training provided in house and by other consultancies. Individual work helped leaders to access potential for working with people. As a result of their duty and preference to provide professional scientific and operational excellence, this aspect of leadership had in many cases been neglected. Personal analytic coaching helped to identify and address personal barriers, often dealing with symbolic material from the personal and collective unconscious. Jung's Word Association Test was selectively used to identify personal complexes which affected thinking and behaviour.

Consultants worked at client team level, facilitating the identification of cultural, business process and subject master barriers to performance. In addition to standard methodologies, consultants were trained to use their feeling responses as participant observers in groups to identify key themes operating at an unconscious level. Each consultant received analytic supervision. Once teams had agreed key themes, these were fed back to a cross group forum with the HRD and Senior Business Leader in attendance and specific issues were identified and action plans were made according to the organizational structures. Often these required escalation to a common line manager where the exercise of good authority was needed to break through tribalised silos.

Inevitably, the problematic themes of the client organization started to be reflected in the consulting group itself. This took the form of a split between concern for production output and the necessity of investment in reflection and learning. The tension was a signal that engagement had been achieved with the client and the insights and reflection within the consultancy were operationalised by the client organization who proved systematic training in 'what and how' 'plan do check view', engagement and so on.

The whole effort was linked to ambitious organizational goals, which were achieved within a short timeframe and allowed it not only to continue without closures but also to expand.

Summary

In summary, the Jungian coaching and consulting approach can form a strong meta-structure which provides safety for uncertainty and discovery within its boundaries. In the last case study, in-depth coaching and consulting took place with individuals, groups (executive, operational, support and specialist) and the organization as a whole. The complex relationships between these systemic levels were mirrored in the hard processes of the company and affected the critical outputs. The themes identified by the consulting group within its own boundaries reflected those of the client, and containment of the former allowed for tension to be held in the latter. There was simply no room for coaches to unwittingly engage with individuals against the organizational and public interest. Neither was there room for coach/consultants to operate without continuous professional self-examination and supervision.

A safe vessel for transformation was provided by the consulting group. Safety in the organization measurably improved. Profitability (in Jungian terms, symbolic available energy) increased. Morale (life energy available to individuals) measured by staff engagement increased at all levels of the organization. None of this was provided by the consulting group, the potential energy which had been siphoned by the complexes impeding the natural individuation of the organization as a whole was simply released. A description of the seminal version of this approach, applied to a US global pharmaceutical company organization was published by O'Brien and Weder (2003).

We know at least that where an individual or group can contain opposites tensions and connect with its symbols, that renaissance takes place. We know that the arena offers communion.

References

Benson, MD 1974, 'Your innate asset for combating stress', *Harvard Business Review*, July–August issue, viewed 19 December 2019, https://hbr.org/1974/07/your-innate-asset-for-combating-stress.

Claremont de Castillejo, I. 1974, *Knowing woman*, Harper and Row, New York, p. 51.

O'Brien, J & Weder, B 2003, 'Stimulating productivity in complex global organisations', *European Business Journal*, vol. 15, no. 3, pp. 112–121.

Whyte, D 1994, *The heart aroused: poetry and the preservation of the soul in corporate America*, Currency Doubleday, New York.

Chapter 19

Making the turn

Individuation, midlife and leadership development

Laurence Barrett

The transition between managerial or specialist roles into senior leadership within organizations can be profoundly unsettling. Managers might discover that the experiences and capability that they have developed over the course of their careers are no longer sufficient to the challenges they now face. They have been rewarded and promoted for supplying practical solutions to well formulated questions from more senior managers, but now their role demands that they must now be the ones to ask those questions of others. For example, they are no longer creating operating systems which are efficient and effective, but instead are being asked to define the parameters of what effectiveness means. They may need to consider why the organization exists, and perhaps even contribute to the future direction of their industry. There are many possible paths ahead and for the first time they are facing them without a clear framework of performance measures and authority figures to validate and approve their choices. Indeed, looking behind them, they discover that they have become the authority figures for others to follow. There are no longer any 'right' answers, and each step just seems to create more questions.

Many managers making this transition often describe a level of anxiety and vulnerability, which threatens to overwhelm their very sense of self. This is an existential threat that goes beyond the psychological, as these new challenges may also threaten their very livelihoods. They know not everyone can make the change successfully, and that the wayside is littered with the corpses of those who have tried and failed: The heroic journeys of senior business leaders often end badly.

Some then fall back on old ways, locking themselves into comfortable, operational habits while the organization loses direction or fails to keep pace with changes to its context. Like Handy's apocryphal frog (2002), they swim in circles while the water around them heats up, never daring to jump out of the pan. Others might simply give up, but as they leave the organization, may discover that the transition has ignited a sense of vulnerability and unease that moves with them. They might discover that their bodies have begun to fail them, in the same way as their experience and knowledge. No longer as fit or as attractive, they may seek to revitalise themselves with a new car, a new partner or drive themselves hard in extreme sports, as they try to recapture the vitality and confidence that seems to be slipping away. Parents may be ageing, and the realisation of parental mortality serves as a further reminder of their own. Children may be becoming independent, living their own lives with a confidence that changes family relationships and perhaps inspires resentment and envy. Work and life seem to be conspiring to make the familiar structures which have given life meaning, increasingly fragile.

These managers have now encountered what Eliot Jaques termed the 'midlife crisis' (1965), an experience that will define the work of most coaches and consultants working with clients at this level and at this point in life. The fact that the term has become commonplace does little to make it more bearable.

Individuation and the growth of the personality

If we are then to support our clients through this period of turbulence, we must understand the psychology of midlife, and its place in the developmental journey that Jung termed 'individuation'. Individuation is central to Jungian thought and describes that lifelong journey of development through which our potential and our full personality emerges over time. Here the conscious and unconscious aspects of the psyche become integrated, leading to a greater sense of wholeness and self-awareness which Jung described as 'an extension of the sphere of consciousness, an enriching of conscious psychological life' (CW 6, para. 762). Through individuation, the psyche may be accessed more completely in support of our development, strengthening our capacity to withstand the challenges we face. With the insight gained through the individuation process, we are able to consciously reform the assumptions which define our sense of self and self-worth; the meaning and quality of our relationships; and the sense of purpose that justifies the time and energy that we invest in our work. We can begin to walk a path that we have consciously chosen, rather than simply assuming the role that society has given to us. Through the gradual integration of both conscious and unconscious aspects of the psyche, the individual experiences a gradual movement towards the 'development of a psychological individual as a being distinct from the general, collective psychology' (CW, para. 757). Individuation may then be seen as the foundation and requirement of leadership, which by definition demands the courage to stand apart from the group mind.

Our lives begin as a *participation mystique* (CW 6, para. 781) in which we are unable to distinguish ourselves from external objects and are bound to our primary caregiver through an unconscious psychological oneness. Our initial sense of self as a distinct being, begins to emerge within the first year of life, and we gradually form the basis of our identity, an unconscious collection of ideas drawn from our environment with which we begin to identify. These identifications play a valuable role in the development of personality in our early lives as it is through this imitation that we learn to solve problems and orientate ourselves within our social context. Identifications allow us to develop the masks or 'personae' which in turn serve as the recognisable and stable markers that position us in society and in time shape our developing personalities.

In the first stage of life, often termed 'containment and nurturance' (Stein 2006b) maternal figures ideally provide us with the emotional support needed for a stable foundation on which we can build our personalities. These figures may be present as our biological mothers, or in the form of any other figure or institution that provides the support, care and shelter we need. The quality of identifications at this stage will continue to shape the developing personality in profound ways and may also be the root of many forms of psychopathology.

We then enter adolescence and begin to experiment with the possible roles we may take up in the world beyond our immediate family circle before crossing over into the second stage of life; that of 'adapting and adjusting'. Here we leave the maternal shelter to find our place in the world and discover consequence and responsibility. Obviously, these lessons may have been learned to some degree before this stage, but at this point we are without the safety net of maternal care. Within this second stage comes the theme of mastery and the ability to operate within the world to shape and define our 'performance' in taking up the roles offered by society. We establish habits and patterns of behaviour, build our careers and look to the judgement of paternal authority figures to validate our capability and progress.

Over the course of these two stages, we establish ourselves as adults and create the foundation of confidence and stability upon which our development continues. However, although we may then be well adapted to our society, accurately representing its values and beliefs, our individuality may remain hidden and we may have become 'a mere mouthpiece for the collective attitude' (Stein 2006a, p. 13). We develop what James Hollis has termed a 'provisional personality' (Hollis 1993, p. 10): a series of strategies chosen to protect us as we adapt to the demands of our world. Inside this protective shell, the range of possibility open to us becomes constrained by our past and present identities and our inner life may remain impoverished. Inertia may still be seductive, as habits create familiar rewards and at worst expose us to familiar risks. Our unconscious, however, compensating for the inflexibility of our ego and prompted by the life's events, may urge us forwards, and at some level we may start to wonder: 'Is this all there is?' If we listen closely to our intuition, we may begin another journey.

Entering midlife

The third stage of life is that of centring and integrating, where we become aware of and then free ourselves from our unconscious identifications with our context. We begin to transcend the social roles we have been given and create space for who we may become. We rediscover our potential and often feel the intangible feeling of wholeness that is associated with that; a feeling that is described in analytical psychology as the emergence of the Self.

It is important here not confuse individuation with individualism, where personality is developed with no regard to the external context. Instead, this stage of the individuation process sees the emergence of a conscious aware-ness of both our potential uniqueness, and our interconnectedness with the world in which we live. When we enter this stage, we become better able to interact with our environment with a conscious flexibility and a change in awareness that 'sees through fixed identities and is able to let them pass into and out of view without clinging to them' (Stein 2006a, p. 19). This allows a balance to be struck between the illusion and hubris of autonomy and individualism on the one hand and a sense of determinism and depend-ence on external objects on the other. We may begin to see these external objects more clearly and relate to them as they truly are, with the result that more genuine intimate relationships become possible. In understanding our-selves we become better able to understand those around us. We are able to make conscious choices about our social context; rather than unconsciously conform to choices that it has made for us. Crucially for leaders, this stage of life allows them to question the operating paradigms of their organization or industry, and perhaps of society itself. Individuals in this stage are able to 'change the game', not just for themselves, but for those around them.

However, to approach this stage we must pass the threshold of midlife, a transition that may in itself last a decade or more as we visit and revisit obstacles and make sense of ourselves and our place in the world. A new way of thinking begins to emerge as the goal oriented 'heroic' thinking of the first half of life, begins to give way to a more balanced and realistic stance (Hollis 1993). As we cross this threshold, we must confront the fanta-sies we had built around the meaning of success and the value of achieve-ment and, on reaching the top of the mountain we had spent so long climbing, we might find the view disappointing. We may begin to wonder whether that the promotion we have worked for, or the wealth we have accumulated was worth the sacrifice. We might experience a profound sense of sadness as we begin to ask questions for which we may have no easy answers, as our identifications begin to fall away, and as we are forced to consider our place in the world without them. This first phase of midlife is a time of separation or analysis. We must begin by 'finding (...) and burying the dead' (Stein 1983, p. 42), recognising aspects of our identity that may have served us well, but that now prevent further development. This may be a difficult process and is referred to in Jung's alchemical metaphor as the 'nigredo' or blackening, a time of heat and suffering when the ingredients of our psyche are heated and recombined, and some parts are burnt away. In the confrontation with the unconscious powerful emotions are surfaced, and the threat of psychological disintegration, the midlife crisis, is very real. In the face of what feels like an existential threat, clients may withdraw and repress the forces of individuation or act out their impulses. Here a coach must be able to recognise the pain of separation and ensure that this experience is not ignored or trivialised. We may become a containing vessel, within which the transformation of identity may occur. Our ability to witness and tolerate the suffering of our clients will define their ability to mourn the loss of the past and move forwards.

For one client, midlife triggered some difficult associations with her childhood, where she had been feted by her father as the 'golden child' whose success would position her family better in their local community. As a result, she had spent much of her career chasing approval from senior male authority figures and upon reaching a senior level herself, she began to resent her feelings of dependence. She left corporate life and pursued a more creative existence as a performance artist, a path she enjoyed but which felt more like an act of raw rebellion than a genuinely new path. In our work together she acknowledged that the anger and shame driving this decision was as much directed towards herself for meekly complying with authority, as with the figures that had guided her. Our work together allowed her to come to terms with both the need to express herself and the need to honour the support and opportunities that she had been given.

During the nigredo, the unconscious provokes us with symbols that may open up new perspectives, the 'prima materia' or raw materials of our transformation. These may come in the form of images or associations and the role of the coach is to help the client to notice these symbols and begin to make sense of them through amplification or active imagination. Some of these symbols may appear not as new ideas but as memories, or childhood fantasies, revealing something that life has repressed but whose time has come again. One client remembered his childhood dream to open a restaurant and, exploring this as a symbolic idea, he revealed a need to create welcoming and nurturing environments. This was somewhat at odds with his rather harsh and abrasive persona, which, with a degree of shame he admitted extended beyond work into his homelife. His life had taught him to be a tough guy and in midlife he discovered a need as a leader to create the more caring spaces that he wished he himself had experienced when he was younger. Midlife might often feel like a break from old patterns, but it may simply be a rediscovery or a reinterpretation, where the myths of our past can be expressed in new ways and new meaning taken from them. The meaning of a memory in the present may therefore be more important than the reality of a memory in the past. As Papadopoulos has suggested (2006, p. 33), 'as the past shapes the present, so the present shapes the past' and as coaches we must therefore help our clients wonder: 'Why this and why now?' Jung suggested that the emergence of the personality through individuation can be considered as the most effective route to psychological well-being, with neurosis being understood 'ultimately, as the suffering of a soul which has not discovered its meaning' (CW 11, para. 497). Through engaging with an innate drive to find purpose an individual may discover that the 'only genuine cure for neurosis is to grow out of it through further individuation' (Stein 2006a, p. 31). For my client, the rediscovery of kindness was the meaning he took from the memory.

Transformation and emergence

Passing from the pain of 'nigredo' clients may then discover a phase of acceptance and possibly depression; what is termed the 'albedo' or the whitening. Here we are truly between states and face the moment of dawn, where we know we are no longer asleep but have not yet fully woken. We know what we are not, but we still do not know what we are becoming. This phase requires patience, and a client must be encouraged to 'sit' with the emotion and observe themselves, allowing something unforeseen to emerge. By trying to force the process of change, perhaps due to our innate narcissism as coaches, we may simply rob the client of a unique opportunity to explore meaning. As Tess Castleman suggests, 'many emotions have hidden within their core a desire for action – the change which is most often resisted' (Castleman 2003, p. 129). In seeking understanding, rather than repressing or overcoming the emotion, we may discover its intent. Perhaps a sense of depression could simply be the mind allowing itself to lay fallow, before new growth begins.

The phase of 'albedo' is an important moment in midlife as it represents an activation of what in analytical psychology is termed the 'transcendent function'. From the tension created by the 'nigredo' a new position or perspective can emerge which has not been available to us before. The transcendent function enables 'individual lines of development which could never be reached by keeping to the path prescribed by collective norms' (CW 6, para. 759). In this phase we gradually realise that the fantasies of success and achievements of youth and early adulthood are illusions and that, if we are truly on a journey of transformation, we cannot know the end. Here the process matters more than the goal.

As we become open to new possibilities emerging, we are then able to enter the final phase of midlife: the 'rubedo' or reddening, a representation of the rising sun and new beginnings. This is a phase of synthesis and recombination, where we gradually become aware of the new possibilities that are open to us and the conscious choices we can make, now we are free from the roles and assumptions that we have unconsciously assumed.

Our focus moves from achievements and goals to the quality and content of the work, and we begin to ascribe meaning to our lives beyond meeting social norms and expectations. We accept that goals and perfection are an illusion and our work becomes a journey of creativity and expression which has a 'sculpted' (Jaques 1965, p. 513) rather than 'engineered' character. In leadership roles we can then express ourselves through our work and cope with the ambiguity we face, as each change just provides a new canvas for that expression. Crucially, the idea of a parental authority figure who validates our judgements begins to dissolve and we realise that we have become the container for others, setting the parameters of what is possible. At midlife permission is to be seized and not requested.

However, the symbolic separation from authority sometimes requires a great deal of courage. A coach may need to support their clients in identifying small experiments or minor transgressions from previous norms, to test new possibilities and build a sense of confidence and agency. These experiments provide the client with a method of enquiry, where they can test ideas and use the results to inform the next steps, refining their messages for themselves and others. They will often involve subtle changes in behaviour or shifts in direction, which may pass unnoticed but represent courageous and often emotionally charged moments for the clients themselves.

A labyrinthine path

As the midlife transition closes, a feeling of psychological stability returns, but we must remember that the passage through the stages of individuation is unlikely to be a predictable process with discrete stages that we pass through in an orderly sequence. Instead, they should be considered as a series of themes or attitudes which predominate through particular phases of the transition and which may recur, particularly if the needs or conflicts from which they arise have not been successfully resolved. Individuation may consist of 'progress and regress, flux and stagnation in alternating sequence' and it may be considered as a 'spiral' or 'labyrinthine path', with the 'same problems and motifs occurring again and again on different levels' (Jacobi 1983, p. 34). Each of us will individuate at a different pace, and in some cases may not progress at all, instead experiencing a blockage at a particular stage, as we become unable to separate from previous identifications.

Our coaching work may be similarly labyrinthine, and the orderly, planned process so beloved by organizations may need to be reconsidered. Clients may need a range of support for different challenges and at different times, depending on where they are in the process and the demands that are placed upon them. A complex world requires emergence and adaption, and as coaches we must respond accordingly. We must be able to walk alongside our clients on a journey, knowing that in doing so they are preparing a path for others to follow. As Jung suggested of psychotherapists:

> He is not just working for this particular patient, who may be quite insignificant, but for himself as well and his own soul, and in so doing he is perhaps laying an infinitesimal grain in the scales of humanity's soul. Small and invisible as this contribution may be, it is yet an *opus magnum* (…)
>
> (CW 16, para. 449)

In helping leaders in a successful midlife transition, we are helping them transform their organizations, creating healthier and more successful containers for others.

References

Castleman, T 2003, *Threads, knots, tapestries: how a tribal connection is revealed through dreams and synchronicities*, Syren Book Co, St Paul.

Handy, C 2002, *The age of unreason*, Arrow, London.

Hollis, J 1993, *The middle passage: from misery to meaning in midlife*, Inner City Books, Toronto.

Jacobi, J 1983, *The way of individuation*, Meridian, New York.

Jaques, E 1965, 'Death and the midlife crisis', *International Journal of Psycho-Analysis*, vol. 46, pp. 502–514.

Jung, CG 1932/1970, 'Psychotherapists or the clergy', in H Read, M Fordham, G Adler and W McGuire (eds), *The collected works of C.G. Jung* (CW), trans. R Hull, CW 11, Princeton University Press, Princeton.

——— 1966, *The practice of psychotherapy*, CW 16.

——— 1971, *Psychological Types*, CW 6.

Papadopolous, RK 2006, 'Jung's epistemology and methodology', in R Papadopolous (ed), *The handbook of Jungian psychology*, Routledge, Hove, pp. 7–53.

Stein, M 1983, *In midlife*, Spring Publications, Chelsea.

Stein, M 2006a, *The principle of individuation*, Chiron, Wilmette.

Stein, M 2006b, 'Individuation', in R Papadopoulos (ed), *The handbook of Jungian psychology*, Routledge, Hove, pp. 196–214.

Chapter 20

Narcissistic leadership[1]

John O'Brien

Who are you then?
I am part of that power which eternally wills evil and eternally works good.
(J. W. Goethe, *Faust*, part 1, scene 3, line 1335)

Narcissistic personality disorder

Narcissistic personality disorder (NPD) poses a serious challenge for human resource professionals and consultants when it is discovered in high performing corporate leaders. It affects around 1% of the population. According to popular psychology, the condition is characterised by 'excessive self-love (...) marked by bloated confidence, vanity, materialism, and a lack of consideration for others' (Twenge & Campbell 2009). The tone of her comments reflects the frustration experienced by colleagues and helping professionals engaging with NPD in leaders. It evokes a feeling of distaste which is quickly translated into dislike of the leader and negative attribution of meaning to the behaviour in question. At a recent clinical discussion on the topic of NPD in corporate leadership in London, a former Human Resources Director of a global international financial services firm reported that he had just been asked for a reference by his former boss, whom he described as an 'undiagnosed NPD'. The contact evoked strong feelings in the HRD who had been terrified by his boss while in his employ. His sleep was disturbed and he reported images of being killed if he did not comply with the reference request. During the same discussion, a psychotherapist reported being 'unnerved' when working with patients with NPD. He described this feeling, as 'without image', as primal fear. NPD evokes a range of feelings such as terror, rage, powerlessness, incompetence and worthlessness in colleagues and subordinates, who are often too afraid either to challenge or to report bad behaviour.

NPD is a mental disorder, which according to the Diagnostic Statistical Manual (DSM) includes the signs and symptoms of grandiosity, a deep need for admiration, a sense of entitlement and a lack of empathy (American

Psychiatric Association, 2013). It is frequently undiagnosed. Sufferers often do not consider themselves to have a problem (Caligor & Yeomans 2015). Features of NPD and related disorders can sometimes be found in certain types of problematic leadership. Taking into account the multiple perspectives of psychoanalysis, cognition and neuroscience, it is pointed out that some NPD patients might be 'excessively goal focused in the service of self enhancement', and 'unable to redirect their attention' (Ronningstam & Baskin-Sommers 2013, p. 191). This facet of the disorder, commonly experienced by patients with psychopathy, is sometimes shared by leaders exhibiting the 'total focus' required to reach the apex of achievement in goal oriented organizations. Excessive emphasis on goals for such leaders is likely to exacerbate matters.

From a management research and consulting perspective, McClelland and Burnham (1995) tracked the natural course of leadership development in corporates, through the career lifecycle. An orientation towards personal goal achievement in early career stages shifted to concern with the benefit of the institution at career maturity. Features of NPD inhibit this process with the result that senior leaders sometimes display behaviours more appropriate to their earlier years. In Chapter 19, Barrett describes the importance of rites of passage from one stage to another. Mature leadership, then, is the exercise of institutional power as opposed to power for personal achievement. This is defined as the direction of effort towards the benefit of the organization. In our experience, value based on short term transactions, such as with incentivised sales operatives eventually accedes to mutual trust between senior executives by virtue of membership of that group. It is contrasted with the motivations of affiliation (need to be liked) or achievement power found at junior levels. While these qualities are often valued and necessary at the commencement of a career, in their extreme forms and at senior levels they can be problematical. The model therefore provides a useful conceptual bridge for ambitious and single minded potential leaders to apply the total focus which drove success at junior levels to a different definition of power at senior levels, one which accords with the natural journey of individuation. The new criteria for achievement include the relinquishment of grandiosity, and the development of empathy. Many coaching techniques have been developed to help smooth this change (Bandler, Grinder, Andreas & Connirae 1982).

Nonetheless, for real progress to be made, difficult feelings must be acknowledged and integrated. Research suggests (Ronningstam & Baskin-Sommers 2013) that unconscious fear is a key factor in NPD and that along with secondary feelings of shame, rage and low self-esteem, it seriously disrupts self-agency and distorts decision making. Jean Knox (2011) emphasises the importance of self-agency in development. Part of the difficulty of getting to grips with NPD, either through self-acknowledgement or through the understanding of others lies in the unconscious nature of the associated feelings. This is often due to the origin of the disorder, the developmental factors of which are found in early infancy.

Certain injuries to self-esteem are of such a deep unconscious nature that they impair the development or the capability of a positive experience of oneself. Healthy self-care is predicated on a sense of being loved. At a simple level, neglected children may appear unkempt as adults and live with continuing rejection which reaffirms an early sense of worthlessness. Such a pattern might be described as a complex (Jacoby 2013). Disruptions to early nurture can cause injury to healthy self-love to the extent that the person is not fully aware of the potential of being loved and to love. These are narcissistic wounds which can occur before the ego is formed. The terror of the infant cannot find expression through words or concepts. It is primal, as in the resonant feelings evoked in the London therapist in the case example given at the beginning of this chapter. It can only be approached through a relationship with a trained professional with the capacity to understand and respond appropriately to the distress in the other. It usually requires careful long term work. At the collective corporate level, narcissistic leadership wounds can deeply affect colleagues and subordinates.

When we encounter narcissism, the symptoms of deep insult and injury frequently evoke revulsion and blame. Natural responses often go without reflection and the problem remains intransigent. We become unwitting participants in a dramatic replay of early rejection. It is that sense of rejection inside us, however distant in our own human experience and that of our ancestors which is evoked. To the extent that we find it difficult to suffer, it is difficult to suffer with andto feel compassion for the other. Wounds can be transformed with compassion, and this requires the light of consciousness to illuminate that dark inner art of self-deception which protects us from the Shadow. The psyche is temporarily defended against traumatic memory by denial, and the same mechanism operates at the collective corporate level in denial of loss of ethics and abuse of power.

The archetype of the Self

In corporate analytical psychology terms, the narcissistic wound creates a complex, which becomes autonomous. At the centre of the complex is an archetype, and in the case of NPD it is not uncommon for this to be described as devilish. But it is important to differentiate between a suffering human being and one's own feeling of primal terror when confronted with coercive and self-centred behaviour. The terror is that which resides unrecognised in the trauma and is felt by resonant projection. In this way professionals are taught to use their own reactive feelings (countertransference) as diagnostic indicators of what remains active but unrecognised in the other. They are in one sense, proxy complex indicators.

Where individuals have been wounded by trauma, the archetype of the Self is activated and provides compensation. This dynamic, precisely observed in clinical practice with individuals, is also observable in corporations. If the ego and relationship with soul are not developed, we can be overwhelmed by the Self archetype and identifying with it, go off on righteous crusades and coercion and oppression, thus unconsciously evoking fear and rage in others. In this way we revive and relive an original power/fear experience which has become a complex. The implication is that as we become aware of the powerful and living reality of these automatic reactions, we develop ego strength and gain humility, allowing space for soul. Furthermore, if we can use the experience of being oppressed to diagnose the suffering of others, we might qualify as agents of change.

The light of consciousness grows with awareness of the Shadow. From the Shadow, all new things are born, lit by the soft and gentle light of the Moon, and not by the harsh glare of the over-interpreting Sun. Self-awareness and ego suffering permits us to take back our projections onto others, refrain from creating aggressors/victims of our colleagues and avoid identification with the Self. To the extent that we can retain humanity in the leadership role we might celebrate the darkness visible. As we approach this natural goal of individuation there is a constant danger of regression to ego control.

From the point of the view of the endangered ego, unmediated by soul, the central archetype is experienced in a negative and persecutory form. Feedback intended to be helpful is interpreted as attack. The ego, however strong, is unable to defend itself against archetypal forces. Such forces channelled through the ego are akin to putting a high voltage charge through a thin wire. The wire gets hot and no longer serves its intended purpose. Rational thinking becomes an unwitting servant in the form of rationalisation.

The soul is the mediator between the rational mind and archetypal forces. But 'soul' has been largely removed from our vocabulary and replaced by given theological systems which seem to have eschewed inspiration in favour of secular power of proponent organizations. Few organized religious movements seem to have enough soul to mediate archetypal forces at a collective level, and cannot in any case replace the individual experience of soul. Hillman (Hillman & Slater 2005) gives a clarifying historical account about how this came about in the 9th century, when the Eighth Council of Constantinople reduced the soul to the level of the rational spirit. Formerly, there had been a threefold understanding of being which included body, soul and spirit. According to Hillman, the church then established itself as intermediary between body and spirit. This left people bereft of personal experience of soul seeking in a manner fitting for each individual. The monastic tradition provided some with personal experience through asceticism but this was largely controlled. Individual experience of sacred images was also persecuted by the early Christian church, which censored those which did not conform to specifications. By hearing the cry of his own soul, Jung acknowledged the wider issue of 'Modern man in search of a soul' (Jung 1933) and through his work, encouraged us to be aware of our own journeys.

The ego's reflection on the Shadow is the primary 'defence against the dark arts'. It enables us to be aware of complexes and archetypal forces of which we would otherwise not be aware. The soul as mediator, presents images of the archetypes, which can be brought to the illumination of consciousness and which can infuse our awareness with meaning. All archetypes are in a sense, representations of the Self, the central archetype of meaning. It is found within, between and around us. It is the wholeness experienced by us of which we are part. The attitude of the ego towards the Self, experienced through the mediating force of the soul defines the positive or negative perception of the image at any point in time.

Incorporation

Many of us recognise the symptoms of NPD in leadership, and the extent that we can help is the extent to which we have recognised the features somewhere in ourselves, and so can have compassion, which transforms. To return to expanded definition, the Mayo Clinic (n.d.) describes NPD as

> a mental disorder in which people have an inflated sense of their own importance, a deep need for admiration and a lack of empathy for others. But behind (...) lies a fragile self-esteem that's vulnerable to the slightest criticism.

From the perspective of analytical psychology there is also the question of what in the organization is thematically represented. We might find clues to this in the legacy issues of the organization and in its foundation. What was incorporated at its founding, and what is now manifesting? What does the organization reflect of the wider collective unconscious? Leads might be found in the corporate myths and legends which illuminate the archetypes at the centre of corporate complexes. What do they tell us about the organizational journey and its successes and challenges? How are the personality characteristics of leaders reflected at the collective, organizational level and so then what is the role of a coach?

The myth of Narcissus

According to the Ovid version of the Greek myth, Narcissus was the son of Liriope who had stayed too long playing in a Thespian field and who was raped by Ceciphus, the river god. As the son of a raped mother we can only imagine the complexities of the early bonding, but it is likely that he would not have been looked upon with the maternal gaze of unconditional love.

He was attractive to others but did not know himself. He only saw his attractiveness in the reflection of it by the other. There was no contained resonance, just a diminishing echo of the yearning for love and Echo's eventual death. The quality of yearning is largely overlooked in considerations of NPD.

When he started to introspect, Narcissus saw his own reflection in the water and fell in love with it. When he touched the water, the image dissolved and the narcissistic wound became apparent. He could not access love. In the myth, there was no mediator between realisation and trauma, no gentle and witnessed discovery in the moonlight, just a harsh confrontation in broad daylight. There followed an enactment of painful self-infliction of wounds to the breast and death. In the Ovid version this is followed by a symbolic return to an earlier vegetative state, an unaware stage of development. He becomes a flower. In this transformation there has been a return to Mother Nature, a regression. But in this we can still read hope, a potential for healing. The narcissus, the flower of spring, represents both death and rebirth and we can consider the possibility of the negative mother complex having been touched by compensating archetypal Mother Nature. The potential for a new cycle with the potential for relationship is there. The narcissus flower has a distinctive cup, and Jung noted that from precisely such images appearing in dreams, the child image sometimes appears, indicating a cycle of renewal in the process of individuation (CW 9i, para. 278). With human nurture, the flower can be made safe, and brought back to humanity.

In conclusion and returning to where we started, if narcissistic wounding is present, then it is likely that archetypal forces will step in to compensate. This 'archetypal love' leads to inflation if the ego is fragile and there is no mediating soul. The individual loses humanity and identifying with the archetype is possessed by cartoon versions of God and the Devil. At the individual level, harsh confrontation of leaders suffering with NPD is unlikely to be effective. An appeal to institutional power ambitions might provide an effective bridge to engagement, but the delicate and long term emotional development work remains to be done and help must be administered softly. At the collective level of organizations renewal is found in the image of the child, which is always vulnerable and frequently requires protection from inevitable attack. Remedies confront us with our own vulnerabilities and defensive reactions are evoked as we engage with understanding. Herein lays the hope for incorporation of new energy which can fuel individual and corporate adaptation and individuation.

Note

1 Reprint: O'Brien, J & O'Brien, N 2019, *Introducing corporate analytical psychology*, Dosije studio, Belgrade.

References

American Psychiatric Association 2013, *Diagnostic and statistical manual of mental disorders*, 5th edn, American Psychiatric Association, Arlington, VA, pp. 669–670.

Bandler, R, Grinder, J, Andreas, S & Connirae, A 1982, *Reframing: neuro-linguistic programming and the transformation of meaning*, Real People Press, Moab.

Caligor, ELK & Yeomans, FE 2015, 'Narcissistic personality disorder: diagnostic and clinical challenges', *The American Journal of Psychiatry*, vol. 172, no. 5, pp. 415–422.

Hillman, J & Slater, G 2005, *Senex and Puer*, Spring Publications, Putnam.

Jacoby, M 2013, *Individuation and narcissism: the psychology of self in Jung and Kohut*, Routledge, London.

Jung, CG 1933, *Modern man in search of a soul*, Harvest, New York.

Jung, CG 1951/1969, 'The archetypes of the collective unconscious', in H Read, M Fordham, G Adler & W McGuire (eds), *The collected works of C. G. Jung* (CW), trans. RFC Hull, CW 8, Princeton University Press, Princeton.

Knox, J 2011, *Self-agency in psychotherapy*, W.W. Norton and Company, New York.

McClelland, DC & Burnham, DH 1995, 'Power is the great motivator', *Harvard Business Review*, vol. 73, no. 1, pp. 126–139.

The Mayo Clinic, n.d. *Narcissistic personality disorder*, viewed 9 October 2018, www.mayoclinic.org/diseases-conditions/narcissistic-personality-disorder/symptoms-causes/syc-20366662.

Ronningstam, E & Baskin-Sommers, AR 2013, 'Fear and decision-making in narcissistic personality disorder – a link between psychoanalysis and neuroscience', *Dialogues in Clinical Neuroscience*, vol. 15, no. 2, pp. 191–201.

Twenge, JM & Campbell, WK 2009, *The narcissism epidemic: living in the age of entitlement*, Free Press, New York.

Chapter 21

A Jungian perspective on the growth of business ecosystems in the Western Balkans

Danijel Pantic

Post conflict business

The societies of the Western Balkans are characterised by the legacy of centuries of conflict, culminating most recently in the Yugoslav wars of the 1990s. The road to recovery is long and hard and the region now faces a serious brain drain problem. 'The Western Balkans will most likely remain an exporter of smart, educated people for years to come, within a migration dynamic that destination countries control' (Vracic 2018). According to the World Economic Forum (2018) in addition to natural reasons foremigration to more prosperous countries, corruption is a significant factor in inhibiting business development. For example, in Serbia, 'Businesses have low confidence in the judiciary's independence and rate the efficiency of the legal framework for settling disputes and challenging regulations as poor' (GCR 2017–2018). Furthermore, 'Serbian Law provides for an independent judiciary, but in practice courts' functions are restricted by corruption, nepotismand political influence' (GAN 2020). Similarly, with regard to Croatia, it is stated in the same report that:

> Contrary to the mainstream view, citizens depart the region not only due to economic hardship and the slow transition but also for more complex reasons. A recent survey in Croatia, which joined the EU in 2013, found that the most common triggers of emigration are corruption, primitivism, religious chauvinism, and nationalism.

Despite such difficulties, there are signs of progress. For example, Serbia, having over the last three years made significant strides, were recognised in the International Monetary Fund report of July 2019, its Standard and Poor's credit rating upgraded from BB to BB+ as of December 2019.

Serbian Monitor cites the Standard and Poor's (2019) comments as follows:

> Our ratings on Serbia are backed by her educated workforce, favorable FDI prospects, government strong fiscal performance, moderate

public debt, and credible monetary policy framework. The ratings are constrained by Serbia's relatively weak institutional settings, low wealth levels, sizable net external liability position, and the banking sector's extensive euroization.

What can we make of these apparently contradictory trends, on the one hand emigration, low business confidence and institutional corruption, and on the other, good management of the economy and improving international relations? What sense can be made of the loss of good authority required for businesses to flourish?

From the point of view of analytical psychology, this is not surprising given the turbulent history of the region. We could consider the current inhibitors arising from as a cultural complex, a trust and confidence barrier to economic and social development. Unhealed transgenerational traumas run deep, disabling individuals and preventing whole communities from leading healthy and balanced lives. The struggle for social dominance is a prevalent theme, overshadowing community and compassion. According to the research stated, official institutions seem to be grappling with the problem of tribalism.

Progress and challenges

Evidence of progress can be seen both in the macroeconomics, in the spontaneous blossoming of private sector firms and in the attraction of international investment to information technology and construction industries. Nonetheless, the World Bank considers that the recent economic growth in the region remains vulnerable, carrying significant downside risk of dependency on consumer spending and we are yet to see significant growth of intraregional and international private sector firms. The growth of such firms is a bellwether of progress towards sustainable growth.

Private sector regional firms are diverse entities who are beginning to follow examples set by their European Union counterparts, acknowledging that they belong to one and the same ecosystem with interlinked economies originating from political bodies which had been archenemies for centuries. Trust is being built from the grass roots (small businesses) up to the central instititions and between businesses from different counrties. What is the nature of the culture complex preventing this movement?

Our history of conflict in this part of Europe poses a challenge to the full realisation of our true natures and collective potential. Ghosts of the past still linger freely in the streets. Their messages can be read in the media headlines and on the subway walls. They ask to be buried with dignity and to be mourned properly. Only then can transgenerational complexes soften and integration take place.

What are these new developments which are struggling to take form? Business ecosystems demonstrate striking analogies with nature which become apparent in post conflict societies such as ours. The transition from centrally planned to mixed and market economies demands a diversity of businesses within a single society and also that these businesses become interconnected with global networks. This mirrors nature's process of creating even more sophisticated, interdependent and mutually reinforcing species. Moore's (1993) HBR article of the year seems as relevant today as it was a quarter of a century ago. He defined the business ecosystem as:

> An economic community supported by a foundation of interacting organizations and individual, the organisms of the business world. The economic community produces goods and services of value to customers, who are themselves members of the ecosystem. The member organisms also include suppliers, lead producers, competitors, and other stakeholders. Over time, they co evolve their capabilities and roles, and tend to align themselves with the directions set by one or more central companies. Those companies holding leadership roles may change over time, but the function of ecosystem leader is valued by the community because it enables members to move toward shared visions to align their investments, and to find mutually supportive roles.
>
> (p. 26)

However, in the societies with foundation myths and histories of collective self-sacrifice (such as Serbia), social energy is hardly being renewed. Cultural renewal seems to be a lengthy cathartic process requiring a psychological sacrifice of ego standpoint rather than of martyrdom. In this way, perhaps progress can be made reconnecting to the Self and restoring good authority. We know when progress is being made when trust in authority is earned back and restored.

For individuals, this restoration journey involves the rediscovery and acceptance of oneself as one really is, before being able to be confronted with historical collective traumatic experiences, and working on their transformation and dissolution. It requires self-reflection in order to overcome inherited traits and attitudes accumulated by unhealed transgenerational trauma. The prize is forward movement, a building of new identity based on the discovery of authenticity and a sense of connection with good authority.

Archetypal forces

How do the members of society create a shared identity over time, and what role does business play in this respect in contemporary societies? Business can be thought of as an emanation of Mercury. Trade is designed for the exchange of goods and services. Energies are being mutually enriched. Trade is essentially emancipating as long as it is fair trade and reaches out to the other, respectful of cultural and other differences. Mercury has a close association with the substance quicksilver, the planet Mercury andthe Greek god Hermes. As a substance, the element mercury exhibits remarkable properties. In Alexandrian alchemy it was used to affect a display of transformation. By crushing and heating a piece of cinnabar ore, a metallic vapour was released. This vapour could then be distilled to yield quicksilver. Reheating the quicksilver transformed it into a red-like crystal, reminiscent of the original cinnabar ore. In effect, it portrayed a transformation mystery whereby a piece of earthly matter could undergo a process of suffering, transformation and renewal. Mercury is opposed as a high damn or barrier towards the impact of Mars, the god of war, which once unleashed, threatens to flood consciousness making us morally numb and indifferent to the suffering of others.

The nations of the Western Balkans have over centuries struggled to preserve, protect and develop their identities, but have to some extent become entrapped in the vortices of forgotten mythological pasts which nonetheless drive, continually narrate and perpetuate historical suffering. Does it not naturally follow that youth is attracted away from these dead and dying societies towards new ventures in a global and multidimensional world, if they can build identity and live its own story?

Is it possible for us to create safe enough conditions to build a holding matrix of interwoven business interests and relationships capable of absorbing the tensions of collective trauma, witnessing them, and transforming them, step by step, transaction by transaction, over years into a prosperous community for our children? Is it possible for us to start to perceive old enemies as potential business partners, fellow craftsmen and women? Or shall we waste our lives instead of watching each other through the sights of loaded guns?

The psychological journey

The region has known great trauma and loss. Atrocities have been committed and suffered. People of the region at the level of collective are seeking ways to find redemption, to ask for and to give forgiveness. We find signs of this in daily conversations with business colleagues in cross-border enterprises. Such business conversations build trust and pave the way to human connection. To some extent this counters the natural tendency to sweep below the carpet the undiscussable traumas, national guilt and shame and our personal uncertainties. It could be argued that it is only the denial of crimes perpetrated in the names of nations which prevents these very weak societies from implosion.

This potentially healing role belongs to new businesses. They are strongly inclined to cross-border collaboration. To cite one young entrepreneur.

'The older generations gave us Srebrenica. They gave us Jasenovac. We do not believe them anymore. We are building something different for our children'.

But as with any individuation journey, the way forward has its challenges. Collectively caught in the grip of the Moses complex (O'Brien 2020), life is potentially suspended in order to cherish the position of eternal victim. If possessed by the Moses complex, individuals can rationalize the mistreatment of those not belonging to an inner tribal group. The process of ethical cleansing, healing and transformation in the Balkans appears a risky one, prone to backlash and exploitation. Like the walker of a steep cliff path on a high mountain, it can only safely go as fast as it can go safely.

Conclusion

Business as a socially transformative force is a unique, valid and unstoppable change agent. It is a force fuelled by pure life energy. Business tends to spontaneously develop into an ecosystem with roots intertwined and branches high up like a rain forest covering the soil and transmuting underworld forces into the ingredients needed for the green growth. It creates a habitat for other, thriving species.

An entrepreneur starts from a blank sheet of paper. It is not practicable to fake the reality surrounding the imagined venture. Reality must be recognised. It is a material and metaphorical container which enables a strong ego standpoint to be filled with the fine matter of dreams, ideas and attitudes generated by the spirit. From this source, the inspired entrepreneur will instinctively feel the needs of the social matrix and an idea will be gradually transformed into being, a corporate body containing and expressing a venture.

An understanding of the hidden forces which govern the deep psychology of individuals, groups and nations can only help us to meet and overcome the serious cultural risks and challenges to process.

References

Viewed on 30 March 2020. GAN Business anti Corruption Portal. https://www.ganin tegrity.com/portal/country-profiles/serbia/.

International Monetary Fund Country Report No. 19/238, July 2019, viewed 19 December 2019, www.serbianmonitor.com/en/standard-and-poors-revises-serbias-credit-rating-from-bb-to-bb/.

Moore, JF 1993, 'Predators and prey: a new ecology of competition', *Harvard Business Review*, vol. 71, pp. 75–86.

O'Brien, J 2020, 'Beyond the Moses complex', submitted to *Culture and Psyche The Jung Journal*. San Francisco.

Vracic, A 2018, 'The way back: brain drain and prosperity in the Western Balkans', *The European council on foreign relations*, viewed 19 December 2019, www.ecfr.eu/publica tions/summary/the_way_back_brain_drain_and_prosperity_in_the_western_balkans.

World Economic Forum 2018, *World Economic Forum's Global Competitiveness Report 2017–2018*, World Bank, Fall 2019, Western Balkans Regular Economic Report No 16, viewed 19 December 2019, www.worldbank.org/en/region/eca/publica tion/western-balkans-regular-economic-report.

Part V

Corporate analytical psychology ethics

Chapter 22

Professional ethics in Jungian coaching and consulting

John O'Brien

What are ethics?

Merriam Webster (2019) defines ethics as

> the discipline of dealing with what is good and bad and with moral duty and obligation a set of moral principles:a theory or system of moral values, the principles of conduct governing an individual or a group, a consciousness of moral importance, a set of moral issues or aspects (such as rightness).

According to the Stanford Encyclopedia (2018), ethics are inextricably bound with moral philosophy. Foundational ideas are found in the Ancient Greek notion of '*arête*', or excellence. This excellence is described as a good of the soul which is expressed in the moral virtue of the individual. Hence the ideas are concerned with the inner psychological world of the person and their relationship to community. In this respect, and in modern terminology, the individual is called 'the agent' and matters such as the justness of the individual are in focus. Modern theories focus more on action, either on the consequences of behaviour or on the conformance of action to law.

Analytical psychology unites ancient and modern approaches in Jung's statement that morality is

> a function of the human soul, as old as humanity itself. Morality is not imposed from outside; we have it in ourselves from the start – not the law, but our moral nature without which the collective life of human society would be impossible.

(CW 7, para. 30)

First, there is the idea that morality is inherent, to do with the character of humans; second, there is the idea that morality is necessary for the group as a whole. The first idea falls within the definition of agent centred Ancient Greek thinking and the second with the two action centred definitions;

consequences and conformance to the law (Stanford Encyclopedia of Philosophy 2018). The perspectives of agency and action are supported by empirical research into the morality of infants. Inherent moral qualities in babies soon after birth are noted by Bloom (2013) and social evaluations of others made by infants are noted by Hamlin, Wynn and Bloom (2007).

The Jungian practitioner is immediately confronted by the issue of ethics. Jungian work is about helping the individual connect to their true nature, which as observed in infant psychology is a recipe for connectedness to society. This is consistent with the Greek idea that excellence, happiness and virtue, including morality, are linked.

What is a profession?

Merriam Webster (2019) defines profession as:

> the act of taking the vows of a religious community, an act of openly declaring or publicly claiming a belief, faith, or opinion:an avowed religious faith, a calling requiring specialized knowledge and often long and intensive academic preparation, a principal calling, vocation, or employmentthe whole body of persons engaged in a calling.

With the above definitions in mind, professionalism can be considered as a declared response to a vocation. The vocation requires extensive knowledge and training. Members of a profession share the calling, commitment, declaration, preparation, training and knowledge.

Codes of ethics

Professional ethics are usually expressed in codes of ethics. A code of ethics is defined by Merriam Webster as 'a set of rules about good and bad behaviour'. They are frequently supported by statements of core values. Codes of ethics relating to Jungian work begin with a commitment to the inner journey.

Accredited Jungian analysts are required to subscribe to the codes of conduct of their professional bodies and the regulations and laws in the countries in which they practice. Additional requirements of the training institute must also be met. For example, The International Association for Analytical Psychology requires its training institute members to meet minimum standards and The United Kingdom Council for Psychotherapy provides a thirteen point checklist of ethical principal and code of conduct. This includes: best interests of clients, diversity and equality, confidentiality, conduct, professional knowledge skills and experience, communication, obtaining consent, records, physical and mental health, professional integrity, advertising, indemnity insurance and complaints. In the case of analysts practising as coaches, it can be reassuring to note that they will have a strong skill set and have subscribed to stringent ethical codes. A typical course of post master's degree training lasts four to seven years.

There is, however, no formal regulation for coaches, but as the industry progresses towards a profession coaches increasingly subscribe to a professional body such as the International Coaching Federation who require adherence to a published code of ethics and who have listed competencies for training providers. Similarly, management consulting institutes require their members to commit to ethical codes of conduct.

Navigation

Returning for a moment to the first definition of ethics as a 'discipline of dealing with what is good and bad and with moral duty and obligations', Jung's perspective provides a useful reference point. 'When we speak of good and evil we are speaking concretely of something whose deepest qualities are in reality unknown to us' (CW 10, para. 860). 'Good and evil are principles of our ethical judgment' (CW 10, para. 864). Jung continues, 'At most we can say cautiously: judged by such and such a standard, such and such a thing is good or evil'. Acknowledgement of the relativity of standards does not, however, relieve the Jungian coach and consultant (JCC) of the responsibility of subjective judgement. As Jung states, in these matters, 'philosophy butters no parsnips'. However, this judgement requires a practical orientation and the deepest self-examination. Our strongest judgements are made from affect when we are in the grip of complex episodes. Practical concern for the client demands that we do not know what is best for the client, defined in terms of their personal journey of individuation towards wholeness. Individuation usually requires digression from the norm and this raises the question of the JCC's ethical stance in working with either or both (individual and collective) parties.

Furthermore, when faced with the deepest challenges we cannot always rely on pre-planned principles to guide action. Only when self-awareness shows both the good and evil perspectives of our own actions, progression is made towards a position which can contain the opposite tensions of the client and allow deeper realities to become known. We might then say that the JCC is obliged to have undergone analysis and is continually engaged in this process to gain a good enough practical ethical position. Jung's view is that the question of absolute good and evil is a secret known only by God. We do not know this secret and should tread cautiously, mindful of both sides of ethical issues and moral judgements. The careful holding of both sides is a distinguishing characteristic of Jungian work.

On the matter of working with individuals in a corporate environment Peltier (2010) explains that coaches must navigate two sets of obligations. If the company is paying the fees there are obligations to the shareholders of the organization generally expressed in terms of the activities required to generate profit. At the same time, there is a duty of care to the individual client. Our view is that both sets of obligations should be accepted by the coach, and that clarity of contract and boundary conditions in advance provided the necessary container for potential tensions which might arise.

Culture transformation ethics

To achieve corporate transformation, it is sometimes the case that coaches work with more than one client in the same team or company and with a team of fellow coaches spread across an organization. The operating model in this case is analogous to family therapy, where structural strategic and systemic approaches might blend with individual ones. This approach is generally unsuitable for analysts unfamiliar with group systems and cultural complexes. Analysts trained in such areas, especially those with additional social/business systems and/or family therapy training can usually adapt more easily to the relevant ethical framework and code of conduct and specific rules of engagement. In complex transformation work it is a natural safeguard for the process to be professionally audited independently of the provider and client organization. The auditors should be at least qualified in the same methodology as the coaching organization and the business disciplines of the client firm.

First, it is important to define the client. If the client is an individual working in a corporation, paying their own fees privately, then the ethic code is determined accordingly. (Note that the obligations of the coach to comply with the moral and legal requirements of the wider system always still apply.) If, however, the client is an employee of the firm, where the contract is arranged with the coach by the Human Resource Director or another agent of the company, a three way contract must be agreed between the Human Resources Director, the client and the coach. The contract will delineate the ethical issues, which include, for example, the boundaries of confidentiality. However, even in cases where a coaching programme is delegated wholesale to the coach, with no reporting requirement to the organization, the coach remains specifically obliged not only to the client and to the law but also to the company. For example, if the client is secretly taking action against the company which is not illegal but harmful to the companies well-being, the conflict of interest must be faced fairly and squarely. This issue sometimes arises with very senior executives who make their own decisions to select a coach, paid for by the company funds. The coach's financial contract with the company carries with it the moral obligation to shareholders for whom the Chief Executive is an agent.

It is also possible, in cases where the commissioner of the programme is not the end user, that requests for assessment reports are made, for example, for selection purposes. If assessment is a competency of the coach and the client is in agreement withthe suggestion, then if the process is transparent, it can be of benefit to all parties. In most cases, clients actively welcome such an arrangement, as development is directly linked to career goals. At the same time, there must be clarity as to what information is reportable and what must remain private. In this respect it is useful to distinguish between competency assessment and personal and group psychology. At its simplest level, MBTI may not be used for selection purposes. Furthermore, bearing in mind the family therapy analogy, an attitude of client optimal self-agency towards the individual client is helpful.

An exception is highly sensitive industries, where safety is paramount and leadership risk management is critical. In such cases, the JCC might participate in the assessment of complexes which, when taken into consideration with other information, might indicate a threat to public safety. An example might be the discovery that a candidate for promotion in a police force is a paedophile or has homicidal tendencies. In these cases, professional boundaries are clearly stated, subject to professional scrutiny and agreed by all parties at the outset. The contract and ethics must be transparent. Deeper consideration is given to ethical codes and boundary management in the case of clinicians working in forensic institutions, and these are comprehensively addressed by Aiyegbusi and Kelly (2012). Familiarity with extreme cases can provide a useful reference point and help to build a safe practice framework for JCC working in 'normal' organizations.

For individual work, questions to consider might include:

Who is the client, what is the contract and what are e the governing ethics to which all parties subscribe?
What if I discover that my client is a homicide or suicide risk?
What if the Human Resources Director prescribes a method of coaching which is not compatible with my personal ethics?
What if the client's boss is behaving abusively and/or unlawfully?
What if the CEO is my client and discusses business secrets which are harmful to the company?
What if I am working with the CEO and the executive team and all parties ask for advice on to influence the other?
What if the client's business is lawful but harmful to the population in general?
What if I discover corrupt or illegal practice?

Right and wrong answers are not provided here, but it is suggested that the coach has a clear and explicit ethical standpoint to which client can refer in the form of code of professional ethics. Whatever contract is agreed the ethics and boundaries must be made as clear as possible to all parties at the outset.

In conclusion, a consideration of professional ethics in Jungian coaching and consulting requires careful definition of terms and invites philosophical and psychological perspectives. However, we can never be certain that our decisions are the right ones for the client or for ourselves. The rigours of personal analysis go some way towards developing a perspective on the natural binary function of concluding 'this' or 'that' with certainty. With contained uncertainty, we can accommodate the psychological reality that wherever one thing seems certain in the conscious realm, its opposite will probably be constellated in the unconscious. This offers a pragmatic, clinically derived rationale for the necessity of analysis for JCCs who are required not only to navigate and abide by codes of ethics but also to be aware of the unconscious complexes which can predispose interpretation and govern judgement.

Example clarification of individual coaching ethics

We have duties of care to both you and to your organization. We will work with you in the overlap of interest between you and the organization.

We will not collude with you to harm the organization. For example, if you were to disclose that you are stealing from the organization, I would be obliged to report this.

We will not collude with the organization to harm to you. For example, if we were asked to reveal the content of our discussions, or private and personal information about you, I would not disclose these. This is agreed with your organization and governed by a professional code of ethics.

We subscribe to following codes of ethics, which govern our professional behaviour (specify these according to the relevant professional associations). I am often asked what happens in the hypothetical case where you might decide to leave the organization or vice versa. As long as you remain in post we will continue to work with you in the overlap of interest between both parties.

References

Aiyegbusi, A & Kelly, G 2012, *Professional and therapeutic boundaries in forensic mental health practice*, Jessica Kingsley Publishers, London.

Bloom, P 2013, *Just babies: the origins of good and evil*, Random House, New York.

Hamlin, JK, Wynn, K & Bloom, P 2007, 'Social evaluation by preverbal infants', *Nature*, no. 450, pp. 557–559, DOI: 10.1038/nature06288.

Jung, CG 1959/1970, 'The Eros Theory', in H Read, M Fordham, G Adler and W McGuire (eds), *Two Essays on analytical psychology*, The collected psychological works of C. G. Jung (CW), trans. R Hull, CW 10, Princeton University Press, Princeton. (CW 7, para 30).

Peltier, B 2010, *The psychology of executive coaching: theory and application*, Routledge, New York.

Stanford Encyclopedia of Philosophy 2018, *Kant and Hume on morality*, viewed on 10 December 2019, https://plato.stanford.edu/entries/kant-hume-morality/.

Chapter 23

Rumpelstiltskin
Archetypal view on ethics

Dominique Lepori

Fairy tales and myths can be entertaining. But they also carry profound meanings and values. They have both obvious and hidden purposes and are intended to reveal certain messages. Myths and stories that attract people of all ages also include such messages. These interfere with matters such as the purpose of life and the morality of collective consciousness. Ethical freedom only can stretch as far as the limits of consciousness:

> No one can flatter himself that he is immune to the spirit of his own epoch, or even that he possesses a full understanding of it. Irrespective of our conscious convictions, each one of us, without exception, being a particle of the general mass, is somewhere attached to, colored by, or even undermined by the spirit which goes through the mass.
>
> (CW 13, para. 145)

Although each fairy tale or myth has a different story, they all give hints of a transformative process expressed through their heroes and heroines which in their abstraction have a connection with our human fallacies. Campbell (2008) showed that the myth of every hero/heroine is experienced on the hero's journey. This journey involves an initial position in society which the hero must leave. The hero will experience a call to adventure. During this process, the hero usually has some sort of a helper along the way. On the road to the main quest, the hero will have to pass many tests. When the journey is completed the adventurer is recognised as a hero/heroine. This path is followed by most heroes in mythology.

According to von Franz (1996), the oral tradition of fairy tales began around 25,000 years ago. The basic motifs have not changed during the more recent 3000 years of written tradition. Archetypal stories originate through individual experiences of an invasion by some unconscious force, for example, a dream. In this way, archetypal content might break through into an individual's conscious life. This can be a numinous experience, which needs to be talked about. Thus, it develops into a saga and when it wanders, it becomes a fairy tale.

Until the brothers Grimm started collecting and publishing fairy tales of the oral tradition around the end of the 18th century, the telling of tales had been a spiritual occupation. Thanks to these collections, an enormous number of strikingly recurrent themes became apparent. In this context Jung (CW 9i) showed how fairy tales are the purest and simplest expression of collective unconscious psychic processes, representing archetypes in their most concise form. Archetypes (for example, Father, Mother and Child) are not in essence intellectual concepts, but can only be experienced. All fairy tales endeavour to describe one and the same psychic fact, but a fact so complex and difficult for us to realise in all the different aspects that thousands of repetitions are needed until this unknown fact is delivered into consciousness. And even then is not exhausted. There is no gradation of value. Every archetype is in its essence only one aspect of the *collective unconscious* as well as the whole. Thus, fairy tales transcend racial and cultural boundaries. Despite their differences, as Fromm (1957) indicated, all myths and dreams have one thing in common. They are all are written in the same language, that of symbolism. The symbolic language is one in which inner experiences, feelings and thoughts are expressed according to a different logic. In this logic time and space are not the dominating categories, but intensity and association. It is the only universal language that humanity has ever developed and is the same for all cultures throughout history.

Fromm (1957) outlines how modern man has forgotten the symbolic language, and with it the ability to wonder, which he says is the beginning of all wisdom. We are capable, but we lack imagination. We refer to what we observe during the day as 'the reality' and we are proud of our 'realism', which enables us to handle it so skilfully.

Naming the issue

With this in mind we can approach the fairy tale Rumpelstiltskin (Grimm & Grimm 2016). In the opening paragraphs the issue is named:

> There was once a miller who was poor, but he had one beautiful daughter. It happened one day that he came to speak with the king, and, to give himself consequence, he told him that he had a daughter who could spin gold out of straw.
>
> (Grimm & Grimm 2016, p. 181)

The initial constellation is known from many fairy tales. Unfeeling, performance oriented, outward looking men press a defenceless, unaccustomed obedient girl. These are all to be seen also as inner figures, as well as archetypes of the collective unconscious. In this case there is exploiting and grandiose father, a beautiful and allegedly talented daughter and a greedy king. What the protagonist might want does not interest this goal oriented world.

Both positive male energy, and female energy symbolised by a mother, big sister or resolute grandmother are missing. These are images of a desperate situation in the masculine. The motif is transactional (if you give me this … then I will trade you that). But then there is the discovery that one has sold the most precious part of one's soul, perhaps the symbolic understanding of this lunar consciousness. Looking more deeply into these archetypal motifs we discover more.

Characters/complexes in the drama

The king is greedy. He represents the dominant collective consciousness where money is the value. When, in the morning, he finds the pile of gold, woven out of straw by the miracle maiden, what does he want? He finds the pile of gold in the morning, woven by the miracle maiden out of straw, and what does he want? More profit! For now, the king gets even more pleasure in the abuse of power. So, what kind of king is he? He simply wants a gold-spinning machine that will benefit the financing of his court (von Franz 2019).

The father is poor. He submits to the king's principle and sacrifices his daughter. Love becomes a business matter. But why is he poor when he is working in the mill and with such a daughter? Is it that children should realise the unfulfilled dreams of their parents? Is she being told that she should become something better? Furthermore, a historical marker of industrialisation can be found in the motif of the mill. After the agricultural revolution, milling enabled the production of flour from wheat using the power of nature.

The daughter is beautiful and desperate, yet clever. She adapts to the situation and at first also sacrifices her child. She has sold her soul to the compulsion to perform and has pushed herself to produce more and more money until she finally exposed in Rumpelstiltskin, the miserable dwarf form of her own alienated humanity. Han (2015) characterises today's society as a pathological landscape of neurotic disorders such as depression, attention deficit hyperactivity disorder and burnout. He claims that they are not 'infections' but 'infarcts', which are not caused by the negativity of people's immunology, but by an excess of positivity. According to Han, driven by the demand to persevere and not to fail, as well as by the ambition of efficiency, we simultaneously become sacrificers and sacrificed, entering a swirl of self-exploitation and collapse. The individual has become what Han calls 'the achievement-subject'. The individual does not believe he is a subjugated 'subject' but rather a project:

> As a project deeming itself free of external and alien limitations, the I is now subjugating itself to internal limitations and self-constraints, which are taking the form of compulsive achievement and optimization.
>
> (Han 2017, p. 1)

This selling of the soul gives the feeling of being separated from life. One feels tortured, unable to go on living. It is important to give this energy a field of action; otherwise, one loses connection to one self. The struggle for her child, which the little demon wants from her, lets her finally take a determined stand.

The test

This testing teaches how to flow with transformative powers. It is not only the outer world that presses us with its demands for performance and obedience. The way we deal with ourselves is often just as ruthless. Especially people who feel inferior or not good enough treat themselves with a cold severity that is in accordance with the king's command: 'If you do not spin the straw to gold, you have to die' (Grimm & Grimm 2016, p. 181). For the miller's daughter, everything comes down to the same thing. She sells her soul to an impersonal performance dictate. But as is often the case in the fairy tale, at the height of despair, when she begins to cry out of sheer fear, a miraculous, unearthly helper enters the scene. An inconspicuous little man, about whom we at first learn very little, compassionately inquiries into the cause of her distress.

So what is the symbolic meaning of making gold out of straw? Straw is an agricultural by product, the dry stalks of cereal plants, after the grain has been removed. And in fairy tales, gold is the noblest, most enduring material on earth, standing for the inmost core of man, for eternity and consciousness. The symbolic meaning of gold connects to money and thus to psychic energy. A classic theory, which goes back to Aristotle (1984), holds that money is a kind of commodity that fulfils three functions. It serves as a medium of exchange, a unit of account and a store of value. Later Adam Smith underlines the meaning of money around the first two functions of money:

> The rich (…) are led by an invisible hand to make nearly the same distribution of the necessaries of life, which would have been made, had the earth been divided into equal portions among all its inhabitants, and thus without intending it, without knowing it, advance the interest of the society.
>
> (Smith 1976, p. 184)

And up to this point money symbolises a means of exchanging life energy. Historically, it is connected first to the agricultural revolution. With industrialisation the importance of money as a store of value became more relevant. Money must be used to fuel both the means of production and labour in order to make commodities. But life energy cannot be stored, it can only be lived here and now, and the gold made out of straw symbolises an illusion of control in which money can buy everything but life itself. 'This is, for example, the situation in cultures that are extremely patriarchal' (von Franz 2019, p. 153). And in the name of this illusion all three protagonists sell their psychic well-being, all are identified with their performance and believe that this is truly who they are, bringing about a split in their personality. And also the daughter plays the game, as at the beginning she could have admitted she is unable to do this (von Franz 2019).

'Three times'

The number three has a logical reason for its important role throughout history. It is the union of oneness and duality. In many religions, three is a special number. For example, in Christianity there is the Holy Trinity and in ancient Greece/Rome espoused the three Graces. The Vikings had the three Norns.

It is the first number that is a combination of different previous numbers. One and two are special as they are representations of oneness and otherness, but three starts the procession of all other numbers following to infinity as the imagined sum of all previous numbers. Numbers do not exist; they are creations of the mind, existing only in the realm of understanding. And three is a crowd, with the three figures becoming anonymous. There is also a theory that 'prehistoric people were able to count only one, two, many' (Stephenson 2008, p. 138). Still, this counting conveys the meaning of a typical average. Three is still so ingrained in our symbolic alphabet that we recognise its meaning in the fairy tale by instinct. And in binary logic, duality connects to the idea of either this or that. Something is either true or false. But life synthesises in the reconciling 'third', which is frequently not neither logical nor foreseeable. This is characteristic of conflict resolution. An anonymous proverb says that 'Only three things in this world are certain: birth, death and change'.

Here the fairy tale starts with three characters, and the transformation process. The peripeteia (sudden reversal of fortune) also follows this pattern. We have the same incident in the story three times. It is neither a single occurrence, nor a coincidence of two. It happens three times, which denotes a pattern. So, the poor miller's daughter has to spin gold out of straw on three different nights, and she barters with her values three times. First, with her necklace, a symbol for threading together also indicating her dignity. Second, she gives Rumpelstiltskin her ring, a tangible manifestation of the circle, representing infinity and eternity, as well as sovereignty and strength. Thus, to bestow a ring is to indicate a transference of power. And third, the last time, she promises him her first child, her vitality. She never says no, she prefers not to confront herself and her split off Shadow.

Rumpelstiltskin: the reliable devil?

So here he comes. Rumpelstiltskin is helpful, reliable and compassionate. He prefers something alive instead of all the treasures of the world. Yet he is also a very good merchant. In similar tales, he is simply referred to as a dwarf. Generally, it has to do with a creative activity, or with some creative fantasy. They are the ones who do all the work for a poor hero/heroine overnight. Linguistically, *Rumpelstilz* means a rumbling poltergeist that rattles stilts or posts to attract attention or annoys people. He is known in many countries around the world. In Denmark, the dwarf is called *Trillevip*; in Austria *Purzini-gele* and *Hopfenhütel*; in Bavaria *Silfingerl*; and in southern England, *Terrytop*. Philosophical depth reveals his Latvian name *Neezinsch* (nothing); *Neezinsch* masters the rare art of being able to spin moss into silk. In African fairy tales, rather than dwarves, it is usually powerful animals that offer their help, under the condition that one guesses their names. These representations of the Shadow belong partly to the personal and partly to the collective unconscious. Rumpelstiltskin represents a creative ability, a fantasy that enables her to get her out of her difficulties. Similar developmental themes with their peculiar processes may be found in many other fairy tales:

> Creativity always comes as a surprise. It is always the thing that we would never have thought of. This is the very essence of creativity itself. If we could think of it ourselves, it would be a conscious discovery. But to speak of the creativity of the unconscious means that the unconscious suddenly serves up an idea, an insight or a fantasy that we would never have thought of consciously. Because when it comes to something unusual or something we are unaccustomed to, we are by nature creatures of habit and we get defensive.
>
> (von Franz 2019, p. 156)

The issue spirals to a climax and the loss of soul is complete the moment the first born child has to be handed over. The child represents the personal core, pulsating life, in contrast to previous docility. From a position of obedience, the character had served the strange expectations of others long enough. Money, prestige and power had become hostile to life.

Freeing the inner child, connecting to creativity

In the enslaved soul achievement orientation, adaptation and heteronomy have become independent and taken the form of the 'dwarf-self', a threatening demon who has to be fought with energy to rediscover vitality. And here she gets another chance. He gives her three days to find out his name, in which case she can keep her child. And for the first time she becomes proactive. She sends out a messenger to help her find out the name. The messenger may remind us of Mercury or Hermes, the god of messages, eloquence and trade, and in particular of the grain trade. Mercury was also considered a god of abundance and commercial success. He was also, like Hermes, a 'psychopomp', leading newly deceased souls to the afterlife. Romans associated Mercury with financial gain, commerce, messages/communication, travellers, boundaries, luck, trickery, merchants and thieves. So, the messenger enhances the exchange in order to find out the name. This means finding the split off parts of one's own soul, through awareness. Whoever knows the name of a thing, a person or an evil power, can disenchant the unknown, gain power over the dreaded and, by redeeming it, integrate it. In the history of religion and culture, the name has always carried deep meaning. The name enables communication, reveals the personality and gives power over the named. But the name cannot be brought out by mere reflection, exploring or guessing. Only by listening to the unconscious, in the deep forest at night, when one allows oneself to be guided to one's own soul can it be discovered. And once his name is found out, the little man cried out, almost in a *rite de sortie* 'The devil told you that! The devil told you that!', and in his anger he split in two, and there was an end of him. Indeed, in this tale, the devil is only vital in the absence of good:

> The real problem, it seemed to me, lay with Mephistopheles (…) At last I had found confirmation that there were or had been people who saw evil and its universal power, and more important – the mysterious role it played in delivering humanity from darkness and suffering. To that extent Goethe became, in my eyes, a prophet.
>
> (Jaffé 1965, pp. 78–79)

Once we overcome the outdated valuing of achievement, the symbolic child (new energy) can grow up with the mother and the father, with the king (conscious ruling attitude) cherishing the spontaneity he brings. So, there is no need for an impeachment. The power play dissolves in the clarity of consciousness of each individual. Fairy tales deal with basic human problems and conflicts and show their symbolic solutions. As a result, the self-healing powers of the soul are activated.

References

Aristotle 1984, 'Nicomachean ethics,' in J Barnes (ed), *The complete works of Aristotle*, pp. 1729–1867. Princeton University Press, Princeton.

Campbell, J 2008, *The hero with a thousand faces*, New World Library, Novato.

Fromm, E 1957, *The forgotten language. An introduction to the understanding of dreams, fairy tales and myths*, Atlantic Books, London.

Grimm, J & Grimm, W 2016, *The original folk and fairy tales of the brothers Grimm: the complete first edition*, Princeton University Press, Princeton.

Han, BC 2015, *The burnout society*, Stanford University Press, Stanford.

Han, BC 2017, *Psychopolitics: neoliberalism and the new technologies of power*, Verso, London.

Jaffé, A (ed) 1965, *Memories, dreams, reflections*, Random House, New York.

Jung, CG 1942/1966, 'Paracelsus the physician', in *Spirit in man, art and literature*, CW 15.

———1942/1968, 'Paracelsus as a spiritual phenomenon', in *Alchemical studies*, CW 13.

———1969, *Archetypes and the collective unconscious*, CW 9i.

———2000, *The collected works of C. G. Jung* (CW), eds. H Read, M Fordham, G Adler and W McGuire, trans. RFC Hull, Princeton University Press, Princeton.

Smith, A 1976, 'The theory of moral sentiments', in DD Rapahael, AL Macphie, (Gen.eds) RH Campbell, DD Raphael, and AS Skinner (eds), *The Glasgow edition of the works and correspondence of Adam Smith*, vol. 1, p. 184. Oxford University Press, Oxford.

Stephenson, M 2008, *The sage age*, Nightingale Press, Mequon.

von Franz, ML 1996, *The interpretation of fairy tales*, Shambhala Publications, Boston.

von Franz, ML 2019, 'Rumpelstiltskin', in A Schweizer & R Schweizer-Vüllers (eds), *Wisdom has built her house, psychological aspects of the feminine*, pp. 103–115. Daimon Verlag, Einsiedeln.

Part VI

Jungian work with institutions

Chapter 24

Jung in jail

Teresa Castleman

Jung

Jung seems to embody the myth of Osirus; the great patriarch of ancient Egypt who is killed and dismembered by his brother and then reconfigured by his sister/wife Isis, who recovers thirteen of his fourteen body parts. All but Osirus' penis is found which allows him to live, not any more as a fertility god, but rather a ruler of the underworld and the land of the dead.

In a similar manner, Jung has been largely discredited, vilified and erased by traditional psychology and psychiatry; yet remains scattered throughout culture in the social and hard sciences, education, business, politics and trends in collective consciousness, creating a myriad of influences, often unknown and overlooked. Jung, unlike Osirus, has not yet been fully restored from absurd rumours, negative projections and superstitious black and white thinking (Bair 2003).

Jung indeed exists in cracks and corners of post modern society and collective consciousness. His fingerprints are everywhere, from psychological research and lie detector tests, to Star Wars films and the Berlin Wall (Bair 2003). Perhaps his work was too vast and influential to remain contained within the psychological textbooks from which he is inexplicably and decidedly absent.

One may not think of a Texas jail, a huge complex of around 10,000 inmates and 900 wardens as a setting for Jungian psychology, and especially for dream circles, but that was the case. In a Buddhist study group, I had met the head chaplain of the jail who discussed the problem of nightmares there with her. He reported that so many people were screaming in the night and disturbing their entire tank that he wondered if a Jungian analyst could help at all. The chaplain told me he really had no hope of the project getting a green-light but since he was retiring in the following year, maybe he could get it approved. And he was right. Somehow the dream group slipped through and was added to the Alcoholics Anonymous meetings and General educational development classes offered to the inmates.

I jumped at the volunteer opportunity because for many years my dream circles had brought surprises and delight. Against the norm, dream circles allowed less affluent people to be exposed to dream work in a safe and respectful process. Their abilities with dreams as well as providing one another with a sense of community had made me curious and eager to take the model to other populations. I had become frustrated with how erudite and privileged Jungian analysis was. As a citizen sociologist, I was very keen to broaden dream groups to the general public outside the clinical setting of my professional office where I had three or four groups running for many years. My clientele extended to a group of chaplains which I had helped to form its own dream circle that met as a peer run group at their hospital, a clique of women who had known each other over fifty years who met in their homes, and an elderly group of people in a nursing home. My publications spawned many more dream circles throughout the world that to date consult with me via email and Skype. I felt very excited to try the experiment.

In jail

The jail itself was an education each time I arrived on Thursday evenings. It was decided that I would work in the women's tank with non-violent offenders. Most of the women were incarcerated awaiting trial for prostitution, theft, drug possession or being present at a crime, usually a boyfriend or husband had apparently committed the crime. I was troubled to hear the women's reports of having been treated harshly by judges. In at least two cases, they were apparently given longer sentences than the men who committed the crime.

On my first evening, I arrived and passed through several rituals to earn passage. Then I entered the anteroom for the tank that housed around ninety women, and waited for a warder to unlock the door and let me in. I waited for forty-five minutes while two warders talked, laughed uproariously and ate the inmates' Christmas cookies which had been brought by nuns earlier. It felt like clear sabotage. Games of this sort occurred almost every time I came. After I was let into the tank, I had to wait for the warder to announce me, so that the women who wanted to could attend. All of this took at least an hour which I saw as a big, 'You are not wanted here' sign.

Stories and dreams

But the inmates came and they absorbed ·the experience in a remarkable way. The women were African American, Latina and one Anglo. The first night, a woman told her story and I was stunned. She was a black version of me. We were the same age and her father was caring for her mother due to

Alzheimer's disease, just as my father was for my mother. She owned a hair salon and was a successful small business owner. My private practice was a remarkable parallel. But here she was in jail and I was not. What had happened?

L had struggled with a crack-cocaine addiction in her youth but for over two dozen years she had been clean, sober, hard-working and successful. One daughter was going to medical school and her younger son was an outstanding student and athlete. In her words:

> One night after work I drove home on the usual route like every night before for years. I don't know what happened but I just took the exit that led to the old crack house. I know I am responsible, but it seemed like another part of me or my car took over and I had no control that night. I got inside the old house, sat down for about two minutes and then the police broke in. They must have been right there ready to make the bust. I was sitting next to the delivery that had just been made. The police arrested me for holding and carrying a large amount of crack since I was sitting next to the drop and had shown up so soon after the delivery. I will be going to prison for a long time.

After the arrest, her daughter, father and son all refused to take her phone calls from jail or connect with her in any fashion. No mail, no visits and importantly, no financial support. I was not aware then that it is imperative for inmates to have someone on the outside to deposit funds in their personal accounts. In this jail, silverware, soap, toothpaste, sanitary items, hairbrushes, underwear, paper, pens and so on are all items that must be purchased. Additionally, a bit of a con game seemed to be run regarding meals. Mouldy bread, foul smelling meat and third tier canned vegetables were customary fare. Most of the women did not eat much or at all due to violent digestive distress following meals. But the commissary cart would roll in the tank regularly with chips, candy bars and coke for sale. They 'survived' on expensive, non-nutritious snacks. L, of course, did not have this option. I was horrified putting L's story together and feeling a white privilege shame that I could not shake. L was at an extremely low bottom and she was struggling. She was absorbing the shock of having her close knit, hard-working family and business all evaporate over a destructive impulse.

A few Thursdays later, L came to dream group and she was beaming. As we all checked in to discuss the week's events, L said, 'Today was a wonderful day for me'.

'Why?' I asked.
'Because someone gave me a bra today and I am so grateful'.
'But I had a dream last night that changed me', she added,

And then she told her dream:

> I entered a golden, light-filled room where there was a huge, just
> a giant-long table piled with the most amazing and delicious foods.
> I cannot really name them all. There were whole fish, turkeys, a large
> standing rib roast, piles of breads, plates of every vegetable and fruit
> anyone could imagine and dozens of cakes, pies and frosted, glistening
> cookies. It was the most remarkable table of abundance I have ever
> seen. Then a voice in the dream said, 'this is the bounty of the divine'.

And then our jail dream group learned that this dream had adjusted her perspective 180 degrees. Before, she had grieved for her losses. Now she cele-
brated a rich inner connection to a source overflowing with nourishment
and grace. Her face beamed and the room of lifted. Tears fell from our eyes.

What happened that evening, which has been repeated countless times in
my practice of working with dream circles for thirty-five years, is that one
dream can affect almost everyone who hears it. In certain circumstances,
such as incarceration, the authentic reality of the dream held forth as the
tincture for transformation. A few months after L's Holy Banquet dream,
I was in the lobby of Lew Sterrit standing in the long, slow line to gain first
entrance to the tank when a young woman approached me. 'Tess!' she
exclaimed. I had to look hard at her to recognise who this teenager in
a fast-food uniform was, with her hair tightly braided in a no-nonsense
style? 'V' she prompted me. Then I said, 'V it's you!'

'Yes, yes', she told me. Then her words tumbled out. 'I am just here to
get mail. I've been out about two months now, gotten a real job and left
my boyfriend'. He was her pimp and there had been a fair amount of discussion in the dream circle that unless she edited him out of her life, she
was doomed.

> I don't know what happened in that group but I can tell you, nothing
> got through to me more than hearing the dreams, they gave me hope
> and an idea I had options and choices. And two more of us from your
> dream group have gotten out and have jobs! Thank you!

I got a big hug that today I can still feel.

One day during this time, at my office, I received a call from another
dream grouper from the jail. She called to thank me. Her grandmother and
mother were boosters and had taught her sophisticated shoplifting techniques, all the while working for an underground criminal network in
Texas. To break free from the prison of jail she had to leave her family. But
this is what she did. She shared a dream one evening of 'being on the outside' but still living in a jail cell. She literally saw herself in the dream as
being free, outside, seeing the sun again, but her living quarters were a jail

cell planted in the middle of a parking lot. She said then, 'I think I'm in jail now but the dream shows my life on the outside is just as much a jail as being in here'. Again, the profundity and authenticity of the image touched everyone in the room.

Hearing that three members of the dream group jail project reported breaking the cycle of theft, poverty, drug abuse and prostitution through the inspiration of sharing dreams made me contemplate what is truly possible through the responsible exploration and sharing of dream material. I never learned what happened to L.

Women in jail understood that dreams were symbolic, subjective, pro-spective and rarely predictive. They told me they had sat at kitchen tables and listened to all of their older female relatives discuss dreams nearly every day. Of all the students, candidates and analysts that I have helped learn the art of dream interpretation this group was the most naturally talented.

Nightmares were neither resolved nor improved by holding a dream circle, but then I had not expected that outcome. Difficult and recurring dream images are not resolved by erasure, but rather can transform when listened to, pondered and courageous change is made (Castleman 2009).

Transformations

Unfortunately, I had to stop the volunteer project that ran for about two years. I was diagnosed with breast cancer which necessarily curtailed my activities. I thought about L's gratitude for a bra and how it led to a truly life changing dream, and her own illness. Like a sentence from the ultimate authority, it would require of me the same courage to find hope again. The women's stories and dreams stayed with me as I recovered; their honesty and forbearance in facing tremendous adversity fuelled my own.

Being diagnosed in my 40s with cancer was a huge confrontation for me. I made changes regarding workload and moved away from destructive rela-tionships, but the primary change regarded my unfinished manuscript that I had not shown to anyone. I knew that I was not prepared to take my last breath knowing that I was too cowardly to face the reception of my work. So, 'the one thing I had to do before I died' was to let the manuscript be seen. And the women from jail gave me an added sense that the story of the dream groups was one that could help people find community, support, spiritual sustenance and courage together.

The gift of the bra, the diagnosis of the diseased breast, the bounty of the divine feast and the manuscript that detailed the power and mystery of dream circles and the tribal field somehow all seemed laced together.

Jung reaches people in their deep soul. It is not really his doing, more likely his recovery of what postmodern humanity has lost over time; the ancient wisdom and spiritual knowledge shut out by science and dogma. In a hungry and bereft world, Jung's contribution to the cracks and corners of collective consciousness feels like dismembered parts being recovered.

References

Bair, D 2003, *Jung: a biography*, Back Bay Books, New York.
Castleman, T 2009, *Sacred dream circles: a handbook for facilitating Jungian dream groups*, Daimon Verlag, Einsiedeln.

Chapter 25

Working with forensic investigators

How corporate analytical psychology can benefit those who serve and protect

Virginia Cochran Angel

First responders are the people on the front line of an emergency response, acting to protect persons and property from damage and destruction. Typically, closely following the first responders are those who are required to investigate and clean up the scene of the crime or disaster. Crime scene or forensic investigators, while not usually the first to arrive on a scene, regularly witness, and must attend to or deal with horrific violence, destruction and carnage. On any given day in any major metropolitan area in the United States, forensic investigators will be called to a bloody murder scene; or a home where a corpse was discovered days or weeks or longer after the individual had died. They might also be called to the location of a tragic plane crash where people both in the aircraft and on the ground were killed. The highly trained investigators are exposed multiple times each day to death, destruction and scenes of unspeakable violence. They must document for the legal record, investigate and then remove bodies or body parts to morgues. Added to these profound stressors, investigators are often confronted with grief stricken or incredulous relatives of the deceased or witnesses of the carnage that they are called to investigate.

In any developed society with sufficient fiscal resources to employ and sustain emergency response services, there is an expectation that the members of the various response teams would have the necessary resources to do their jobs. Firefighters, paramedics, law enforcement officers and forensic teams need certain tools of their respective trades to perform theirs effectively and efficiently. In addition to specialised equipment, education and training, for sustained performance at optimal levels these responders require resources for the psychological health which supports resilience.

By definition first responders and forensic investigators, are exposed to trauma on a repeated and ongoing basis. Such exposure chips away at the reserves of psychological strength and resilience of the personnel that, in turn, paves the way for the development of psychological symptoms and disorders including debilitating PTSD. Adults who experienced one or more traumatic events in childhood are even more inclined to develop PTSD. Unaddressed, it can push a sufferer into deep depression, substance abuse and addiction. In its severe and complex forms it can result in psychosis or suicide.

Symptoms

The American Psychiatric Association gives a summary of the DSM 5 diagnostic criteria for PTSD:

> Criterion A (one required): The person was exposed to: death, threatened death, actual or threatened serious injury, or actual or threatened sexual violence, in the following way(s):

- Direct exposure
- Witnessing the trauma
- Learning that a relative or close friend was exposed to a trauma
- Indirect exposure to aversive details of the trauma, usually in the course of professional duties (e.g., first responders, medics)

> Other symptoms can include:

- Re-experiencing the trauma in flashbacks and nightmares
- Avoidance, even changing routines to avoid reminders of, or feelings related to, the experience
- Cognition and mood problems, forgetfulness, feelings of guilt or blame, loss of interest in enjoyable activities, isolating
- Arousal and reactivity, including angry outbursts, risky behavior, hypervigilance and exaggerated startle reaction, sleep difficulty.
> (Veterans' Administration 2019)

As with any mental health disorder, PTSD in first responders and forensic investigators can be debilitating and lead to work related burnout. The World Health Organization, in its current diagnostic manual, the ICD-11, also includes burnout as an occupational phenomenon:

> Burnout is a syndrome conceptualized as resulting from chronic workplace stress that has not been successfully managed. It is characterized by three dimensions:

> 1) feelings of energy depletion or exhaustion;
> 2) increased mental distance from one's job, or feelings of negativism or cynicism related to one's job; and
> 3) reduced professional efficacy.
> (World Health Organization 2019)

Understanding the problem

Looking at it from the perspective of analytical psychology, violent crime reflects the shadow side of a cultural, national and/or ethnic psyche. It is part of a cultural complex. The meteoric rise in hate crimes (Federal Bureau of Investigation Uniform Crime Reporting 2019) and mass shootings (ABC News 2019) in the United States in recent years is symptomatic of the current political and cultural Zeitgeist, which invites understanding and intervention on multiple levels if meaningful impact is to be made. The Jungian approach takes into account multiple psychological layers of the individual as well as historical and collective aspects of the cultural content.

Humans seek and make meaning. We seek to understand, to comprehend and, most importantly, to connect. Analytical psychology, developed by Swiss psychiatrist Carl Gustav Jung, is a relational, depth psychology that expresses and explores the complexity of the human psyche. Thus the connection with oneself, the other, family, ancestors, society and nationhood, are all fertile soil to be tilled in the personal and collective unconscious, in the analytical process. When psychological health is compromised by traumatic experiences, people lose their sense of connection to themselves, to others and to something larger. Jungian analyst Donald Kalsched notes that 'related to this dimension of meaning, and rarely discussed by clinicians, is that animating spirit at the center of all healthy living' (1996, p. 37). If humans feel no connection with something larger than themselves, we lose a sense of meaning, become dis-spirited and lose connection with their personalities or, as Jung would also call them, 'souls' (CW 6, para. 797). Perhaps the loss of soul is one way to describe mental illness.

Trauma, complex and psyche

In performing his Word Association tests, which revealed archetypal ideas or images accompanied by emotions and thoughts, Jung formulated the concept of the complex. He discovered that when a word triggered an emotional affect, that an individual might not be able to consciously control, this was a clear indication that the person was being visited by a complex. 'It is the image of a certain psychic situation which is strongly accentuated emotionally and is, moreover, incompatible with the habitual attitude of consciousness' (CW 8, para. 201). He noted that as a result of the normal psyche's tendency to split, parts of it 'detach themselves from consciousness to such an extent that they not only appear as foreign but lead an autonomous life of their own' (CW 8, para. 253).

> When one is in the throes of a complex triggered by a presently occurring situation linking back to something in one's personal psychological history, it is as if one becomes possessed. The complex almost invariably

is formed around a core traumatic event that occurred in the life of the individual. Reality sees to it that the peaceful cycle of egocentric ideas is constantly interrupted by ideas with a strong feeling-tone, that is, by affects. A situation threatening danger pushes aside the tranquil play of ideas and puts in their place a complex of other ideas with a very strong feeling-tone. The new complex then crowds everything else into the background. For the time being it is the most distinct because it totally inhibits all other ideas; it permits only those egocentric ideas to exist which fit its situation, and under certain conditions it can suppress to the point of complete (momentary) unconsciousness all ideas that run counter to it.

(CW 3, para. 84)

The 'situation threatening danger' thus triggers the complex, based in fear, which may lead to aggression against or flight from a situation by which one feels threatened. Even if the situation is not rational, the complex will manifest behaviour that supports only those thoughts that are congruent with the complex and none other for a time. This may then lead to a chaotic, volatile psychological state.

When repeatedly subjected to traumatic images or experiences, at some point the human psyche begins to defend itself from the threat of annihilation. Initially it may attempt to explain or interpret the trauma in a way that is less incomprehensible, creating a narrative that makes more sense. Failing that, it may turn to compulsive thoughts or actions, repetition compulsion, to allay fear and anxiety that has been triggered by the traumatic event. In more extreme situations, ego consciousness dissociates from the reality of the trauma and turns inward in an effort of self-preservation. If the process continues, if the onslaught of trauma does not relent, the dissociation can devolve to a point of complete disintegration and psychosis. Kalsched (1996), who explores the internal world of traumatised people, explains it well:

The traumatized psyche is self-traumatizing. Trauma doesn't end with the cessation of outer violation, but continues unabated in the inner world of the trauma victim, whose dreams are often haunted by persecutory inner figures. (...) The victim of psychological trauma continually finds himself or herself in life situations where he or she is re-traumatized. (...) Something more powerful than the ego continually undermines the progress and destroys hope.

(p. 5)

Kalsched explains that when trauma overwhelms our normal ego-based defences, archetypal defences are triggered. These can be maladaptive, but nevertheless have a life-preserving nature. Analytical psychology is well positioned to work in and with the imaginal, archetypal material that impacts the traumatised psyche to shift the course and move it in a direction of integration, healing and wholeness.

Forensic investigation, trauma and healing

In 2017 and 2018 I had the privilege to work with and observe members of the Harris County Forensic Science Institute, in Houston, Texas, in the United States of America. In association with the staff of the C.G. Jung Educational Center Houston, the year-long series of group sessions with the forensic investigators was intended to inform and educate the investigative personnel about the psychological and physiological stress involved in their work and their effects on the individuals, teams and the organization as a whole; to build and enhance relational connections and healthy modes of communication in and with the members of the Institute in order to provide support and foster emotional strength and resilience, and to teach them various techniques of self-care that they might incorporate into routines that bolster the individual's and the group's psychological and physical health. Taking into consideration the complexity of the endeavour and sensitivity of the material, I will provide a small vignette of this work which will outline the framework, modalities used and themes constellated over a year.

The work began with an informal polling of the investigators to determine the levels and impact of work related stress they were experiencing. The participants generally reported high levels of stress and difficulty to varying degrees with coping with the traumatic events that they regularly experienced. It became apparent that helping them connect with and nurture their own interior worlds while at the same time building connections with each other and with the larger organization was of high priority. To begin the process, it was important to create a safe holding environment, a temenos of both space and time, within which the investigators could begin to open themselves and express their inner thoughts, fears and fantasies related to their work and the relationships with themselves, each other and the organization.

Modalities utilised included lectures, group discussions, meditations, creative writing, artistic expressions and other experiential exercises. The forensic investigators and staff social workers would attend the hourly sessions which took place monthly. Supervisors and department heads did not participate in order to foster a non-hierarchical, non-threatening environment to allow the personnel to more fully engage with the material presented. Jungian themed work included dream interpretation, utilising active imagination, and working with images and narratives. Concepts which were explored included shadow, complex, symbol, the unconscious and its impact on consciousness and archetypal patterns.

Themes that were constellated in the group included concern about effective job performance, being perceived as incompetent, fear of expressing strong emotion to colleagues and appearing weak. In our opinion, active imagination and the re-working of narratives through writing and sharing with each other, seemed most helpful for the participants. Our experience of working with the forensic investigators for a year so far supports the hypothesis that over time, helping the investigators to symbolise and work their dream material will continue to enhance their psychological resources and resilience.

A way forward

The provision of safe space, or *temenos* allows individuals to share of themselves and be vulnerable, through each of the modalities offered. Movement of psychological energy takes place. This is energy that has been dammed up or split off from consciousness in response to traumas.

In releasing this energy in a contained manner, the investigators are able to process and make meaning of their individual and shared experiences which, in turn, facilitates a sense of communitas, of mutual support and identity. In the release and transformation of this energy (initially generated by traumatic events) psychological growth and restoration are fostered and the systems, intrapsychic, interpersonal and corporate, may then function more optimally.

While the application of corporate analytical psychology to people and organizations that are routinely exposed to traumatic events is in its nascency, it is an ideal mechanism to assist in recovering psychological health and resilience, and to promote robust reserves of these resources to weather future storms.

References

ABC News 2019, *There have been at least 21 deadly mass shootings in the US so far in 2019*, viewed 21 October, 2019, https://abcnews.go.com/US/deadly-mass-shootings-month-2019/story?id=63449799.

Federal Bureau of Investigation Uniform Crime Reporting 2019, *Hate crime*, viewed 21 October 2019, https://ucr.fbi.gov/hate-crime.

Jung, CG 1907/1960, 'The psychology of dementia praecox', *The psychogenesis of mental disease*, CW 3.

——— 1921/1971, 'Definitions', *Psychological types*, CW 6.

——— 1948/1960, 'A review of the complex theory', *The structure and dynamics of the psyche*, CW 8.

——— 1959/1969, 'Concerning the archetypes and the anima concept', *The archetypes and the collective unconscious*, CW 9i.

——— 2000, *The collected works of C. G. Jung* (CW), eds. H Read, M Fordham, G Adler and W McGuire, trans. RFC Hull, Princeton University Press, Princeton.

Kalsched, D 1996, *The inner world of trauma: archetypal defenses of the personal spirit*, Routledge, New York.

U.S. Department of Veterans Affairs 2019, *PTSD and DSM-5*, viewed 10 August 2019, www.ptsd.va.gov/professional/treat/essentials/dsm5_ptsd.asp.

World Health Organization 2019, *ICD-11 Mortality and morbidity statistics*, viewed 10 August 2019, https://icd.who.int/browse11/l-m/en#/http://id.who.int/icd/entity/129180281.

Chapter 26

Association football

John O'Brien

Mass event

C. G. Jung, writing of the symbolisation of the Mass, argued that the event is a ritual which has its fundamental existence in an eternal realm, and which becomes manifest in earthly form through the ministry of the priest and congregation, who are participants in this expression:

> The ordinary man is not conscious of anything in himself that would cause him to perform a mystery. He can only do so when it seizes upon him. This seizure, or rather the presumed existence of a power outside consciousness which seizes him, is the miracle par excellence, really and truly a miracle when one considers what is being represented.
>
> (CW 11, para. 379)

Perhaps the most frequently quoted comment on English football displayed on the Liverpool Football Club website was made by Bill Shankley, their former manager. 'Some people think football is a matter of life and death. I assure you, it's much more serious than that'.

Football today is not only a game but a serious global industry. It is the most popular sport in the world, officially played by more than 4% of the world's population, with 265 million registered male and female players and 5 million referees in more than 200 countries. In 2019, more than 1 billion people watched the World Cup on television.

We can only speculate on the number of the 1.9 billion children in the world who play every day with friends. Any child in any part of the world can create a makeshift ball and start a game of football with other children in the street or on a rough patch of ground. It is not even necessary to speak the same language to play. It is sufficient to be able to kick a ball, and to imagine being a famous player scoring a goal for a favourite club. Football is a truly international language.

This chapter examines the game from the perspective of analytical psychology, describes the perspectives and potential contribution of analytical psychology to coaching.

Origins

Arguably, early prototypes of football can be found in the games played by the Egyptians, Greeks, Romans (Crowther 2007), Mesoamericans (Reichard 2009), Lenape Indians (Dean 1971) and English Medieval Mobs (Hornby 2008). But the game as we now know it was founded in 1863 by the Football Association at Freemasons Tavern in London. From the original code was developed a set of governing Laws by the International Football Board in 1886. While the IFB remains the guardian of the laws, the overseeing body today is FIFA which was founded in 1904. Its statutes protect accessibility, integrity and fair play and it has the objective of growing the sport internationally.

Bread and circuses

The importance of the game can be diminished by reference to it as 'bread and circuses'. Around 100 CE, the Roman satiric poet Juvenal coined the phrase to describe the vote winning strategies of the politicians of that time. It generally applies to the distraction of the masses from important political issues by diversionary emphasis on basic needs and entertainment.

But why do these strategies work? People need bread. And there are equivalent profound individual human and collective psychological and cultural needs which are met by games (nowadays, football). The exploitation of needs is certainly a testament to the fact and importance of those needs. And it should be noted that the English game (local Derby) was not originally played in stadiums, but was a rough week long competition between whole towns trying to get a ball into each other's town Square! (Hornby 2008). The game might be exploited in different ways but its history and universal appeal point to a deep psychological phenomenon, on a par with our daily bread.

The 'bread and circuses' criticism is itself a potential distraction from realising the profound importance of the game which gives insight into the deepest unconscious workings of individual and collective human nature, and which can potentially most fully contribute towards both national and international social stability and advancement.

Trauma and tribe

We owe our existence to the opposite forces of conflict and cooperation. We represent the hopes and dreams of ancestors who since the beginnings of our race have fought countless wars, who have bonded together in tribes for protection and mutual support, and who on precious rare occasions experienced transcendent moments of human unity, somehow inspired by mysteries and visions greater than themselves. This is our genetic inheritance. But the work is not finished. We ask what we might yet become, and what do we wish for our children? Another war? At the very least, we wish for a peaceful and stable world.

Recent discoveries in neuroscience and analytical psychology suggest that we can do more than wish. We can act. The Zurich epigenetic research informs us that we not only individually and collectively carry the traumas of our ancestors, but we repeat them without our conscious awareness. The key mechanisms are:

Transgenerational transmission and repetition of individual and collective trauma. (This accounts for repeated cycles of violence and warfare.)
Individual and collective Shadow projection (This accounts for fear, hatred and aggression towards of 'otherness'.)

There is growing evidence that transgenerational trauma can be genetically repaired at the genetic level with safe conditions being provided for suffers.

Football training

Probably one of the most influential forces in the repair of collective transgenerational trauma and the transformation of raw instincts and related defences is the football training of children and young people. The rituals and methods trains reality perception, decision making and constructive behaviour.

The symbolic importance of football in civilisation is illustrated by those precious moments of peace and humanity during the Christmas truce in WWI when in many places along the battlefront opponents met in no man's land to exchange souvenirs and to play football. It is now regarded as a counterpoint to the glorification of war. On the terraces of many international football matches can still be heard popular chants evidencing active traumas of the past. They are not politically correct. But like the writing on the wall, they evidence psychological facts, a gradual working through of collective trauma, and they are ignored at the politician's peril.

Trauma recovery is a process. It begins with concrete, literal psychological and physical replays of the trauma and projection of our fears and aggression onto the other. Through safe space and structured physical play, it can progress towards symbolisation and empathy. The key requirements are containment and engagement.

Containment

At the most primitive level, children will mark out a territory to create a safe space for the game. There are boundaries. There are also goals. Then there are opposite teams, which are generally evenly and fairly matched. It is frequently observed in playgrounds that, without referees, children will self-organize but spend as much time arguing about the rules as they do playing the game! The aim is to provide boundary conditions within which fair play can happen.

Engagement

When children are left without engagement, chaos reigns. When parents and children are left without engagement, then chaos can also reign. It can be highly disturbing to see parents howling instructions at their young children from the sidelines of a children's football training pitch and even more disturbing to see such behaviour modelled by trainers. We observed at a recent match between teams of 8-and 9-year-olds, an aggressive trainer pulling a child from the pitch by his ears while berating him for his poor performance. The parents were too busy screaming for victory to comment. What are the archetypal roots of this madness?

Football madness

The motif of child sacrifice was recognised by Jung. In an active imagination, one of Jung's patients had produced an image of a child being picked up by a bull and thrown into the air and caught by a maiden. He remarked that 'The game of ball with the child is the motif of some secret rite which always has to do with "child sacrifice"' (CW 9i, para. 324). In a dream seminar given in London (1928/1984, p. 25), he commented on the same motif in relation to a dream presented by a patient:

> They really used to play ball games in churches, the *jeu de paume* and this gave rise to the rumour that Christians killed a child by tossing it to one another like a ball till it died.
>
> (p. 25)

Furthermore, in the same lecture, Jung explained that 'the centre of a social group is always a religious symbol' (p. 24) which has historically progressed from totem to the slaying of the bull in Mithraism to more recent religious sacrament. He noted that people in communion 'turned their faces towards each other' as in the ancient English stone circles. Ancestors were thought to be watching, occasioning a communion uniting collective consciousness and the collective unconscious. Jung noted that Mithras was represented as a 'toreador, like a Jesus of the boxing ring or the football match. These games were communions (…)' (pp. 24–25).

The motif of ritual child sacrifice and the reality of child sacrifice can be found in many ancient cultures as well in parts of the world today (Bukuluki 2014). Communally, it is regarded as a means of connection to or appeasement of a god. It is associated with loyalty to a tribe or nation, or sometimes or as part of a belief in witchcraft.

These darker aspects of human nature, particularly manifest at the collective level are not so distant from the civilised cultures. It is not so long since the world wars when millions of people were collectively 'sacrificed', motivated by tribal and national loyalties and blessed by their respective religions. In the game of football can be discerned these psychological realities. Sometimes they have been acted out in riots, violence and murder. are the fires of good and evil. It is the containment of these opposite forces, which supports the natural progression towards psychological wholeness.

Football sanity

When they are engaged properly, children of all abilities give their best for themselves and their teams, perform and learn well and flourish as human beings. Above all they smile! In these best case situations, the trainer's passion is communicated, and uninvolved involvement is total. The trainer is completely engaged but can at the same time reflect upon what is going on for all parties and act accordingly. For example, when seeing a child running to tackle, the encouragement 'no foul' is given in advance. When the child is afraid of an oncoming striker, the instruction 'focus on the ball' is given. When children have difficulty in playing, they are included, supported, helped and encouraged. Parents are involved and all parties commit to working together to support the trainer to support the potential of the child.

Bora Stankovic and his wife Dragica were unremarkable football players from former Yugoslavia. Their son, Dejan, was not regarded as talented enough to play for his local football club, in Zemun, Serbia. However, Dejan, aka 'Deki' went on to become the only football player to play for three different nations in three different World Cups. An attacking midfielder, he scored 114 goals in 647 appearances and achieved many honours with his clubs; Red Star Belgrade, Lazio and Inter Milan, with whom he won the European Champions League in 2009/2010.

A small children's summer camp, called 'Deki 5' now operates at altitude in Serbia. Deki runs it. The camp is a model of excellence for the nurture and development of children. Above all, the trainers, professional pedagogues actually care, and in doing so inspire children of all abilities and all walks of life to overcome personal dragons and succeed.

Fair play

In fair play, transformation can take place. Play de-traumatises. There is movement from the acting out of violence to the symbolic, for example, from the unarmed life and death combat of Brazilian slaves through the development of Ginga to the Brazilian World Cup victories. Its evolutionary function is the transformation of trauma into culture and at the individual level the child moves through a series of initiations to symbolic warriorship and tribal belonging. At good football training camps it's the childish instincts (*the symbolic child*) which are sacrificed during the rites of passage to adulthood. In the stadium all participants, including parents, spectators and so on take part in the transformation ritual at a deep unconscious level.

Football like other team sports can help to foster a growing sense of physical, mastery and confidence which provides the basis for secure individual identity which extrapolates to the tribe and nation. The greater tribes such as FIFA, by containing many contradictory aspects of human nature, have the potential to transform trauma into conscious responsibility health and well-being and empathy and respect of self and other.

Dodgy refereeing decisions teach us that life is not always fair. People make mistakes and we have to continue regardless from a position of integrity. We are not perfect but we improve by emulating those we admire and by paying attention to our mistakes as learning opportunities. And as we evolve, we rely more on transparent justice such as that provided by the video assistant referee (VAR).

While it is possible to draw obvious analogies between sports and corporate life, it is sufficient to note that corporate coaching was derived from sports coaching and that football clubs are in any case corporations. The JCC interested in individual, team organizational and national individuation does not have far to search for the common fire in the symbolism and reality of football.

References

Bukuluki, P 2014, 'Child sacrifice: myth or reality?', *International Letters of Social and Humanistic Sciences*, vol. 41, pp. 1–11.

Crowther, NB 2007, *Sport in ancient times*, Praeger Publishers, Santa Barbara.

Dean, NT 1971, 'Pahsahëman – indian football', *Newsletter of the lenape land association*, New Hope.

Hornby, H 2008, *Uppies and downies: the extraordinary football games of Britain (Played in Britain)*, Historic England, London.

Jung, CG 1928/1984, *Dream analysis. Notes of the seminar given in 1928–1930 by C.G. Jung*, ed. William McGuire, Routledge, London.

Jung, CG 2000, *The collected works of C. G. Jung* (CW), eds. H Read, M Fordham, G Adler and W McGuire, trans. RFC Hull, Princeton University Press, Princeton.

———— 1959, *The archetypes and the collective unconscious*, CW 9i.

———— 1969, *Psychology and religion: West and East*, CW 11.

Reichard, JD 2009, *Life and death overtime: sacred play of the Ancient Mesoamerican rubber ball game*, American Academy of Religion Midwest Region, viewed 19 December 2019, www.academia.edu/400019/Life_and_Death_Overtime_Sacred_Play_of_the_Ancient_Mesoamerican_Rubber_Ball_Game.

Chapter 27

Realities yet unknown

Corporate analytical psychology and the New Zeitgeist

Nada O'Brien

Recovery and death. Conscious and unconscious. Duty and fun. Primitive and civilised, freedom and automatism. Power and love. Being and having. Moving and stopping. To achieve and to care. To dance and to sleep. To survive and play. To sleep and dream.

> The play's the thing
> Wherein I'll catch the conscience of the king
> (William Shakespeare, *Hamlet*, act 2,
> scene 2, line 565)

Crisis

Individual life brings a tearing asunder, a split. The split sparks a search for meaning and reconnection to the whole, the individuation journey towards the realisation of the central archetype of meaning, the Self. There are natural points in life when the search lapses under the illusion of permanency, times when we forget that health and stability are temporary as change is eternal. The search receives fresh stimulus when there is a life crisis. Crises occur at specific points in fairy tales, the blueprints of life.

We leave these in the drawer of our children's bedside table, or every now and then are reminded of a book from childhood, of the voice of a parent or grandparent conveying the wisdom of ages which cannot be made explicit. But we generally forget them. When there is no search for meaning any more, we suffer 'dis-ease'. There is a loss of soul. Recovery is not easy. The conscious ruling attitude says 'Cancel the offsite. Why are we wasting resources on jollies?' 'I will work just another few hours and I will be home'.

According to the Online etymology dictionary (2019) 'crisis' denotes a 'vitally important or decisive state of things, point at which change must come, for better or worse'. It derives from the 'Latinized form of Greek *kri-sis* turning point in a disease, that change which indicates recovery or death' (used as such by Hippocrates and Galen). The literal meaning is 'judgment, result of a trial, selection, from "*krinein* to separate, decide, judge"'. Most interestingly, 'a German term for "mid-life crisis" is *Torschlusspanik*, literally "shut-door-panic", fear of being on the wrong side of a closing gate'.

Jungian work engages with crises individual and corporate. It recognises the opposites of differentiation and wholeness, which must coexist as opposites until they unite in the squaring of the circle. The search for meaning lifts a veil from a garden of colours and sets them in motion. It animates. One of the greatest theorists and magicians of colour, Paul Klee, considered light as a movement of colours (Johnson 2010, p. 107). The search for meaning brings light in the form of many-coloured consciousness. It puts new and vital energy at our disposal for the creative incorporated ventures of life.

Play

In our early years, our natural method of engaging with the split is play. It seems that a great depository of spiritedness just waits to be allowed an arena in children's play.

Into the circle of play come all the actors of humanity's past, present and future. There are warriors, tricksters, kings and queens, princesses and princes, dwarves and giants, animals of all kinds, fools, magicians, witches, traders, bus drivers, doctors, friends, enemies, postmen, priests, shopkeepers, astronauts, famous footballers and more. Yet, the prerequisite for play is *symbolising*; that ability to be in the known and unknown, here and there, reality and imagination.

Symbolisation is the foundation for making the unconscious conscious. Time and space to play open a liminal realm where we are both in the imaginary world and also aware of everyday reality. In play, traumas are healed and patterns are formed for adult life. According to Davis (1992) the approach to play developed by Margaret Lowenfeld (a close associate of Winnicott) was close to Jung's. She felt that in play the child is accessing an in-built ability to make meaning through symbolisation. In other words, the patterns are already there, in the form of archetypes. They carry the inherited wisdom of ages in the structure of the brain. At playtime, the secrets of lost civilisations are recovered as the child organizes material objects to reflect inner realities.

In this way, fantasy is pre-scribed by an invisible hand. 'This explains why even fantasy, the freest activity of the mind, can never roam into the infinite (…) but remains anchored to these preformed patterns' (CW 6, para. 512). To be engaged with our archetypal foundation and yet not to lose the ground of everyday reality is the utmost artistry of life. It allows openness for the flow of the archetypal potential through our human existence. It opens up a new space for humanity to progress led by the light of the individual. However, if the early formative conditions were not 'good enough'

(Winnicott 1973), there is not yet capacity to stand on the ground of consciousness and we are swept away by the potent archetypal energy and are lost in the unconscious. The prerequisite for play is the creation of safe space in time and place. Mature and spirited individuals can sometimes create this subtly and informally, for example, by timely interventions which stimulate an exchange of wit as a counterpoint to serious boardroom discussion.

Reflecting upon the themes constellated in our work with organizations over decades, without exception, the underlying red thread is the attempt to retrieve and (re)create the ideal conditions for play. If not a form of play, what else is the opportunity to freely associate ideas? What else is the highest form of science?

This may be a core reason why clients commission our coaching and consulting services; to somehow bring forth their own symbolic playmaker, in their own language. Their internal and archetypal 'Magister Ludi' is realised. Beneath all the effort and industry of corporate life can be discerned a game. It is described lyrically in Herman Hesse's imaginative story of life in the 23rd century.

We could say that there are only two types of clients: the ones who can play and the ones who cannot play *yet*. This is equally true of coaches and consultants. The ones who can play, in the sense of having had good enough safe time/space to grow through the formative cycles of their lives, engage with their own images which guide them, time and time again, through the rites of passage into the new cycles. Those who cannot play, cannot play yet. The symbolising function may gradually develop through the positive experience of a safe relationship.

Zeitgeist

The maturation process, or individuation, is a series of rites of passage. In the lives of individuals, they are mastered through the rituals of play. When the environment has not been good enough, the mastery of play is interrupted, and maturation skills are partially impeded. Children become adults too soon. This keeps them in childhood when they are adults. Then they need to keep coming back to that particular play, to that particular role which was skipped, not learned and not lived for adult life to continue satisfactorily.

Collectively, the rites of passage take form in accordance with the Zeitgeist. In recent history two world wars interfered with collective maturation cycles. Those wars also had their antecedents. Collective development was impeded. The present Zeitgeist is impregnated with images of past holocausts. It is as if their unseen, un-mourned, unredeemed gravity affects every single aspect of our time. We find potential repetition in the prospect of destruction of the planet and denial in detachment from the issue. We also find the prospect of revitalisation, of creative ways forward.

Thinking in Jung's terms, what is that which is not seen? What is again and again so forcibly kept in the unconscious so that it comes back as global outburst of violence and destruction? What needs to be given a proper gradient in the conscious dimension of the collective human life in order for a higher degree of balance to be restored in the collective dynamics? If we do not know, then where are the arenas of play which can provide symbolic understanding?

The answers can be found by asking the question, 'Where is the greatest energy stored and expressed?' We can immediately recognise corporations' radiant sources of energy. We can also appreciate the collective libidinal charge of global sports, especially of football. They are symbolic arenas, where the attempts of rites of passage to new stages of maturity are enacted. It is astonishing to see the intensity, ingenuity and skilfulness, in corporate life. Many of our brightesst chosen the pursuit of corporate leadership careers.As for football, it has never ceased to enchant millions with the simple drama of twenty-two individuals on a pitch and a ball. At the outset, one is a stage for the finest, most developed intellectual aspects of humanity, and the other, for the superb bodily (corporal) mastery of play. In fact, both arenas engage the entire human being in play. Both constellate tensions between fair-play and the goal, the beauty of playing and winning by any means, artistry and brutality and honour and corruption. The tension between the 'child' and 'warrior' actors (archetypes), of the collective psyche, is constellated in attempt to come back and catch up and master the play that was missed when the 'child' was forced into 'warriorship' too early. If the safe space was destroyed, then the referee failed. Just as justice fails post war societies. (see Chapter 21). The initiation rites must be performed three times before passing. After two world wars, maybe the third attempt is now.

The child archetype is always the treasure of the individual, group and collective. It is the image of new life, future, vital energy itself. The positive and protective Warrior archetype needs to be equipped with all its different kinds of energies (Knight, Trickster, Amazonian Woman, Enkidu, Dwarf, totem animal and so on) in order to secure space for future life to grow. Or at least a stable might be provided (CW 11, para. 267).

The 'child' in the narrative of this book appeared on the stage with autistic features (which in many indigenous cultures signifies connection to the divine). The flow of images brought music as a way for the child to bridge the realities. The 'silence' in the case example of the multinational corporation had apparently stopped the music flow. Yet, the new music could start playing silently.

The closing line in Hamlet is: 'The rest is silence'. The rest is a musical rest, of space and time in the music flow which allows listening. Listening to the narratives.

References

Davis, M 1992, *Play and symbolism in Lowenfeld and Winnicott*, Dr Margaret Lowenfeld Trust, viewed 21 December 2019, http://lowenfeld.org/wp-content/uploads/2014/06/Play-and-symbolism-in-Lowenfeld-and-Winnicott-MadeleineDavis.pdf.

Johnson, G 2010, *The retrieval of the beautiful: thinking through Merleau-Ponty's aesthetics*, Northwestern University Press, Evanston.

Winnicott, DW 1973, *The child, the family, and the outside world*, Penguin, London.

Index

For Product Safety Concerns and Information please contact our EU
representative GPSR@taylorandfrancis.com
Taylor & Francis Verlag GmbH, Kaufingerstraße 24, 80331 München, Germany